# Hall of Mirrors

David Sinclair is the author of seven previous books, including *The Pound, Edgar Allan Poe, Dynasty: The Astors and Their Times* and *Two Georges: The Making of the Modern Monarchy*. He has enjoyed a long career as a senior Fleet Street journalist and newspaper executive, a former editor of the *Sunday Times Review* and *News Review*, arts editor of the *Sunday Telegraph*, deputy editor of the *Sunday Express*, and editor of *Financial Mail on Sunday*.

His website address is www.nvo.com/davidsinclair

# Hall of Mirrors

David Sinclair

ARROW

Published by Arrow Books in 2002
This edition published by Arrow Books in 2001

1 3 5 7 9 10 8 6 4 2

First published in the United Kingdom in 2001 by Century

Arrow Books
The Random House Group Ltd
20 Vauxhall Bridge Road, London SW1V 2SA

Random House Australia (Pty) Limited
20 Alfred Street, Milsons Point, Sydney,
New South Wales 2061, Australia

Random House New Zealand Limited
18 Poland Road, Glenfield
Auckland 10, New Zealand

Random House (Pty) Limited
Endulini, 5a Jubilee Road, Parktown 2193, South Africa

The Random House Group Ltd Reg. No. 954009

www.randomhouse.co.uk

A CIP catalogue record for this book
is available from the British Library

Papers used by Random House UK Limited are natural, recyclable
products made from wood grown in sustainable forests.
The manufacturing processes conform to the environmental
regulations of the country of origin.

ISBN 0 09 941495 3

Typeset in Ehrhardt by MATS, Southend-on-Sea, Essex
Printed and bound in Great Britain by
Bookmarque, Ltd, Croydon, Surrey

# *Contents*

The defining moment of the twentieth century is not so much the Great War of 1914–1918, but the signing of the peace treaty that followed it.

Most historians agree that the war was an accident waiting to happen. It was a battle of political dinosaurs, the crumbling empires of Austria-Hungary, Germany and Turkey – characterized as the Central Powers because of their web of alliances – and, on the other side, the so-called Entente Powers of France, Russia and Great Britain, bound together by the 'Entente Cordiale' of supposed mutual interest and obligation. There was no real reason for the war, other than as an impromptu trial of strength among outmoded systems of government that knew no other way of surviving, and as the ritual bloodletting of a world – and especially its ruling classes – in mortal fear of revolutionary change.

The peace treaty, by contrast, negotiated in Paris during the first six months of 1919, and signed on 28 June that year in the Hall of Mirrors at the Palace of Versailles, was something deliberate and calculated. It had been thought about, discussed and planned long before the tide of the war had turned in favour of its eventual victors. But if the Great War was a tragedy, the Treaty of Versailles was a travesty. Far from guaranteeing, as it claimed for itself, the peace, stability and prosperity of a new and better world, the treaty ensured that the remainder of the century would see horror, brutality and suffering unparalleled in human history.

Looking into the glass of the Hall of Mirrors, it is possible to see, reflected back at us, images of the shadows that would darken the rest of the century: the heedless idiocy of the 1920s; the Great Depression of the 1930s; the terrors of fascism and of Soviet Communism and the rise of an imperialism even more destructive than its nineteenth-century ancestor; the cataclysm of the Second World War, the paranoia of the Cold War and the threat of Armageddon implicit in the race to build bigger and better nuclear weapons. Even as the century ended, peculiarly gruesome conflicts in the Balkans could be traced right back to the Treaty of Versailles.

These may seem large and even fanciful claims. Surely it is simplistic to blame the travails of a particularly troubled century – perhaps the most chaotic and painful since the grim fourteenth century, the age of the Black Death – on the actions of a handful of men in the confused aftermath of the greatest war the world had ever seen. Well, the fact is that the Treaty of Versailles was an utter failure even before the ink was dry on its signatures. It was a failure of vision, a failure of courage, a failure of common sense and a failure of competence. It was cobbled together largely by three men who had very little idea of what they were doing and even less of what they should have been doing.

They liked to think of themselves as statesmen, but in truth they were merely manipulative politicians whose horizons were no broader and whose principles were no higher than the limited national and personal interests that kept them in power. In trying to satisfy their voters and their own egos, they satisfied nobody. Such was the comprehensive nature of their failure, that few of the articles of the treaty were ever observed in practice – and those that were turned out to be frighteningly temporary. America failed to ratify the treaty, Britain and France turned their backs on it, and the League of Nations – which was designed to be its centrepiece – turned into an ineffectual talking shop.

Overall, the powerful men behind the Treaty of Versailles resolved nothing and instead created a novel set of problems, the effects of which – from Eastern Europe to Africa, from the Middle East to the Balkans – still trouble the new world that is finally, painfully, emerging from the political quagmire of the old.

This book is the story of those three men: Woodrow Wilson, twenty-eighth President of the United States of America; David Lloyd George, Prime Minister of Great Britain; Georges Clemenceau, Prime Minister of France. With the somewhat reluctant and occasional addition of Vittorio Emanuele Orlando, Prime Minister of Italy, this group formed what became known as the Big Four. It was a misnomer. For a start, with the exception of Wilson, they were all physically small men – and, with no exceptions, the scale of their approach to the task they had confidently set themselves could not be said to be large. They fussed over minute details, indulged in petty squabbles, pursued personal vendettas, shrank from telling the truth to their colleagues and their public, engaged in shabby intrigues and compromises in order to achieve their own selfish, misguided ends. The fate of the world was in their hands, but the members of the Big Four were not nearly big enough to carry the responsibility.

Woodrow Wilson was, on the one hand, an impractical and self-righteous idealist who believed that his vague ideas for the League of Nations would be sufficient to persuade powerful nation states to set aside their rivalries and share the power they had spent centuries striving to achieve. Yet on the other hand, he was a calculating and partisan politician with an ambition to lead America into a new era of international influence, replacing the imperialistic domination of the likes of Britain and France. He saw the peace conference as an opportunity to achieve both these aims, and equally to demonstrate to the belligerent and – in Wilson's view – outmoded European powers the error of their ways. It was this arrogant belief in America's superiority that helped to bring about his undoing and render the treaty unworkable.

David Lloyd George went to Paris with no such grand design. His main concerns were to maintain the British Empire as the world's first superpower and to prevent Germany from rising again to challenge it, as it had done with remarkable success before the war. At the same time, however, his keen intuition had alerted him to a new and dangerous spirit of radicalism unleashed by the war, and he began to fear the prospect of international revolution on the Bolshevik model. Dependent for his survival as prime minister on former political opponents, he found himself trying to placate both right and left, which meant that his approach to the international settlement the treaty was intended to achieve varied wildly from one day to the next and helped to make its ultimate failure inevitable.

Georges Clemenceau was motivated principally by a desire to crush Germany and ensure it could never in the future threaten France, as it had done in 1870 and again in 1914. Despising the Germans, jealous of British power and suspicious of the Americans, he was a man rooted firmly in the nineteenth century, wedded to the old balance of power maintained by intricate alliances and backed up by military force. He was dismissive of the League of Nations idea and uninterested in the establishment of any new world order. For him, the Versailles treaty represented little more than the underpinning of the Allies' – and notably the French – victory over the Central Powers, and for such a limited aim he was prepared to compromise international stability.

As for Vittorio Emanuele Orlando, he was the prisoner of a corrupt and severely fragmented political system that desperately needed to restore its credibility on the world stage. Italy had long resented being overshadowed by the imperial powers of Europe and had joined the Entente after the outbreak of the war mainly in order to enhance its international standing, and on the promise of its own imperial rewards to come. Those rewards became the Italians' obsession at the peace conference, overshadowing all other considerations in their eyes, but the effect was merely to diminish Italy's influence on the wider settlement – and to ensure that, when its demands were not met, it marched heedlessly into the false dawn of fascism.

With such irreconcilable agendas dominating the proceedings, the disaster of Versailles unfolds through the
characters of the main participants, the other people who most
influenced their thoughts, feelings and actions, and the events
and pressures to which they were subject. Based on official
documents, once secret reports, letters, memoirs, diaries,
historical studies, eyewitness accounts and other records, this
is a careful reconstruction of what really happened, what was
said, what was perceived, and the reasons why the treaty
negotiations and their outcome proceeded as they did. For the
sake of the narrative, events have been dramatized, much
imagination and some invention have been employed in the
re-creation of important scenes – for which detailed
documentary records often do not exist – and a number of
conversations and exchanges have been either transposed out
of their original contexts of recollection or constructed from
dry, sometimes less than complete official minutes. In some
cases, the conversations took place in private, so that what was
said has to be deduced from what subsequently happened,
while in other instances, it must be assumed that there was
such an exchange because of the statements or events that
followed. Although the participants appeared at the outset to
commit themselves to open diplomacy, much of the
negotiation of the Treaty of Versailles was carried on in the
deepest secrecy. But while the words on the page may not be
actually those that were spoken, the main events described
really did take place, and every effort has been made to
describe, reflect and explain accurately the opinions and the
behaviour of the people involved.

Although the conclusion is well known, the process of the Treaty of Versailles is a fascinating story when told in terms of the flawed human beings who orchestrated it, and who ultimately became its first victims. It is intended to be read as just that: a story, and one that is all the more gripping because of the effects it has had on all our lives. This is less of a history book than a book about how history came to be made, and, more particularly, about the people making it.

If the story has a moral, it is that politicians, whom we trust with decisions that shape our future, are fundamentally no different from the rest of us. They are just as fallible, just as unreliable, just as uncertain, ambitious, fearful, selfish, vain and prejudiced – except that the illusion of power and the assumption of superior wisdom produce in politicians an even greater capacity for self-delusion.

Georges Clemenceau once said: 'War is too serious a matter to be left to generals.' As an architect of the Treaty of Versailles, he might have done well to reflect that peace was too serious a matter to be left to politicians.

The history of the world, wrote Thomas Carlyle, is but the biography of great men. All too often, though, the course of the world's history is set by men who are merely deluded, and encouraged by the rest of us, into believing that they are great.

# When the War Is Done

*And when the war is done and youth stone dead*
*I'd toddle safely home and die – in bed*
SIEGFRIED SASSOON
*Base Details*

# CHAPTER 1

# Twilight of the Gods

*I*

The chill of approaching winter was already notice-
able in the little town of Spa, more than eight
hundred feet up in the heavily wooded mountains
south-east of Liège. Soon, the bare slate peaks above the
treeline would receive their first dusting of snow, and the
narrow river running through the town, by the Boulevard des
Anglais, would swell and surge as the high moors of the Hohe
Venn shed their excess moisture. In the northern Ardennes of
Belgium, the temperature rarely rises above sixty-five degrees
Fahrenheit, even in mid-summer, and this year had not been
as good as most. Ordinarily, that might have been a matter of
regret in Spa, the *Ville d'Eaux* whose name had, over the
centuries, become a generic term for the sort of health-giving
mineral springs on which its livelihood depended.

But 1918 was no ordinary year. In fact, it had been quite
some time since Spa had seen its customary summer influx of
the crowned heads and aristocracy of Europe, come to restore
themselves at the springs named after Peter the Great and
Queen Marie-Henriette, or to drink the clear but evil-smelling

water of *la Géronstère*. Instead, the hotels of the continent's most famous health resort were playing host to the Imperial German Army.

Spa was not alone, of course. The Germans had invaded Belgium in August 1914 on the pretext of the Belgian government's refusal to allow their troops to cross the country for an attack on France, which had declared its support for Russia in its conflict with Germany's close ally Austria-Hungary. By the end of 1914, almost all of Belgium and a large swathe of northern France were under German control – and that remained the position in September 1918, as the bloody stalemate of the First World War reached its climax. The *Ville d'Eaux*, however, had been singled out for special treatment, an honour its inhabitants naturally regarded with a certain ambivalence.

At first, it was the casualties of the carnage on the Western Front, where Germany was locked in battle with the armies of France, the British Empire and Belgium, who colonized the town. Wounded and shell-shocked soldiers arrived by the trainload from the lethal trenches of Flanders to the west, from the deadly mud of the Somme valley farther south, from the charnel-house of Verdun. Frock-coated doctors and white-aproned nurses turned the elegant hotels of Spa into convalescent homes for the battle-scarred, who took the waters and regained their strength on leafy walks along the Promenade des Artistes, or more taxing expeditions to Warfaaz lake. The *Spadois* treated them kindly, accustomed to serving the needs of the sick, and relieved to be far away from the violent convulsions that produced such pain and suffering.

By the autumn of 1918, though, the war had come

somewhat closer – not with its guns and tanks and corpses, but in the imposing figure of General Erich von Ludendorff, commander-in-chief of the German army. Early that year, he had stepped from a special train at Spa railway station and made his way by car to the renowned Hôtel Britannique. The irony must have made him smile, though the Prussian officer class was not well-known for its sense of humour. The Britannique was to be the headquarters of the Imperial General Staff for the last great battle of the war, the spring offensive that would take the Germans to Paris, drive the British back to the Channel ports and make the lately-arrived American forces wish they had never set foot in Europe. The Chief of the General Staff himself, the legendary Field Marshal von Hindenburg, also took up residence at the Britannique and even the emperor, Kaiser Wilhelm II, graced Spa with his presence, settling himself in the nearby Château Neubois to await victory. All was bustle and excitement as epauletted, heel-clicking staff officers scurried to and fro, field commanders came to discuss tactics and receive their orders, government officials arrived from Berlin for conferences that would settle the fate of Europe.

But that had been back in the spring. Now, as the trees in Spa's little valley began to shed their leaves and chilly nights foretold the coming of the first frosts, the mood inside the Hôtel Britannique was very different. Officers wore worried frowns and spoke in hushed voices. The sudden ringing of a telephone on an orderly's desk would bring anxious glances and cause the office to fall silent. Everywhere the tension was almost palpable.

General Ludendorff, never an easy man to deal with because of his excessive nervous energy, had become impossible of late. There were not many on his staff who had escaped his famous temper tantrums when things did not turn out as he wished, or his violent outbursts of frustration at delays in accomplishing the tasks he had ordered and achieving the objectives he had set. Those explosions usually served only to increase efforts to satisfy him, such was the almost godlike regard in which he was held by his subordinates. He was an inspired commander, a master strategist, and he was no harder on others than he was on himself. Now, though, the officers closest to him were beginning to have their doubts. His demands were becoming ever more hysterical, often completely unrealistic. Members of his personal staff were beginning to fear that the strain was stretching to breaking point the always taut nerves of the commander-in-chief.

On 28 September 1918, those nerves finally snapped.

For more than a month, the news coming back to the Hôtel Britannique from the Western Front had been almost entirely bad. Not only had the great spring offensive been stopped in its tracks without achieving the expected gains, but also the enemy was now counter-attacking vigorously right along the front, relentlessly forcing the German armies back towards the position from which they had launched their assault in March. Ludendorff had been working day and night, his manic energy on full power, studying maps, barking orders, moving up what reserves he could muster to plug gaps in his defensive line, stiffening the resolve of his field commanders.

He was exhausted, but his willpower and an innate optimism that sometimes bordered on the lunatic kept him going. This was a crisis, certainly, but it was not a disaster.

After a snatched lunch of local smoked ham, Ludendorff called into his large, wood-panelled room two of the officers responsible for liaison with the War Office, the *Kriegsamt*, back in Berlin. He wanted to brief them on the latest reports from the front, to ensure that the right messages went to the paper-pushers and the politicians. He was short of men, of munitions, of tanks, of fuel, but all he got from Berlin were bland reassurances, with no follow-up. How did they expect him to carry on the war when they would not send him what he needed?

'We're holding on,' Ludendorff told the two officers. 'The enemy has pierced our line in certain places, but there has been no general breakthrough – and there will not be one. We're still in a position to do them a lot of damage with local offensives, but overall my strategy is a defensive one. We can hold out for months. We can sap their will to go on fighting. Soon they will have outrun their supply lines, and that's when we'll strike back. We'll force them to make peace.'

It was a far cry from the great ambitions of the spring. They had expected to be occupying Paris by now and to be dictating peace terms to the Entente powers. Instead, they were merely counting on their ability to fight the enemy to a standstill, when they would be able to negotiate terms that would at least recognize what they had achieved so far.

'We still hold Alsace and Lorraine,' Ludendorff said, 'we're still in control of Belgium, and we're still occupying part of

France. We have preserved our honour and we shall continue to do so. And Marshal Hindenburg, I may say, takes the same view. He himself told the Kaiser that we could succeed in maintaining ourselves on French soil and by so doing we would eventually subject the enemy to our will.'

He was pacing about the room, stopping occasionally by its tall windows to look out, his hands clasped behind his back, the fingers knitting with each other.

'And what about the Austrians, General?' asked one of the officers.

They had all seen the reports of a week ago that the chief minister of Austria-Hungary, Count Burian, had issued a statement calling upon all the warring states to arrange a high-level, confidential meeting in neutral territory with a view to establishing the principles on which a peace treaty might be based. The Austrians were ready to give up, in other words.

'I'm afraid we can't rely on them any more,' Ludendorff said. 'We did our best to persuade them not to take this defeatist course – but, in any case, I don't see the Entente jumping at their suggestion.

'Our policy remains what it was when the Vice-Chancellor outlined it at the beginning of the month. We are ready and willing to make peace, but only on certain conditions, such as those we laid down in the treaty we signed at Brest Litovsk with the Russians and the Romanians last year. Now we have peace in the east, whether the British and the French like it or not. We are not unreasonable. If they give back all the territories seized from us in the course of the war, and they do the same for Austria and Turkey, then we are prepared to negotiate the position of Belgium. If they want disarmament, then of course we'll talk about it, so long as it is on the basis of complete reciprocity – and it includes reductions in the British navy. And if the Americans persist in their ideas for the protection of small nations, then of course we'll take part in any international arrangements, provided they apply to countries now dominated by Britain.'

But could such an aim be achieved with the enemy now in full attack on the Western Front?

'We can still paralyse their will to fight,' Ludendorff said. He even managed a smile. 'We're going to chop a hole in their line. Then we'll see what happens next.'

And on the southern front, where they were reliant on the Turks and their Bulgarian allies? The French had attacked near Salonika just a few days ago, and already they seemed to be making substantial gains. There had been reports that the Bulgarians had fallen back twenty miles.

'It is a weak spot,' Ludendorff admitted, 'and I'm worried about it. But it's difficult country and the enemy won't have things all his own way. General von Mackensen is there, well-armed and with some veteran troops. He's an excellent commander, Mackensen. He'll put some steel into those Bulgarian peasants.'

There was a knock at the door. An army clerk entered and saluted, standing to attention.

'An urgent message, General.'

He handed the paper to Ludendorff and withdrew. The general began to read the message. Almost at once, the heavy jowls of his mastiff-like face began to quiver and he turned deadly pale. Then a flush of redness spread upward from his neck, darkening as it rose past the small eyes towards the close-cropped white hair.

'This can't be true!' he roared, smashing his fist into the centre of the paper he held. 'I don't believe it. This is not happening!'

The two officers exchanged sidelong glances.

'General! What is it? What's happened?'

Ludendorff flung the message aside and raised his arms in the air, his face turned upwards as if in appeal to the Almighty.

'Betrayed!' he almost screamed. 'We've been stabbed in the back. It's a disaster. It's shameful. Surrender! My God, we're ruined! What are we going to do?'

As the general continued to screech, one of the officers retrieved the piece of paper from where it had fallen and took it over to his colleague. They bent their heads together to read the message that had caused such distress.

The seventeen Bulgarian divisions on the Salonika front had surrendered to a French general two days ago. The soldiers had simply thrown down their arms and gone home. The Bulgarian government had told an American envoy in Sofia that it was ready to demobilize all its troops unconditionally, surrender all means of transport, hand back all occupied areas, and make its own territory and its railway system available to Entente forces for their further military operations. In the circumstances, General Mackensen had withdrawn his troops, which were now available to the commander-in-chief. The Bulgarian armistice would probably be signed tomorrow, the 29th, or the next day.

Ludendorff was now shaking as he marched back and forth across the room, clenching and unclenching his fists, or waving his arms wildly.

'We're finished!' he roared. 'I am humiliated. This should never have happened. It's those damned politicians and their defeatist talk. They're gutless, the lot of them. Even the Kaiser! He pretends to listen to us, but all the time the civilians are whispering in his ear, spreading sedition, preaching defeat. I don't believe he even cares any more.'

He wheeled to face the two shocked officers and gesticulated violently at them.

'The *Kriegsamt* is to blame for this,' he shrieked. 'They and the rest of the armchair generals back in Berlin. They don't know what war is. We're the ones who have faced everything and never flinched, Hindenburg and I. Who turned the tables on the Russians at Tannenberg? Who knocked the enemy sideways at Amiens and at Soissons and on the Chemin des Dames? We're heroes, and they're all jealous. For months they've been undermining us. Where are my tanks? Where are my guns? Where in the name of God are my reinforcements?

'They want us to be defeated. All they had to do was hold their nerve. But, no! They listen to the enemy propaganda. They flinch from sinking his merchant ships. Hah! And what about the great Imperial German Navy? What have our heroic admirals been doing while we have been taking the punishment?'

He was becoming incoherent. The watching officers did not know what to do.

Suddenly, as they stared at him, a line of foam appeared along the strong curve of the general's protruding lower lip. His face turned chalk white. His eyes rolled upwards. His body went rigid, then seemed to crumple. As if in slow motion, the commander-in-chief of the Imperial Army crashed unconscious to the floor.

For a few seconds, the liaison officers appeared to be rooted where they stood. One, recovering himself, made for the door.

'No!' shouted his colleague. 'Get water. On the desk.'

They knelt down and forced a little of the famous Spa water into Ludendorff's open mouth. Then they patted his cheeks. His eyelids fluttered briefly.

'Brandy! There'll be some somewhere.'

They found a bottle in a cupboard and wetted the general's lips with a little of the spirit. He opened his eyes and emitted a long, racking sigh.

'It's all right, General. Don't move. You've had a sort of seizure.'

Gradually he pulled himself together, and the officers sat him up, propped against a leather sofa. He raised his right arm weakly, motioning at the officers, and tried to say something.

'For God's sake, don't . . . You mustn't . . .'

'Calm yourself, General. Everything is all right.'

Finally, they got him to his feet. Ludendorff pulled down the skirts of his tunic, straightened the Iron Cross on its ribbon at his throat. Some colour had returned to his face.

'I'm better now,' he said quietly. 'I was just . . . I'm so tired.'

He shivered slightly.

'It was the shock, General. The news from the Balkans. It's very bad.'

Ludendorff nodded slowly.

'I must send a message to Mackensen,' he muttered almost to himself. 'I must go and see Hindenburg. We have to . . .'

He stopped speaking and stared at the two officers, as if he had forgotten they were present. Then he straightened his back and thrust out his chest.

'I'm all right, now. It's over. I'm myself again. Thank you. You may go.'

The officers stood to attention, clicked the heels of their highly polished riding boots and inclined their heads sharply in salute.

'Don't . . .' Ludendorff said, 'don't say anything about . . . what happened here. That's an order. Please, gentlemen.'

'Of course, General.'

But whatever he had said, Erich Ludendorff was not himself again. All the optimism, the self-confidence, the energy and the discipline seemed to have deserted him. He sat for a while in the big chair behind his desk, staring out of the window. Soon it would be dusk, he observed – the end of Germany's darkest day. It was a defeated man who, in the gathering gloom, entered Hindenburg's office.

'The war is lost,' Ludendorff said flatly.

The old field marshal – the Kaiser had recalled him from retirement to put some fire into the war effort – showed no emotion.

'I'm afraid,' he said, 'that I have been forced, reluctantly, to the same conclusion myself.'

'You've heard the news from the Balkans, then.'

'Naturally. But, I must say, I have been half expecting it since the attack at Salonika began.'

'Do you think there's anything we can do?'

'Well, our strategic position is not all that bad, really. We are still denying the enemy a final breakthrough on the Western Front. France and England are visibly tiring, and, as for the Americans, they are simply bleeding in vain. But, as you know better than anyone, our resources are diminishing all the time. With this news from the Balkans, they might soon fail altogether. And with Bulgaria gone, who will close the gap? There's still a great deal we can do, but we can't, absolutely cannot build up a new front.'

'You're right, of course,' Ludendorff said. 'We don't have many options.'

'It seems to me,' replied Hindenburg, 'that we have only one option. Look at it this way. With Bulgaria gone, Austria is exposed and, as we've seen, already wobbly. Oh, the Austrians are sending some Czech troops to prop up the new front, but I am not confident they have any more will to fight than the Bulgarians had. And with this success for the Entente, we might even find that Romania will join in against us once more. Those Romanians are still smarting from the fact that we forced them to capitulate.

'Then there are the Turks. Not much to hope for there, I fear. The British have been doing pretty well in the Middle East, and I don't think the Bulgarian surrender will do much for Turkey's resolve to continue the struggle.'

But the Western Front, where the main enemy attacks were

concentrated, was holding up extremely well, Ludendorff pointed out.

Hindenburg agreed: 'It's a magnificent example of the skill of our commanders and the courage of our men. I'm very proud of our fierce resistance. On the other hand, we have to assume that the enemy attacks will continue indefinitely . . .'

The conclusion was left hanging in the air.

'So we must bring things to an end,' Ludendorff said.

Hindenburg leaned forward in his chair.

'We must bring things to an end. But an honourable end, my dear Ludendorff.'

He sat back again and lowered his eyes. 'No one will say it's too soon.'

They agreed that the Chief of Staff would telephone the Kaiser and arrange a meeting for the following morning. It was Sunday, but the war would not wait.

Before he made the call Hindenburg looked quizzically at Ludendorff.

'By the way, are you feeling all right?' he asked. 'You don't look very well to me.'

That night, Ludendorff was too disturbed to sleep. He sat up late in his office, brooding about the course of events that had brought Germany to this desperate pass. The more he thought about it, the worse his depression became.

Only a couple of months ago, at the end of July, when Admiral von Hintze, the new Secretary of State in the Imperial Office of Foreign Affairs, had arrived at General

Headquarters, Ludendorff had been able to assure him categorically that the current offensive was certain to defeat the enemy completely and decisively.

'*Nach Paris!*' the triumphant soldiers had cried. 'On to Paris!' The shouts echoed eerily now in Ludendorff's mind.

It seemed to be going so well at first, he thought.

At the end of March, they had smashed the British Fifth Army before Amiens and forced the Third Army to abandon its defensive positions and retreat four miles. In a lightning strike, they had routed the French east of Amiens and brought Paris within range of their biggest guns. Four weeks later, they had driven the British out of territory they had held for three years and in May they had overrun six French and three English divisions on the Aisne-Marne Canal, bringing the German forces back almost to the position they had reached with their first invasion of France in August 1914.

To be sure, the Germans' position in July 1918 was still very far from the crushing victory they had envisaged as they swept west and south in that heady summer of four years earlier. Ludendorff's predecessors had somehow squandered the tremendous advantage they had achieved in so short a time. But he and Hindenburg had agreed that a successful spring offensive in 1918 would allow Germany to offer peace to the Entente Powers on terms very favourable to itself, consolidating its territorial gains and leaving it the undisputed master of Europe. That would be a victory. The four years of sacrifice would still be amply justified and the two presiding military geniuses would be celebrated as having saved, even enhanced, their country's honour.

'Where are the celebrations now?' Ludendorff thought bitterly. 'Where is our honour?'

Unfortunately, the offensive had not quite succeeded in all its aims, a fact that had become apparent within only a week or two of Ludendorff's confident assertion to Admiral von Hintze. They had been advancing over ground already devastated in the battles of the previous four years, and that had made almost impossible the strategic and logistical mobility upon which Ludendorff's plans depended. Quite simply, they had become bogged down, short of the ultimate objectives the commander-in-chief had identified. Worse still, they had become victims of their own success in the sense that they had forced their enemies to do something they had never done before – act in unison. Taking their model from the Germans, the Allies had established their own Supreme Command, so that when their counter-attack came, it was extremely well co-ordinated. The German forces, struggling with their supply lines, had lacked the firepower to turn back the assault, and had been forced to retreat themselves.

Ludendorff remembered his bitter disappointment – but, he told himself, I was not downcast. War is a risky business, and one's gambles do not always pay off in full. Those had been difficult days for the German army, but it had still been in an extremely strong position. The Allies suffered heavy losses, especially the Americans. The Supreme Command had calculated that all Germany needed to do was continue to resist strongly, and it would still be powerful enough to dictate the peace. The real problem that had faced the generals lay in selling that concept to the politicians and the public back home. They had to be convinced that this would be victory.

Ludendorff recalled that, in the middle of August, he had tried to make the position clear to Hintze in advance of an important meeting of the Kaiser's Crown Council at the Château Neubois.

'Listen, Admiral, in July I told you that I was certain that the present offensive would break the enemy's will to fight and force him to make peace,' the general told the minister when they met privately at his office in the Hôtel Britannique. 'I have to say that, now, I am no longer absolutely certain about this.'

Hintze's eyes narrowed: 'In that case, General, how do you imagine the war can be continued?'

Ludendorff described his defensive strategy and patiently outlined the counter-attacks he was planning in order to give the Allies a bloody nose.

'It's important that you fully understand the situation,' he said. 'We must be prepared to offer peace terms to the enemy when the time is right. But we must not be defeatist. This has to be made clear at the Crown Council tomorrow.'

At the time, Ludendorff hoped he had set the Foreign Secretary's mind at rest and that there would be no political pressure for precipitate action in the face of what was, admittedly, a delicate situation. But, as he now realized, that was when things had started to run out of control.

Hintze, he reflected, had become too much the politician. The Admiral had refused to take Ludendorff's assessment at face value and had apparently concluded, as his subsequent actions showed, that the Supreme Command was covering up the real nature of Germany's predicament. He had been too willing to listen to the rumblings of discontent in Berlin at the lack of outright victory. But instead of urging more support for the army, Hintze had sought to undermine it by arguing for urgent peace negotiations. Regrettably, the sombre mood of that Crown Council meeting back in August had rather played into the Foreign Secretary's hands.

Ludendorff pictured the scene on that Wednesday morning.

The little Kaiser sat at the head of the long, rectangular table and listened gloomily as his Chancellor, Count von Hertling, spoke of the restiveness of the parliamentary parties in the Reichstag, the war-weariness of the population and the growing warnings of political unrest.

'The longer the war goes on,' he added, 'the more the sympathy we have among the neutrals drains away. They no longer understand what our war aims are. As for our allies . . .' The old Bavarian fox glanced up the table in the direction of the Emperor of Austria, who had been invited to the Council with his chief minister. 'As for our allies, I think it would not be overstating the case to suggest that there are signs of despair among them.'

The Austrian minister, Count Burian, stared at the table.

'We have to be realistic,' he said. 'Our people are suffering greatly from the shortages of food. In some places, they may be close to starvation. I'm not sure how long we can go on. It might be . . . It might be that we have to consider reaching some sort of accommodation with our enemies.'

The Kaiser, as always, looked to his generals. They knew he

trusted them not to let him down, not to do anything to damage the honour of the Fatherland.

'What is your assessment of our military posture?' he asked Ludendorff.

'Well,' the commander-in-chief replied, 'it is true that we have suffered some serious reverses. As you know, Sir, the offensive we mounted in the spring, though brilliantly successful at first, did not quite achieve its desired objectives. Since then, the enemy has counter-attacked strongly at various places along the Western Front and, to be frank, we are no longer in a position to mount another major offensive.'

'Which means?' asked Admiral von Hintze.

'Which means,' Ludendorff said, 'that my present strategy is one of strong defence, combined with local offensives. This, I believe, will mean that we remain in a powerful position, with options other than outright victory.'

'And in your opinion, General,' Hintze said carefully, 'outright victory is no longer possible?'

'Not by military means alone. But may I remind you of the memorandum prepared by Colonel von Haeften, which I sent to the Chancellor in June, and which suggested that we consider what the colonel called a "peace offensive" that would undermine the morale of the English in particular, causing a surge of popular sentiment against the government. England is tired of this war, and if we showed a desire for peace, I'm sure the people would jump at it, even if the government resisted. France and Italy would follow, and we would be left in the position of achieving our aims just as if we had been overwhelmingly victorious in the field.'

The Kaiser crossed his legs and stroked his curling, waxed moustache reflectively. The generals were aware that he was as frustrated as they were by the fact that victory always seemed to be just beyond their grasp. They had noticed signs that he was growing tired of the war. At first, he had enjoyed it as a great, exciting game, but by now a degree of boredom had set in, as it usually did when Wilhelm II did not enjoy the rapid gratification of his desires. The question was, would his growing sense of wishing to bring it to an end lead him to accept that victory might now depend on more than military action?

'And these local offensives you mentioned,' the Kaiser said to Ludendorff. 'Are they possible? Are they likely to be successful?'

'Absolutely, Sir. We are planning them at this moment. I am confident that we'll be able to give the enemy a fright or two.'

'Perhaps, then . . .' The Kaiser hesitated. The generals waited anxiously for him to continue. 'Perhaps the best course would be to watch for a favourable moment for coming to terms with the enemy.'

'I agree, Sir,' said Count Hertling. 'I recommend that steps be taken at the opportune moment to arrive at an understanding . . . perhaps the moment of our next success on the Western Front.'

Ludendorff remembered exchanging relieved glances with Hindenburg. Hertling was one of the old sort. You could rely on him.

The Foreign Secretary, however, had proved to be

somewhat less reliable so far as the Supreme Command was concerned.

It was no good, Hintze had told the Council that day, waiting for the right moment. He himself was not convinced that Ludendorff's so-called defensive strategy would achieve the desired result, and at this point who could tell when there might be a German attack punishing enough to make the enemy respond to a peace offer?

'I should like, Sir,' he told the Kaiser, 'immediate authority to initiate the work of peace by diplomatic means. And if that involves something of a reduction of the war aims we had set ourselves, then so be it.'

Ludendorff's body tensed as he remembered his reaction to those chilling words.

'We cannot agree to that,' he snapped. 'The Supreme Command would not countenance anything that might suggest we go back on the goals we have set ourselves. There would be no question, for instance, of modifying our demand that Belgium must remain under German influence.'

But Hintze's intervention had struck a chord with the Austrian Emperor, Ludendorff recalled.

'I agree with the Foreign Secretary,' the Emperor Karl said suddenly. 'I believe we should do all we can to achieve a negotiated peace.'

The generals had tended to disregard this slight young man with the prominent ears and receding chin, who had succeeded the grand old Emperor Franz-Josef barely two years ago, a few months short of his thirtieth birthday. His presence at the Crown Council was really no more than an accident of the war, since his accession would never have come about had it not been for the assassination of his uncle, Archduke Franz-Ferdinand, which had provoked the conflict in the first place. But now, with his obvious lack of willpower and moral fibre, he was becoming dangerous.

'I would go so far as to say that, rather than waiting for this "opportune moment" we have spoken about, we should take steps to open negotiations with the Entente Powers as soon as possible.'

Count Burian supported him.

'I should like to take soundings from our allies in Turkey and Bulgaria,' he said. 'They have a role in all this, too. I think you will find they are in favour of negotiation.'

Ludendorff threw up his hands in a gesture of despair. The Kaiser hesitated.

'We wouldn't approach the enemy, directly, of course,' he said. 'We could work through the neutral powers – the King of Spain, perhaps, or the Queen of the Netherlands.'

This was too much for the veteran warrior Hindenburg.

'Gentlemen,' he said, 'there really is no justification for this sort of talk. All we have to do is maintain our present position, keep our footing on French soil, and in the end we shall, I hope, impose our will on the enemy.

'In the view of the Supreme Command, the military situation gives no grounds for depression. We'll only be defeated if we give up hope of victory. In our opinion, there is every reason to hope that we shall reach a military position that enables us to achieve a satisfactory peace.'

'Quite right,' said Chancellor Hertling. 'There is only one

approach, and that is to say to our enemies: "You see you can't beat us, and we are always ready, as we've told you, to conclude a peace based on honour."'

The Kaiser brightened up.

'Very well, then. My decision, Chancellor, is that I authorize you to make all necessary arrangements for diplomatic overtures with the purpose of negotiating peace with the enemy, in the expectation of the favourable opportunity that will be created by our next military success – and bearing in mind, of course, the legitimate aims we set out in this very room in July.'

If only, General Ludendorff thought despairingly as he finally went to bed on that dreadful night only a little more than a month later, if only it had been that simple. They had managed to hold the line at that Crown Council, in spite of Hintze and the Austrian Emperor. All the Supreme Command had needed was continuing support for their strategy and a little luck. As it had turned out, both those things had been denied them.

## II

—

Admiral von Hintze was a man who liked to be sure of his facts before deciding on a course of action. Accordingly, on the morning of 29 September, the Foreign Secretary arrived at the Hôtel Britannique in good time to confer with the Supreme Command about the proposition they would later place before the Kaiser.

He had not been entirely surprised by the previous evening's telephone call informing him that Hindenburg and Ludendorff had finally been driven by the course of events to endorse his opinion that an offer of peace negotiations should be made to the enemy. The Austrian Emperor had consulted Hintze before issuing his own peace proposal a fortnight earlier, inquiring about the prospects for continuing German resistance and the possibility of counter-attacks on the Western Front. The admiral's questioning of Ludendorff on the Emperor's behalf had not produced the unequivocal assurances that would have been the only means of dissuading the Austrians from pursuing their attempt to end the war.

'Our basic intention is to stay where we are,' had been the best that Ludendorff could offer, along with a lot of complaints about the pathetic numbers of tanks coming off the production lines in Germany, his troops' shortage of food and his dwindling supply of reserve divisions. Now, it seemed that even the limited ambition of a couple of weeks ago was beyond Germany's capacity.

'So what has changed in our military situation,' Hintze

asked the commanders that morning in Spa, 'to convince you that we should make an urgent appeal for peace?'

Ludendorff was agitated, pacing ceaselessly about the room, his hands working furiously in a washing motion.

'What's changed?' he almost shouted at the Foreign Secretary. 'I'll tell you what's changed. First of all, the Americans have taken the St Mihiel Salient south of Verdun. The British and the Belgians are pushing us back in Flanders. Two British armies are advancing steadily in the Douai-Cambrai area and the French are driving forward massively along the front from Montdidier almost to Reims. We are on the defensive, Mr Secretary. We are holding our chosen defensive position. But I don't know for how long.

'My troops are taking a tremendous battering all along the Western Front, and the way they are being used up means that all we can look forward to is being beaten back again and again. I'm having to split up perfectly serviceable reserve divisions to make good the losses in the others – and there seems to be no hope of any further reinforcements from home.

'The simple fact is that our position is bad and it can only get worse. It can never get better.'

Hintze frowned. This was not the sort of talk he was accustomed to hearing from Ludendorff. The man seemed to be on the verge of hysteria. The admiral took Hindenburg aside.

'Is the general quite well?' he asked in an undertone.

'I don't know,' Hindenburg muttered. 'The strain is beginning to take its toll. I'm just hoping his nerves will hold up.' Then, more loudly: 'Look, Mr Secretary, both General Ludendorff and I, quite independently, came to the conclusion yesterday afternoon that the military situation, especially in the light of the news from the Balkans, demands that we use all means at our disposal to bring this war to a speedy end.'

'But, Field Marshal, we could have used those means a month ago. Then, you were implacably opposed to it. I wanted to put peace negotiations in hand, and so did the Austrians, but you told the Kaiser there was no urgency. We should wait, you said, for a successful counter-attack in the west, which would provide a favourable moment for proposing the peace that we all now desire. And the Kaiser listened to you, as he always does.'

'The Austrians didn't listen, though, did they?' Ludendorff snarled. 'They stabbed us in the back. And after that, look what has happened in Bulgaria.'

'I did my very best to prevent it,' Hintze said. 'I spent a week in Vienna trying to convince the Emperor Karl to keep faith with us. But even if they had kept faith, it now seems, from what you're saying, that it would only have had to be for a matter of weeks. What you are suggesting is what the Austrians – and I – proposed at the Crown Council in August.'

'Not quite,' Hindenburg retorted. 'Then, the idea had the smell of defeatism about it. And that is apparent in Austria's appeal. We have not been defeated.'

'Not yet,' Ludendorff broke in.

Hintze stared at the general. 'Are you seriously telling me that if we don't make peace moves now, we're suddenly going to lose the war?'

'What I'm telling you is that we aren't going to win it.'

Ludendorff's troops had withdrawn to what the army called the Siegfried Zone, a complex series of earthworks, pillboxes and barbed wire fortifications that had been specially built in 1917 between Arras and Soissons to serve as a shortened defensive line behind what had then been the battlefront. The Allies called it the Hindenburg Line.

'I'm telling you,' the general went on, 'that there could be an enemy breakthrough in the Siegfried Zone at any moment. I'm telling you that I don't give a damn about peace negotiations, but what I do want is a ceasefire as soon as possible. We are in a situation that we do not have the strength to reverse. In fact, we're barely holding on. We must cease hostilities before the line breaks.'

'And,' added Hindenburg, 'yesterday's news from Bulgaria makes the matter even more urgent. As we speak, the Bulgarian government is concluding the terms of its surrender. Within weeks, at most, the Entente will control the Danube and the Black Sea. Its forces will be in a position to cut our communications with Turkey and our only remaining route for bringing in oil supplies. Our tanks and transport are already short of fuel and the stocks we have for our aircraft will run out in two months. We'll be completely at their mercy – especially since they will also be poised to attack Austria directly.'

'Well, as it happens,' Hintze said, 'we are making progress on the peace front, on the basis of the Kaiser's instructions to Chancellor Hertling in August. Only yesterday the Netherlands agreed to host a peace conference as soon as it can be arranged.'

'Not good enough,' said Ludendorff. 'We need an armistice first. We must have it now. There's not a moment to be lost.'

'And this is what you intend to tell the Kaiser?'

'That is our recommendation,' Hindenburg responded.

'Well, in that case, we had better go and make it.'

The Kaiser seemed calm, almost unconcerned, when they arrived at the Château Neubois. But as Hindenburg reprised the vital parts of the conversation that had taken place back at the Britannique, the colour drained from Wilhelm's face and he sank into a chair, staring at the three men in disbelief.

'This is terrible,' he cried. 'Don't you realize what this means for the honour of Germany?'

'Sir,' said Hindenburg, 'it is precisely to protect the honour of the Fatherland that we are proposing this course.'

'At this moment,' added Ludendorff, 'we remain in an honourable posture. I cannot guarantee how long that will continue to be the case.'

'Peace with honour is possible,' Hindenburg went on, 'if we act now.'

'But what will our enemies think of us?' the Kaiser protested. 'Surely we are placing ourselves at a disadvantage by such precipitate action?'

Hintze, after all his quiet preparations for a diplomatic offensive following the change of heart he had detected back in August, was ready for this. 'That depends, Sir, on how we go about it. We do not need to make a direct approach to the British or the French. Remember, the American President has already set out the principles for what he would see as a just peace. Peace without victory, he calls it. America wants this war to end. It will be to our credit with President Wilson if we offer the means by which it can be ended.'

The Kaiser stood up and walked over to the window. 'I don't know,' he said slowly. 'America is on the side of the Entente, after all.'

'Not quite, Sir, with respect,' Hintze countered. 'It is not actually part of the alliance. President Wilson has been careful to make that clear. America has intervened in order to bring about the peace in Europe that the President so earnestly wishes to see. I think that if we approached Mr Wilson and expressed our willingness to accept the sort of broad terms he has outlined, it would leave us in a strong position.'

'Just so long as we achieve an armistice in short order,' Ludendorff said. 'My troops cannot go on as they are.'

Still the Kaiser was unconvinced. 'What makes you think Mr Wilson would be favourably inclined towards us? Americans are so proud of their democracy, aren't they? From what I have heard, they don't think much of the way we do things in Germany.'

'That's true, Sir,' Hintze admitted. 'You will recall that I have already proposed some changes in our constitution . . .'

'What changes?' Ludendorff demanded.

'Changes that will involve the leaders of the political parties in the Reichstag, as representatives of the people, more closely in the formulation of policy. I sent you a copy of my memorandum yesterday, General.'

Ludendorff grunted. 'It wasn't a very good day yesterday.'

'I think,' Hintze continued, 'that such changes are a vital preliminary to any peace offer we make, especially to the

Americans. I'm sure you will agree, General, when you have the opportunity to consider my proposals.'

'If that's what it takes,' said Ludendorff grimly. 'I'm more worried about my boys on the Western Front. They must have relief, and soon. Anyway, it's about time the damned politicians took some responsibility. The point is, whatever we do, it has to be done quickly.'

'But changing the way we govern ourselves . . .' the Kaiser mused aloud, '. . . just to please some queer American notion . . .'

'There will be no great change, Sir,' Hintze reassured him. 'My proposal is simply that the leaders of the main parties in the Reichstag should be given seats in the Cabinet appointed by the Chancellor.'

'Ah, the Chancellor,' said the Kaiser. 'He will be here shortly. We must obviously consult the Chancellor before coming to any decision about changes to the government.'

'But not about the armistice,' Ludendorff said sharply. 'That's a military matter. I repeat, Sir, that we must . . .'

Hintze interrupted him. 'General, the two things go together. There would be no point in our appealing to the Americans without offering them something. They have characterized us as an old-fashioned imperial power – as a military dictatorship, even. They have made it clear that they do not trust us. If we are going to have peace, which is what we all now want, then we have to show some willingness to embrace the principles Mr Wilson has set out in his speeches. It seems to me that we are no longer offering peace, which was the strategy that had been agreed, but we are now seeking it.

I'm sure we'll be able to negotiate a treaty that is satisfactory to us, but that will involve some sacrifices on our part.'

'Just so long as we get the ceasefire,' Ludendorff repeated.

'We must wait for the Chancellor,' said the Kaiser.

'Every hour of delay is dangerous,' Ludendorff insisted.

Hintze glanced meaningfully at Hindenburg. The commander-in-chief really did seem to be on the edge.

It was about noon when Count von Hertling arrived from Berlin. He was shocked and dismayed when the generals told him their story.

'This is absolutely terrible,' the old Chancellor said. 'I never imagined, not for a moment . . . How could this have happened? You are now telling me that we must ask the Entente for peace *as soon as it can possibly be done*? But this is defeat, surely? And yet they have taken nothing from us. We still have Belgium, we remain well established on French territory. Our line is still holding . . .'

'They are attacking it even now,' Ludendorff shouted, 'and I cannot be certain that it will continue to hold. Don't you understand, I haven't got the divisions to fill any gaps that might appear? So far we have withdrawn in good order, fighting every inch of the way, but at any minute a serious breakthrough could provoke a general retreat.'

'What about our troops in the east?' asked the Kaiser. 'We have peace with the Russians, and they are in no position to attack us again with this dreadful Bolshevik revolution of theirs. We could bring men back to reinforce the Siegfried Zone.'

'It would be useless, Sir,' said Ludendorff. 'They might not arrive in time. The situation is changing every hour. And, frankly, I can't be sure we would be able to maintain them. At least, where they are, they can be fed.'

The portly Hindenburg rose to his feet. 'The Supreme Command has considered the situation very carefully and we see no alternative but to seek immediately a cessation of hostilities. Our military position demands it. The honour of the Fatherland demands it.'

'The honour of the Fatherland!' snorted Hertling. 'Where is the honour in giving up?'

'We are not giving up, Chancellor,' Hintze reassured him. 'We are merely taking the opportunity of pursuing the diplomatic alternatives we discussed at the Crown Council in August. The urgency arises from the fact that, since then, our Austrian friends have taken it upon themselves to ask for peace and the Entente has frightened the Bulgarians into submission.'

'That,' Ludendorff interrupted, 'and the fact that we are in an extremely dangerous position on the Western Front. I cannot emphasize strongly enough . . .'

'Yes, yes, General, we understand,' said Hintze testily. He turned back to the Chancellor, who now slumped despairingly in a chair.

'Count, what I propose is to send a note to the American President requesting him to set in train a process that will bring peace to Europe, to host in Washington negotiations aimed at settling our differences on the basis of the speeches he has made in relation to the desirability of a fair and just peace – a "peace without victory", as he called it.'

'With an immediate ceasefire, of course,' said Ludendorff.

Hintze ignored the general and continued, picking up a sheaf of papers from the table and skimming through them: 'I have here a copy of the speech the President made on 17 August last year, in which he says, and I quote, that "peace should rest upon the rights of peoples, great or small, weak or powerful, their equal right to freedom and security and self-government and to participation in the economic opportunities of the world – *the German people, of course, included*". That seems to me a basis on which we can deliver an appeal.'

He glanced round the room and selected another piece of paper before going on: 'Here is the speech the President gave at a meeting of the American Congress last January, in which he talks of the establishment of what he describes as an association of nations for the purpose of affording mutual guarantees of political independence and territorial integrity. I believe that is perfectly sensible, and I see no reason why Germany would not wish to discuss participation in such an association.'

Hertling stirred himself in his chair. He might be getting on in years, but his memory was still good. 'Wait a moment,' he said. 'That is the speech in which Mr Wilson laid down his so-called Fourteen Points, if I recall it correctly. He demanded the evacuation of Belgium, for instance, and the restoration to France of Alsace and Lorraine. Surely you are not suggesting that we go along with such demands?'

The Foreign Secretary shook his head. 'I don't think we need refer to the Fourteen Points at this stage. They are clearly nothing more than a basis for negotiation. Our intelligence reports suggest that the British and French are less than happy with them in any case. And, as I believe you yourself have indicated, Chancellor, it is not out of the question for us to withdraw from Belgium eventually if certain guarantees are obtained and our natural economic links are recognized.

'Look, the Supreme Command tell us that we are in the midst of a military crisis and recommend that we take immediate action to secure an armistice. This is the most sensible and honourable action we can take, in my view.'

'And the Supreme Command will support you,' said Hindenburg.

The Kaiser had said little since the Chancellor's arrival. He was in his usual chair at the head of the long table, hugging his withered left arm and staring distractedly into space. His short stature and his deformity had provoked in him, as a young man, an excessive regard for his dignity and a desire to present himself to the world as an heroic figure. Maturity had not tempered those psychological traits. The war was to have been the hour of his greatest glory. He now regarded with something approaching horror the prospect of its ending in his humiliation.

During the silence that followed Hintze's brief monologue, the Kaiser sat forward and leaned his elbows on the table.

'Chancellor,' he said flatly, 'Admiral von Hintze has a proposal to make with regard to our position in making any approach to the Americans.'

The Foreign Secretary appeared to have taken charge of the meeting, which he found a somewhat unusual situation with the Kaiser's beloved generals in the room. This sudden military diffidence emboldened him.

'I took the liberty, Chancellor,' he said to Hertling, 'of sending you a memorandum outlining the changes we must make in our constitutional arrangements in order to demonstrate to the American President the seriousness with which we take his democratic principles.'

'I read it,' Hertling snapped. 'And such changes are out of the question. They would destroy the Empire created and defended by the late, lamented Prince Bismarck. What you are suggesting is nothing short of revolution, and I will have no part of it. The very idea! The Reichstag must support the Chancellor appointed by the Kaiser, not become his master.'

'Nevertheless,' Hintze persisted, 'some changes are necessary. We must approach the Americans on the basis of the will of the people.'

'Will of the people be damned,' Hertling sneered. 'The people are quite content to do what they are told. I'll have none of it. We simply cannot have other countries telling us how to run ours. If you insist on this, Your Majesty, I shall have to resign.' He paused, rose somewhat unsteadily to his feet and bowed to the Kaiser. 'With your permission, Sir, I don't think I have anything else to add.'

With all the dignity of his years, he left the room. The Kaiser examined the faces of his two military commanders.

'And what do you have to say now, gentlemen?' he asked coldly. 'We appear to be on the point of losing another Chancellor.'

'So be it,' said Ludendorff. 'We cannot afford to let

anything stand in the way of our pursuit of an armistice in as short a time as possible.'

'And me? What am I supposed to do? Throw myself on the mercy of the Reichstag?'

He was becoming irritated in that juvenile way of his. Hindenburg adopted an almost fatherly tone: 'Of course not, Sir. Your own constitutional position is unchanged. You must simply choose a new Chancellor, someone you can trust but who, at the same time, will inspire confidence in the Americans. It will then be up to the new man to deal with the Reichstag – and, after all, there is a long tradition of support among the political parties for the Kaiser's choice of Chancellor.'

The Kaiser's face brightened. He even managed a thin smile. 'Yes, of course, you're quite right. We don't want any damned Bolsheviks, do we?'

He looked for help from Hintze, but the Foreign Secretary had seated himself at the far end of the table and was busily writing on a sheet of paper. Ludendorff, meanwhile, was pacing up and down in front of the windows, his broad shoulders hunched, muttering to himself, occasionally punching his left palm with his right fist.

The Kaiser turned to Hindenburg. 'If I am to appoint a new Chancellor, we must discuss who he might be. Do you have any suggestions, Field Marshal?'

The old warrior looked up at the ceiling. 'It would be best if the man were entirely unconnected with the present government, I suppose. He must be a man of honour, naturally, but he must also have a reputation that the Entente will recognize – a man of unimpeachable character.'

'But also,' the Kaiser said, 'a man who will vigorously defend the interests of the Fatherland.'

'That goes without saying, Sir. I have no doubt there are difficult times ahead.'

Suddenly, Hindenburg struck the table with the flat of his hand. Ludendorff stopped pacing and turned to face him. Hintze looked up from his writing.

'I have it, Sir! You must appoint the Prince von Baden.'

'Max?'

'Absolutely. He is the perfect Chancellor for the circumstances in which we now find ourselves.'

'Do you think he'll do it?'

'Prince Max is a patriot, Sir,' Ludendorff said. 'He is extremely popular with the army because of his work on behalf of our prisoners of war.'

'And he is equally respected by the Entente,' added Hindenburg, 'because he has been meticulous in ensuring the proper treatment of enemy prisoners, too. He has spent the whole of the war working with the Red Cross, and that has given him an excellent international reputation.'

'What do you think, Admiral?' the Kaiser inquired. 'You're the diplomat in this room.'

Hintze laid down his pen. 'The best possible choice, Sir. The Prince is known throughout Europe as an intelligent, reasonable man – a man with impeccable humanitarian credentials. I'm sure he will be more than acceptable to the other side, yet at the same time he can be relied upon to uphold the honour of Germany.'

Hindenburg said: 'He's old enough to have wisdom, but

still young enough to be open to modern ideas. He will also have the confidence of the parties in the Reichstag, and that will make it easier to ensure public support for our initiative.'

'Excellent!' said the Kaiser. 'I'll speak to Max immediately. Thank you, gentlemen, and now I think . . .'

'With respect, Sir,' Hintze interrupted him.

'Yes, what now?'

'Sir, if the Chancellor is to be replaced and the government to be reconstructed, I feel it is my duty also to tender my resignation as Foreign Secretary, to make way, perhaps, for one of the senior figures in the Reichstag.'

'What? You resign too? Out of the question, my dear Admiral. You cannot possibly desert the Foreign Office at this critical moment. I won't hear of it.'

'Don't forget,' Hindenburg said, 'that this is your peace plan.'

'But it's the Supreme Command that's pressing for it with such urgency,' Hintze retorted.

'Enough,' ordered the Kaiser. 'We have made our decision, and that's an end of it. We'll proceed as we have agreed.'

He stood up and the two military men jumped to attention.

'We must get back to Headquarters,' Ludendorff told Hindenburg. 'I need to find out what's happening. God knows where we are now.'

The Kaiser was heading for the door, but Hintze caught up with him, brandishing the paper on which he had been writing.

'Sir,' he said in low tones, 'I must have more if I am to act on the Supreme Command's request for an immediate approach to the enemy. Before we establish contact with the Americans, we have to make it clear that we have the support of the German people. I'm sure Prince Max will be more than acceptable as Chancellor. That will help a great deal. However, we must emphasize that he is also the choice of the people's representatives in the Reichstag. This is not a revolutionary step, Sir, as Count von Hertling was suggesting – not by any means. It is a matter of presenting ourselves in a favourable light.

'I have taken the liberty of drawing up a draft decree to settle the matter, and if you would sign it before you leave, it would be of enormous help to me and, of course, to the new Chancellor.' And he added slyly: 'It will also make it easier to act immediately on the advice of the Supreme Command, before there is any further deterioration in our military situation.'

The Kaiser read the document Hintze handed to him. It was addressed to Hertling and it began by accepting his resignation. Then it continued:

> I desire that the German people shall co-operate more effectively than heretofore in the determination of our country's fate.
>
> It is therefore my wish that men who are supported by the confidence of the people shall take part in wide measure in the rights and duties of the Government.
>
> I ask you to conclude your work by carrying on the business of government and initiating the measures

which I intend to introduce until I have found your successor.

I look forward to your proposals in this matter.

The Kaiser looked quizzically at his Foreign Secretary.

'It's my intention to return to Berlin tonight,' Hintze said. 'It would be enormously helpful if I might show this to Prince Max. I'm sure it will influence his decision about the Chancellorship. I could also use it to ensure the compliance of the Reichstag. More importantly, however, it will permit me to act quickly in regard to our peace proposal.'

The Kaiser looked over towards his generals, but they were absorbed in military matters.

'Very well.'

He strode back to the table, picked up the pen Hintze had been using and signed the draft decree. Then he left the room.

Hintze turned to Hindenburg and Ludendorff. 'Well, gentlemen, with any luck, you'll soon have your peace.'

'It can't come soon enough,' Ludendorff said.

*III*

———

A shadow passed over the open, honest face of Maximilian von Baden as the import of the words he had just heard seeped into his brain. The Prince was seated in the lofty, imposing sanctum of Admiral von Hintze at the Foreign Office in the Wilhelmstrasse.

'You can't be serious,' he said finally. 'An immediate appeal to the Americans for an armistice? That looks like the act of a defeated nation. We can't behave like the Austrians. The Entente will scent complete victory and treat us accordingly.'

'The Supreme Command insists on it,' Hintze told him. 'They say our military crisis is so acute that we cannot afford to wait.'

'That cannot possibly be true,' Prince Max protested. 'We would have to have been pushed all the way back to our own frontiers before it was that desperate. But as I understand it, on the Western Front we're now not very far from where we were at the end of 1914.'

'Nevertheless, the Supreme Command feels we shouldn't risk a dangerous breakthrough by the enemy. General Ludendorff seems to think it could happen at any moment, and he fears being forced into a disorderly retreat.'

'And what do you think?'

'I think we should have proposed a peace conference a month ago, when it became clear that our offensive was not going to take us right to Paris. At that stage, the Entente was in disarray and I'm convinced that if we had made an approach it would have given us an advantage. But the Supreme Command wouldn't hear of it.'

'And now?'

'Better late than never, I suppose. I mean, we all want an end to this damned war, don't we? I've been in touch with the Austrians inviting them not to proceed with their own proposal, but to join us in approaching President Wilson with a view to arranging a peace conference in Washington. I've also asked Turkey to take part. It seems to me to be the best course of action.'

Prince Max fiddled with his curling, dark moustache.

'And this,' he said, 'is the moment when the Kaiser wants me to become Chancellor?'

'You've seen his draft decree. He wants *you* to replace Hertling, because the Entente powers respect you, and he wants you to include the leaders of the Reichstag in a new Cabinet so that the change of regime is obvious to the Americans. That's something our old Bavarian friend would never have done, of course. Seek advice from people such as socialists? He could never bring himself to do it.'

'And the Supreme Command is happy with this approach? They're really willing to share power with politicians?'

'Absolutely. I heard it from their own lips.'

'Things must be worse than I thought,' Prince Max said.

'So you'll do it? You'll take the Chancellorship?'

'I don't know. To be frank, I would be very worried about rushing into this peace proposal you're talking about. I think I need more information before I come to a decision.'

'Very well. Why don't you discuss it with Hindenburg? Not

Ludendorff, by the way. I think he's on the verge of a breakdown. He doesn't seem to know what he's saying half the time.'

But it was Hindenburg who got in touch first. The very next morning Hintze arrived in the Wilhelmstrasse to find on his desk an urgent telegram from the field marshal, demanding news of progress with the reformation of the government and the message to be sent to the American president. The harassed Foreign Secretary telephoned Prince Max and read out the message.

*If by seven or eight o'clock this evening it is certain that Prince Max von Baden will form the government,* Hindenburg's telegram concluded, *I agree to postponement until tomorrow morning. If, on the contrary, the formation of the government should be in any way in doubt, I consider it desirable that the declaration should be issued to foreign governments tonight.*

'This is becoming ridiculous,' Prince Max said. 'Look, I'm going to see the Kaiser at the Château Neubois tomorrow. I'll take it up with him then. I presume you agree that nothing can be done until we've dealt with the question of the new government.'

Hintze did agree.

The following day, Wednesday, was 2 October. It was a cool, crisp evening when Prince Max was driven through the golden-leafed trees of the park at the château. There was an air of unreality about the place. Among these wild and beautiful mountains, the war seemed very far away.

He was greeted warmly by the Kaiser, who was anxious to

know when he would take up the duties of Chancellor. In Wilhelm's autocratic mind, decision was as good as action. It was also a comforting prospect to have one of his own kind, the heir to the Grand Duchy of Baden, ready to seize the reins of government at this critical moment. The honour of Germany would be in the safe hands of one brought up in its traditions, unlike those little politicians in the Reichstag, many of whom these days were actually working class. Certainly, it was important to have the support of the people – Wilhelm had actually fallen out with the old 'Iron Chancellor', Bismarck, on that very subject. But having the people run things was an entirely different matter.

'It's important that we act quickly,' he told the Prince. 'Hindenburg and Ludendorff are most anxious to conclude an armistice to preserve the integrity of our armies on the Western Front.'

'So I see,' Max said. 'As you know, I am not familiar with the details of our military position, but it seems to me there are grave dangers in acting out of a sense of panic.'

'Panic? What do you mean, panic? This is the considered opinion of the Supreme Command. You must be aware that we have been reflecting for some time as to the advisability of making an offer of peace. The Supreme Command judges that the moment has come to do it. We must not miss that moment.'

'I'm sure that is the case, Sir. But there is a difference between acting quickly and acting with careless haste. No doubt the Supreme Command has very good reasons for their attitude, but they are soldiers. There are political and diplomatic aspects to making any peace proposal that must be taken into account.'

'The advice of the Supreme Command is based on an assessment of our military position,' the Kaiser said firmly. 'This is a war, and in a war, military considerations must come first. We have to respond to the needs of our generals. They are the ones who are fighting the war and who know what is required.'

'Yes, of course, I appreciate that. But all I need is a week in order to formulate our peace proposal properly. What difference is a week going to make to our military situation?'

'It might make all the difference, according to Ludendorff. At present, we remain in a position of strength. We cannot risk damaging that position in any way. The Supreme Command believe we should act immediately to obtain an armistice and arrange a general peace conference. I am of the same opinion. I want you to go back to Berlin, make any political arrangements you and Hintze think are necessary, and make an approach to the American President through our embassy in Switzerland at the earliest possible opportunity. Now, what do you say? Will you do it? I'm depending on you.'

This, Prince Max thought, was all wrong. He knew that the British and the French, after four years of stalemate in which Germany had barely given an inch, were desperate for some sort of significant breakthrough. So far they had failed to achieve it militarily, and even their latest advances on the Western Front seemed to hold little prospect of definitively weakening German strength. But they might make that breakthrough politically, with Austria confessing its weakness,

Bulgaria out of the picture and the Turks under severe pressure in the Middle East. A German demand for a ceasefire, on top of all that, would play right into their hands. The consequences for Germany could be catastrophic. These were things the generals were not considering. Their reasoning was purely military, but as usual they had imposed their will on the Kaiser. They had to be stopped.

'Very well, Sir,' he said at last. 'I will go back to Berlin and form a new government. But the matter of the ceasefire and the peace conference will require further discussion.'

'There is no time for that,' the Kaiser insisted, his natural impatience beginning to show through again. 'You must do what the Supreme Command thinks is necessary.'

On his way back to the capital, Prince Max struggled to understand the motives of Hindenburg and Ludendorff. Could it be that Germany's position was very much worse than they were revealing? He doubted it. There were no signs of a general collapse, though there had clearly been reverses. But why was the Supreme Command so insistent that a ceasefire should be called immediately? He would have to find out. He dictated a telegram to Hindenburg.

The reply from Spa arrived the next morning. It was short and pointed: *The Supreme Command insists on its demand of Sunday 29 September that a peace offer to our enemies be issued at once.*

Now installed in the Chancellery, Prince Max was irritated by Hindenburg's arrogance. The field marshal appeared not to realize that the army was no longer in complete charge. As of today there was what, by German standards, was a democratic government in place which would determine the course of events. Admiral Hintze had been busy negotiating with the parties in the Reichstag, and even before his visit to the Kaiser, Prince Max had been able to assure himself that the leaders of the Centre Party, the Democratic Party and the Social Democrats would join his new Cabinet. The generals could no longer simply rely on bullying the Kaiser. They were now accountable to the politicians. The new Chancellor felt confident enough to summon a liaison officer from the Grand General Staff to brief him on the true state of military operations.

It was a Major von dem Bussche who arrived at the Chancellery. He had been in touch with his colleagues in Spa, and he seemed anxious to deliver a professional assessment.

'The attacks along the whole of the Western Front have obliged us to scatter our reserves,' the major said. 'We did have a plan to transfer some divisions from the Balkans, but seven of those have been immobilized by the events in Bulgaria. Meanwhile, the enemy has been able to deploy a great many more tanks than we thought he had available. Our troops have fought well, but the strength of our battalions has fallen to 540 men – and that's in spite of the fact that we have broken up twenty-two divisions for replacements. It seems we cannot count on any reinforcements. The Allies are certainly taking heavy casualties, but, thanks to the Americans, they are in a position to make good their losses.'

'Yes, yes,' said Prince Max, 'I can see we are in some difficulty. But what I want to know is what the military forecasts are. Is the situation really so bad that we have to call for an immediate ceasefire?'

The major fiddled with the stiff collar of his tunic and shifted his feet uneasily.

'Well, Sir, I think it is clear that the German army is still strong enough to withstand the enemy for months. We can still force the Entente to make sacrifices, and I believe we will still be able to win local successes.'

'Then why . . .'

'Sir, the Supreme Command believes – well, so far as anyone can judge – that there is no longer any possibility of forcing the enemy to make peace.'

'But we are not talking about *forcing* the enemy to make peace. We are talking about *asking* the enemy to make peace. I presume you understand the difference.'

Major von dem Bussche lowered his eyes towards his boots.

'Well, Sir, what seems to be happening . . . That is . . . To be honest, Sir, I spoke to one of our staff officers in Spa and he said . . . well, he said that everyone there seemed to have lost his self-control.'

It appeared to be precisely as Prince Max had suspected. For reasons which he could not yet work out, the Supreme Command had suddenly lost its nerve. Either that, or they were up to something and this demand for an immediate armistice was a ploy. This time he telephoned Hindenburg, but the bull-headed old field marshal was obdurate.

'The German army remains firm and we are repulsing all attacks,' Hindenburg said, 'but the situation is becoming more critical every day and it may well develop in a way that will force the Supreme Command to take measures that would have serious consequences.'

What exactly did he mean by serious consequences? the Prince asked.

'I mean that in certain circumstances, such as a general breach of our defensive line, the military necessity may be to withdraw to our own frontiers. Were that to happen, we would have no alternative but to ask for peace, but we would have been placed at a very serious disadvantage. What would we have to negotiate with?'

'I think,' Prince Max said wearily, 'that I'd better come back to Spa to settle this once and for all.'

Hindenburg and Ludendorff were waiting for him next morning, 4 October, when he arrived at the Hôtel Britannique.

'Have you brought the text of the message you intend to send to the Americans?' Ludendorff demanded.

'First, I have some questions, General.'

'My God! More questions? What does it take to get some action from the Chancellery?'

'General, I must have answers so that I can act accordingly. Do you, for instance, expect our defensive line to give way?'

'Let me make myself very clear, Chancellor. My assessment is that we are still in an honourable posture, but our line could be broken through at any moment. If that happened, it would be a most unfavourable time to propose an end to the fighting. We are playing a game of chance here.'

'You are certainly playing a very dangerous game, General. Do you not realize that if peace negotiations are begun under the pressure of a critical military situation, it might well lead in the end to the loss of Alsace and Lorraine, possibly our Polish provinces – even our colonies overseas?'

'If we don't begin moves towards an armistice now, we run the risk of losing them anyway. If we do achieve a ceasefire quickly, we'll be in a position where we might have to give up Belgium, but at least we'll be capable of defending our pre-war frontiers.'

'Well, let us suppose we are able to insist on maintaining our pre-war frontiers. How long would the army be able to hold them?'

'Indefinitely. We would withdraw in good order with the bulk of our arms and equipment, destroy any installations that might be of use to the enemy, paralyse railway lines and roads, and dare them to take us on at our own borders. Our army would be intact.'

Prince Max began dimly to understand what was in the general's apparently confused mind. Ludendorff had given up hope of defeating the Entente, and he was now considering the military options available to him. This pressure for a ceasefire was simply to buy him time. He was not interested in peacemaking, only in preserving his military strength. And it was obvious he did not appreciate the risk Germany would be running.

The Prince said carefully: 'General, if what you are really doing is preparing for an orderly withdrawal, would it not be better for us to emphasize our strength rather than our weakness by proposing a peace conference without seeking an armistice? We cannot know what conditions might be attached to an armistice. By suggesting a conference, we merely show that we are prepared to negotiate a settlement.'

'Not possible. The fighting must end. My troops desperately need a rest.'

'Give me forty-eight hours to get some diplomatic advice,' the Prince pleaded.

'Forty-eight hours!' screamed Ludendorff. 'The army can't wait another forty-eight hours.'

Hindenburg ushered the Prince out of the room as Ludendorff continued raving.

'You're going to have to do something about him,' Max said quietly. 'He's going to blow up.'

'It's just his nerves,' Hindenburg replied. 'He's under terrible strain. Anyway, I *have* done something. I've sent for a psychiatrist in case he completely loses control.'

The state in which he had found Ludendorff served only to confirm Prince Max in his opinion that any peace proposal, with or without an armistice, should be delayed, but when he returned to Berlin he discovered that matters had been taken out of his hands. His desk was littered with telegrams and messages from members of the Reichstag demanding an immediate approach to the enemy with proposals for an armistice and peace talks. He sent for Friedrich Ebert, the leader of the majority Social Democrats and now a member of the Cabinet. He was a plodding, unimaginative sort of man, but one who liked order and was unlikely to give way to panic.

'Has the Reichstag been robbed of its reason?' Prince Max demanded irritably. 'Suddenly the deputies seem to be behaving as if we've lost the war.'

Ebert's lugubrious face, with its heavy, drooping moustache, told its own story. 'Haven't we?' he retorted. 'According to Colonel Bauer, our only chance of avoiding disaster is to obtain a ceasefire at once.'

'Bauer? Who is Bauer?'

'Colonel Max Bauer. You must know him, Chancellor. He's on General Ludendorff's staff.'

Prince Max began to realize that he had been outflanked. The Supreme Command was still behaving as if it were the government.

'Colonel Bauer came to see us yesterday,' Ebert went on, 'and, I tell you, everyone was deeply shocked by what he had to say. We had no idea that things were going so badly. If we had known before what we know now, this war would have been over months ago. We've only managed to keep the people behind us because they believed we would win. Now . . .'

The little man shrugged his shoulders expressively.

'But we mustn't be panicked into starting a process we cannot control,' Prince Max said, almost desperately. 'If we issue a peace proposal now, the outcome will be in the lap of the gods. It's an enormous gamble. We could lose everything we believed we were fighting for.'

'I'm not panicking, Chancellor. But when the news of our true position comes out – as it will, of course, and soon – I'm afraid there could be serious trouble. People are already sick of the war, the casualties, the shortages, the misery. If they think there's no hope, I don't know what will happen. Already there are Bolsheviks mobilizing for a revolution. We have to give ordinary, decent people something to hope for. And all we can give them, it seems, is peace.'

'And your colleagues agree with you?'

'Absolutely. You have brought us into the government, and our opinion is that we should follow the advice of the Supreme Command and ask for a ceasefire and a peace conference with all speed. I understand that's what the Kaiser wants, too. You won't find support in the Reichstag for any other course of action.'

It was clear to Prince Max that he had no choice, in spite of his deep misgivings. With an overwhelming sense of trepidation, he composed a note to be sent to Washington through the Swiss government. Its terms, and the language in which they were couched, were as vague as he could make them:

> The German Government requests the President of the United States of America to take in hand the restoration of peace, acquaint all belligerent states with this request, and invite them to send plenipotentiaries for the purpose of opening negotiations. The German Government accepts the programme set forth by the President of the United States as a basis for peace negotiations.
>
> With a view to avoiding further bloodshed, the German Government requests the immediate conclusion of an armistice on land and sea and in the air.

President Wilson had portrayed himself as a sort of honest

broker, forced reluctantly to take up arms in this war, but only in order to achieve a just and lasting peace. He gave the impression of being an idealist, a man to whom philosophy was more important than politics. Well, Prince Max thought, we shall see now how far his idealism goes. For himself, he was less than optimistic.

The President's response, on 8 October, seemed to confirm the Prince's fears:

> The President of the United States deems it necessary to assure himself of the exact meaning of the note of the Imperial Chancellor.
>
> Does the Imperial Chancellor mean that the Imperial German Government accepts the terms laid down by the President in his address to the Congress of the United States on 8 January last, and in subsequent addresses, and that its object in entering into discussions would be only to agree upon the practical details of their application?
>
> The President feels bound to say, with regard to the suggestion of an armistice, that he would not feel at liberty to propose a cessation of arms to the governments with which the United States is associated against the Central Powers so long as the armies of those Powers are upon their soil.
>
> The good faith of any discussion would manifestly depend upon the consent of the Central Powers immediately to withdraw their forces everywhere from invaded territory.

> The President also feels that he is justified in asking
> whether the Imperial Chancellor is speaking merely for
> the constituted authorities of the Empire who have so
> far conducted the war.

That did not sound like peace without victory. Prince Max called Hindenburg and Ludendorff to Berlin for an urgent meeting at the Chancellery.

'Well,' he said, 'I warned you. What do you have to say now?'

Ludendorff, tired, anxious and defensive, tried to put on a brave face, but it soon became clear that he could not fully grasp the situation.

'I see no immediate danger for the Lorraine frontier,' he replied when the Chancellor asked him for his latest assessment. 'Our provinces west of the Rhine can be held for a long time yet. Once we are back on our own frontier the army will be able to repulse any enemy attack.'

He was apparently still assuming that an armistice would involve the withdrawal of his troops to Germany's pre-war frontiers, and that these would be defended if they were not respected by the Entente. Did that mean, Prince Max wondered, that the Supreme Command had given up hope of holding the position it still held on the Western Front, well to the west of the pre-war frontiers?

'Our present defensive line has not given way, has it?' he asked.

'Well, no,' said Ludendorff. 'The danger of a break-through, though, is always there. I'm not expecting it, but it's possible. It could have happened yesterday, for example – the whole thing hung on a thread.'

'None of this,' Max said acidly, 'is helping us to decide how we should reply to President Wilson's note.'

Ludendorff ran his fingers through his cropped grey hair.

'The point is this,' he said. 'I am anxious to save the army so as to be able to have it as a means of pressure during the peace negotiations.'

'So does that mean you think we should respond positively, in spite of the demands Wilson is making?'

'Oh, I don't think we can possibly give up German fortresses. And if the demand for evacuation includes Alsace and Lorraine – which I know the French regard as invaded territory – then we have to draw the line at that. It's a point of honour for us.'

Prince Max sighed. This was getting nowhere. Ludendorff did not seem to know what he wanted. Having forced the peace conference proposal only for the sake of a ceasefire to preserve his forces, he now showed himself prepared to reject armistice terms he found unacceptable and to continue fighting. Was he actually losing his mind? Something would have to be done about him. He turned to Hindenburg in an effort to make some progress.

'Field Marshal, how would you react if I suggested that we accept the American note at face value and agree to proceed on the basis of the President's statements it refers to? I mean, they're fairly vague and we should have plenty of room for manoeuvre. Obviously there's a problem with the demand for evacuation, if it means our giving up Alsace and Lorraine. But

I would counter that by suggesting the establishment of a joint commission to discuss the matter.'

'I think it's a good idea,' Hindenburg said. 'I'm not opposed to eventual withdrawal to our pre-war frontiers, provided we have the time to organize a methodical evacuation. That would give us time to regroup and rebuild the army.'

'Very well,' said Max, adding slyly: 'I'd like the agreement of the Supreme Command in writing.'

He was not going to let them outmanoeuvre him again, especially with Ludendorff apparently prepared to say anything that came into his head. The Chancellor had not forgotten Colonel Bauer. He was by no means convinced that they would get away with such a disingenuous reply to the Americans, but at least it bought him some time. He would use it to neutralize the Supreme Command, and then he really would have the freedom to develop the idea of a negotiated settlement of the conflict. He composed his second note to the Americans.

President Wilson's response, sent on 14 October, came as a thunderbolt:

> Any armistice will not be considered by a joint commission, but will be on the basis of conditions drawn up by the military authorities of the Allies – and those conditions must include absolutely satisfactory guarantees of the maintenance of the present military superiority of the armies of the United States and of the Allies in the field.
>
> The President feels he must add that no Allied government will consent to consider an armistice so

long as the armed forces of Germany continue the illegal and inhuman practices which they still persist in. Submarines are engaged in sinking passenger ships at sea. In their present enforced withdrawal, the German armies are pursuing a course of wanton destruction – cities and villages, if not destroyed, are being stripped not only of all they contain but often of their very inhabitants. The nations associated against Germany cannot be expected to agree to a cessation of arms while acts of inhumanity, spoliation and desolation are being continued which they justly look upon with horror and with burning hearts.

And finally, there can be no negotiations with the same authorities that have conducted this war in such a manner. The only way to achieve a merciful peace is for real change to emerge in the way Germany is governed and for negotiations to take place with a genuine representative of the German people.

Prince Max was appalled, though not entirely surprised. He had foreseen the possibility that any peace approach from Germany would be seen as a sign of weakness, but he had clung to the hope that the American President would maintain the even-handed approach to peace about which he had made so much noise. It was now clear that would not happen. If Wilson ever had been as high-minded as he pretended, he had obviously set aside his idealism and given way to the demands of the British and the French. The Supreme Command had led Germany into a trap.

Ludendorff was summoned to appear before the Cabinet in Berlin to explain himself. The ministers were astonished by the sudden change in his mood.

'We cannot accept these terms,' he declared. 'They are completely unjustified. Look, they did pierce our defensive line, it's true, but there has been no general breakthrough. My commanders in the field have fought very skilful defensive actions, and the Allies have now outrun their supply lines with their advance. The attacks are already slackening. The worst that can happen is that we shorten our defensive line again, to our own frontiers, and those we can defend.'

Prince Max finally lost patience with this general who seemed to swing from black despair to utter confidence without any reason.

'Are you mad?' he asked. 'Fifteen days ago, you demanded that a peace offer be made, and much against my will I was forced into doing what you said. Now you're telling me we can carry on fighting the war. Perhaps you could explain what has changed in fifteen days.'

All the arrogance of the Prussian officer class rose up in Ludendorff.

'I have already told you, Chancellor, that I consider an Allied breakthrough possible, but not probable. That's all I can say. I do not fear a breakthrough. If I'm given reinforcements, I look upon the future with confidence. If the Army holds for four weeks and winter arrives, we'll be out of difficulty. If our battalions were at normal strength, we wouldn't be in this position.

'If armistice negotiations were to begin, the undertaking to evacuate occupied territory would in itself constitute a real aggravation of our military situation. Yesterday and the day before, the enemy made little progress. Instead of meekly accepting conditions that are too harsh, we ought to say to our enemies, "Come and take them by force." '

This was too much for one of the other ministers at the meeting: 'But you, General, were the one who asked for the armistice in the first place. What are we to make of your attitude now?'

'You should have sent me reinforcements when I asked for them,' Ludendorff snarled.

One of his aides, Colonel Heye, cut in: 'When the General Staff decided to make the offer of an armistice, we believed that an honourable peace could be concluded. But we're ready to accept the decisive battle if the conditions imposed upon us touch our honour.'

Ludendorff added: 'I will take the responsibility if our refusal to accept these terms leads to a breakdown in negotiations with Wilson. You should be aware that I have telegraphed to my commanders in the east to organize the diversion of troops to the Western Front.'

'That does not reassure me, General,' said Prince Max coldly. 'The last time the question of reinforcements from the east was raised, you said it was an impossibility. I fear we have no choice but to accept the terms President Wilson has laid down.'

'That is not an option so far as the Supreme Command is concerned,' Ludendorff snapped. 'It would be a betrayal of the Fatherland, and your own position, Chancellor, would be untenable if you were to take such a step.'

'Then what am I to say?'

The note that went back to Wilson was largely composed by the Supreme Command:

Evacuation of occupied territory – *Germany will agree to withdraw from Belgium and France.*

The armistice – *Germany recognizes its terms must be left to the Allied military authorities, but the present relative strength on the fronts must be made on the basis of arrangements that will safeguard and guarantee it.*

Illegal acts committed by the German forces? *This is a war, and such destruction is normal and necessary in a retreat, as permitted by international law – however, instructions will be given that private property should be respected.*

Sinking of passenger ships – *yes, but these were not deliberate acts, though U-boat commanders have now been warned not to attack passenger vessels.*

The government? *The military is no longer in charge and legislation is being introduced to give the Reichstag direct power over decision-making.*

It was Ludendorff's last throw – but the Americans hurled it straight back in the Germans' faces.

'The Armistice will be concluded,' the President said, 'only if the military advisers of the Allied governments deem it possible from the military point of view. That means it will render impossible any resumption of hostilities by Germany and leave the Allies in a position to enforce any arrangements entered into.'

He had seen through the Supreme Command's crude tactic. But that was not all.

'The peoples of the world have and can have no confidence in the word of those who have hitherto been the masters of Germany,' his reply stated baldly. 'If the United States has to deal with the military masters and the monarchical autocrats of Germany now, or if it is likely to have to deal with them later in regard to the international obligations of the German Empire, it must demand not peace negotiations, but surrender.'

*Surrender*. It was the first time the dread word had been mentioned. That sent a shiver down Prince Max's spine. There must be no surrender. They must do whatever they had to do to placate the American President. There was still a chance that they could avoid complete humiliation – even if it meant that the past four years would have proved to have been a pointless sacrifice. He conferred with Friedrich Ebert and Matthias Erzberger, the young former journalist who now led the main Roman Catholic group in the Reichstag, the Centre Party. He was relieved to find them both in relatively optimistic mood.

'President Wilson won't let us down,' Erzberger said. 'We simply have to prove that we have turned our backs on the old ways, we've kicked out the Prussian military élite, we don't want to dominate Europe and we are ordering our affairs like any other democratic country. We can draw the President's attention to our Reichstag resolution of last year, when we said there should be a negotiated peace with no territorial gains. That will show it was only the discredited old regime that wanted to carry on the war.'

'You realize what you're saying, don't you?' said Prince

Max. 'The implication is that the Kaiser will have to be stripped of his power to govern.'

'Regrettably, yes,' Ebert agreed. 'We're getting reports from all over that people are demanding his abdication. They're blaming him for the war, but, more importantly, they're also blaming him for holding up the peace. They just want an end to it all now. They've ceased to care why we went to war in the first place.'

But General Ludendorff had not forgotten, and so far as he was concerned now, the war had to go on. With reserves finally on their way back from the east, he ordered the army to stand fast and appealed to the troops to signal their utter rejection of President Wilson's terms.

It was too much for Prince Max. He telephoned the Kaiser.

'This is not only utter folly,' the Chancellor said, 'but it is in direct opposition to the will of the new government. Ludendorff is acting on his own. He has gone mad. He will lead us into the abyss unless we put a stop to his lunacy.'

Ludendorff had threatened to remove the Chancellor, but it was Prince Max who had the commander-in-chief removed. The Kaiser dismissed him from his post on 26 October. Next day, Prince Max replied to President Wilson's latest missive. The necessary constitutional changes were being put in hand and the German government *now awaits proposals for an armistice, which shall be the first step towards a just peace, as the President has described it.*

With or without Ludendorff, the German armies were still in the field and still inflicting punishment on the enemy. The war had not been won, but neither had it been lost. There was

still, Prince Max judged, an honourable way out. The main
stumbling block was the Kaiser. The Chancellor would have
to go to Spa and persuade him to step down. But it would have
to wait. Max was feeling unwell, hot and cold by turns, with
moments of dizziness. There was a lot of influenza about, and
it would be unwise to make the journey into the mountains as
winter began to set in.

The Prince's temperature was not helped by the news he
received from Ebert the following afternoon, 29 October.

'There's a serious crisis in Kiel,' Ebert told him on the
telephone. 'The navy has mutinied.'

'My God! What's going on?'

'It appears that Admiral Scheer is as deranged as our former
commander-in-chief. He said he would be damned if he would
hand over his fleet to the enemy and he ordered the ships to
sea to attack the British. The sailors refused and Scheer
arrested their leaders. Now the rest of the sailors have armed
themselves and are holding out in the port. They've formed
what they call a local government and they're demanding the
abdication of the Kaiser and the immediate conclusion of an
armistice.'

'We must stop this before it goes any further,' Prince Max
said. 'I'll send the Secretary of State to Kiel to keep the
admiral quiet, but it would be as well if one of your Socialists
could go and sort out the sailors.'

'Gustav Noske's the man. They'll listen to him.'

By evening, Prince Max knew for certain that he had
influenza and he retired to his bed. But he could not rest and
took a sleeping draught. Next day, groggy from the medicine

and his fever, he did his best to keep in touch with events. Desperate for rest and relief from the aches and pains of the virus, he took regular doses of the soporific drug. On the Friday morning, 1 November, he did not wake up.

'He's in a sort of coma,' the hastily summoned doctor pronounced. 'He's taken an overdose. He'll be all right, but I'm afraid it will be some hours before he wakes up.'

The doctor was right. It was the early hours of Sunday morning before the Chancellor recovered consciousness, to learn, as his strength began to return, that Turkey and Austria had each signed armistice agreements with the Entente – and that Germany appeared to be on the brink of revolution. Throughout that day, and the next, the reports came in hour by hour:

*There is serious rioting in the streets of Hamburg. The signs are that it is being organized by Bolshevik elements.*

*Naval ratings in Wilhelmshaven have formed a political council and taken control of the base.*

*There are significant disturbances in Munich. The local authorities are in danger of losing control. Bolsheviks are to blame. They are forming workers' councils and demanding the foundation of a people's republic. Soldiers are joining in the demonstrations.*

Friedrich Ebert, now effectively in charge of the government, came to see the ailing Chancellor.

'We're in danger of losing control,' he said. 'People don't think we're moving quickly enough, and Bolshevik agitators are whipping them up. I hear reports that the Red forces are arming themselves for a full-scale revolution. They want a republic, like the Austrians have got now that the emperor has gone. You must persuade the Kaiser to abdicate, and quickly, or else we'll find the country being run by workers' soviets. It'll be anarchy.'

There was also a new message from President Wilson to the effect that the Allied governments had agreed on the military terms for an armistice and were ready to communicate them to representatives nominated by the German government.

'Erzberger is the man to lead our delegation,' Ebert said. 'He's got a head on his shoulders.'

'Organize it,' Prince Max said. 'We have no choice. I'll speak to the Kaiser about his abdication. I hope the generals aren't still filling his head with nonsense. Look where that has got us.'

'It's a sad day,' said Ebert. 'The end of the empire.'

The Kaiser did not seem to be making much sense when Prince Max got through to him on the telephone.

'I have my loyal troops round me,' he said grandly. 'I shall return to Berlin at the head of my army and personally restore order. Germany will remain intact.'

'The people won't support you, Sir. They are demanding a republic. They require you to abdicate. And unless you do, the Entente will not negotiate with us.'

'I am no longer to be Kaiser?'

'No, Sir. Your position is no longer tenable. You must allow me to announce your abdication.'

'But I may at least remain King of Prussia . . .'

Next day, 7 November, extreme left-wingers in Bavaria declared an independent republic and occupied the important military headquarters in Munich. Prince Max received the news at about midnight. All day he had been hearing that councils of workers and soldiers were setting themselves up as local authorities in cities right across the land. It seemed like the end of the world. Then came a telephone call from the General Staff.

'It's only a matter of time before sections of the army mutiny. Officers are reporting that their troops are prepared to go on defending Germany, but they will no longer fight for the Kaiser. It's chaos on the Western Front. Whole units are surrendering to the enemy.'

'Get in touch with your colleagues in Spa,' Prince Max said. 'They must impress upon the Kaiser that if he wishes to save Germany, he has to announce his abdication now. I've tried to make it clear to him, but, as always, he'll only listen to the officer class. They *must* make him do it.'

As he spoke, Matthias Erzberger and his delegation were arriving at a railway carriage parked in the forest of Compiègne, some forty miles north of Paris, and within shelling distance of the Siegfried Zone. They were met by the Allies' supreme commander, Marshal of France Ferdinand Foch.

'Gentlemen,' Foch said affably enough, 'what can I do for you?'

Erzberger said: 'We have come to receive your proposals with a view to arriving at the conclusion of an armistice.'

Foch, his *képi* at its accustomed jaunty angle, smiled through his substantial moustache.

'I'm afraid I have no proposals to make, gentlemen. We are quite happy to go on fighting.'

Erzberger was nonplussed. 'But we must have your terms,' he said. 'We cannot continue with this conflict.'

'Ah, so you are *asking* me for an armistice. That's an entirely different matter. You will find the terms we require in this document. You have seventy-two hours in which to signify your acceptance of them.'

He handed the document to the Germans and they withdrew to quarters prepared for them. As Erzberger quickly read the Allies' demands – evacuation of occupied territory, withdrawal from Alsace and Lorraine, the handing over of huge quantities of weapons and *matériel*, surrender of the fleet – his face turned deathly pale. This was not the just peace the American President had promised. It looked like abject and humiliating surrender.

# CHAPTER 2

# *The Man Who Won the War*

*I*

It was raining steadily in London that Monday evening, 11 November 1918, but nobody cared or even seemed to notice. Since eleven o'clock in the morning, the streets of the capital had been a heaving mass of people – singing, dancing, hugging each other, some even making ecstatic love in full view of the crowds. Except in the pubs and restaurants, all work had stopped the moment Big Ben had finished striking the hour of the armistice. At first, as the booming chimes were accompanied by explosions in the grey skies overhead, some people scuttled from offices and shops to shelter in cellars or underground railway stations. Then they remembered. This time the signal rockets were not warning of the approach of enemy aircraft. This time they meant that the war was over.

As the day went on, the celebrations became ever wilder, especially when thousands of soldiers, sailors and airmen, liberated from their duties for the day – or in many cases simply feeling liberated – arrived in the city to join in the festivities. Buses were commandeered to become the venues for mobile champagne parties. Anyone in uniform was seized, hoisted aloft on shoulders, subjected to ordeal by handshake, made to dance and sing, treated endlessly to food and drink and kissed, it seemed, by every woman in the street.

Young Captain Moody, of the Royal Welch Fusiliers, was shocked by the state of abandon among the female population he encountered in Soho. He did his best to avoid the women of all ages who roamed the streets in groups, looking for servicemen on whom to unleash uninhibited and not always comfortable displays of affection. But he could not escape the press of men who wanted to express their admiration for the army, and before long his hand was swollen and sore from the number of times it had been shaken.

With three other officers, Moody retreated to a French restaurant in Wardour Street, where they hoped they might be served dinner. After the fish course, however, all thought of food was abandoned as the over-excited – but still businesslike – proprietor pressed champagne on his customers so that they might drink repeated toasts to the *entente cordiale* between Britain and France. The officers were impressed by the fact that nobody expected them to pay for anything: they were the honoured guests of the grateful civilians.

As the wine flowed, the singing began, the French competing with two Scottish officers in Moody's party who offered ear-splitting renditions of every Highland ballad they could remember. Then the tables were pushed aside and the increasingly inebriated customers began to dance. It was all too much for the hungry soldiers, who forced their way out into the street, only to find the crowds even more dense than they had been before. One of the Scots, much the worse for drink, was last seen by Moody disappearing through the throng as he performed a Highland fling on the roof of a limousine. The second Scotsman simply disappeared, while the third officer threw himself enthusiastically into the task of teaching parade-ground drill to a group of policemen.

By now desperate for something to eat, Moody made his way to the grill room at the Piccadilly Hotel, but as revellers danced on tables and challenged each other to hurdle races over chairs, all he was offered was more champagne.

In Trafalgar Square, revellers led by a group of Canadian soldiers scoured the surrounding streets for anything combustible with which they would build a huge bonfire. To give it a good start, they drove a lorry to the base of Nelson's Column and set the vehicle ablaze, greeting the sight with a deafening cacophony from whistles, dustbins, an array of musical instruments and everything else that could be used to make a noise.

The din carried along The Mall to Buckingham Palace – where earlier in the day King George V had appeared on the balcony before a rapturous, flag-waving throng – and down Whitehall to Westminster Abbey and Parliament Square, where the mood of celebration was considerably more muted. In the House of Commons that afternoon, there had been a solemn silence as the Prime Minister, David Lloyd George, officially announced the signing of the armistice.

'At eleven o'clock this morning,' he said, 'came to an end

the cruellest and most terrible war that has ever scourged mankind. I hope we may say that thus, this fateful morning, came to an end all wars. This is no time for words. Our hearts are too full of gratitude to which no tongue can give adequate expression.'

It was not often that words failed the little Welshman, the country solicitor whose agile brain and skills of oratory had propelled him to the realization of a boyhood dream, and ultimately to the highest office in the land. But on this day, Lloyd George's heart was full of more than gratitude, and he had no vocabulary with which to express the confusion of his thoughts and feelings. The Members of Parliament who followed him across the square for a service of thanksgiving in St Margaret's Church, next to the Abbey, noticed that the Prime Minister's customary energy and ebullience seemed to have deserted him. He appeared strangely down-cast, and almost indifferent to the congratulations showered upon him for the leadership that had driven the nation to victory. Afterwards, they gossiped about it in the corridors of the House.

'He's not long recovered from the influenza, of course,' said one MP. 'That takes it out of you.'

In September, Lloyd George had fallen victim to an especially virulent strain of the disease that was now sweeping the world, killing people in their hundreds of thousands from Melbourne to New York. He had recovered reasonably quickly from the worst symptoms, but they had left their mark.

'You can see it in his face,' the MP went on. 'His eyes have a sort of hooded look and they're all black underneath. And, you know, I'd swear his hair and moustache are whiter than they were before.'

'It's the strain, too, I expect,' a colleague said. 'Don't forget, things were very bad when he took over in 'Sixteen. I mean, we've all been through hell, but him more than most. Imagine if we'd lost!'

Others were less charitable. 'Credit where it's due,' put in one of the small number of Labour Party representatives in the House of Commons, 'but he could get away with behaving like a dictator while the war was on, couldn't he? Ride rough-shod over Parliament, and never mind the voters. It's all changed now we've won. He's going to have to face the music. And things are going to be very different from now on, you mark my words. People didn't fight this war for nothing. They won't just go back to the way things were before, bowing the knee to the ruling class. Lloyd George is going to have to watch himself, and he knows it. No wonder he's a bit down in the mouth. Whatever else he might be, he's not stupid.'

There were howls of disapproval from most of his hearers, but an elderly Conservative MP intervened in support.

'I wouldn't bet on his staying prime minister unless I got very good odds,' he said. 'After all, it was my party that put him in the job over the heads of his own party. Oh, he's done very well, I admit. Perhaps we wouldn't have won the war without him. But don't forget, he counted on us while the half of the Liberal Party he'd turned his back on was in opposition. Now, of course, there'll be a general election and *we'll* decide what happens to him. I can't see him being able to make it up with the Liberals after the way he's treated them.'

The Labour man laughed. 'Don't be so sure *you'll* be in charge,' he said. 'After this war, everything's going to change, and you lot won't escape. Anyway that Lloyd George is a tricky little devil at the best of times. I've no doubt he'll have something in mind to outsmart you Tories. It's the voters he won't be able to get round.'

But it was not his own Liberal Party, or the Conservative Party, or the electorate that weighed on the mind of Lloyd George during that momentous day. Of course, he felt enormous relief, and a sense of satisfaction that he had held his nerve throughout what must surely be the worst months of his life.

'I'm the only one of them who has been closely involved in the conduct of this war from the day the first shot was fired until the signing of the armistice,' he said to himself as he made the short car journey from the Houses of Parliament to the Prime Minister's residence in Downing Street. 'I saw it through. That must count for something, by God!'

Yet the thought did nothing to lift the eerie depression that had settled on him so soon after the news had been delivered, shortly before seven o'clock in the morning, that four years of unimaginable bloodshed would cease abruptly within a few hours. Curiously, he had felt the thrill of victory in the days leading up to the armistice, but now that it had actually come to pass, there was only a sense of anticlimax, of lethargy, uncertainty.

'I'm so tired, *cariad*,' he told his wife, in Welsh, in the seclusion of his private quarters at 10 Downing Street. 'Four years and more of devoting all our energies, all our intelligence, to the work of destruction and pain. It seems like a nightmare.'

Margaret Lloyd George had spent little time with her husband in London. Though she supported him as best she could, she was not a political wife. Her home in North Wales and her responsibilities to her two sons and three daughters always came before the demands of a career that in many ways offended her deep Methodist sensibilities. But she had been at Downing Street during those final, frantic days when victory had at last seemed assured, and she had been beside him in the corner bedroom on the first floor, overlooking St James's Park, when the messenger banged on the door to rouse them with the confirmation from Paris that the armistice had been signed.

'And we never thought the war was going to happen at all, did we?' Margaret said.

Lloyd George shook his head.

'No, we didn't. I remember what I said – it keeps coming back to me – at the height of the war fever in 'Fourteen, when the Austrian ultimatum had gone to Serbia, and the Russians and the Germans had got involved, and the French were rattling their sabres. I said the government was confident that we could solve the problems facing us with common sense, patience and goodwill. Common sense, patience and goodwill, eh? We haven't seen much of any of those things in the last four years.'

He shivered.

'And I . . . I turned out to be the butcher's boy who led the lambs to slaughter.'

'You mustn't blame yourself.'

'No. No, you're right, of course. I had to play my part, even though it was a terrible burden and it caused me pain to do it. But we're all to blame, you know, all of us who had any authority. I'm still horrified when I think about it. And I can't stop thinking about it, today of all days. Yes, we can say we've won the war, but really what we've done is stagger along a path stained with blood, recklessly, stupidly, barely able to avoid catastrophe and saved in the end mainly by the incredible folly of our enemies.'

Margaret was well used to his flights of rhetoric.

'But we did win,' she said firmly. 'And thank God I still have my Richard and my Gwilym at the end of it.'

'Amen to that, certainly. But there are too many mothers and fathers whose sons aren't coming back, too many wives who'll never see their husbands again. Thanks to the so-called military experts – *inexperts* they really were. They hadn't an idea of what they were doing. You know, I believe they were actually trained *not* to master the methods of modern warfare.'

'You're in a very black mood this afternoon,' Margaret said.

It was a mood that continued well into the evening, despite the growing clamour of revelry elsewhere. Far from celebrating, the Prime Minister had arranged a quiet dinner for a few of his close colleagues. Among the first to appear was Winston Churchill, like Lloyd George a politician to whom party meant less than policy. Once a Conservative MP, he called himself a Liberal now, and had held Cabinet office in pre-war governments, but it seemed to be the war, and the coalition government it had produced, that brought out the best in him. Lloyd George had made him Minister of Munitions, and it was he who had done most to promote the tank as the decisive weapon it had proved to be.

'The scenes out there are absolutely extraordinary,' Churchill said. 'The British are a remarkable people. After all they have been through, all they have sacrificed . . . They are so brave, and so generous. In spite of everything, they never lose faith in their country, they never lose sight of its destiny. And in the end they forgive us our mistakes.'

'So it seems,' Lloyd George said. 'But there was nothing I could say to them. When the hour had finished striking, the whole of Whitehall was thronged. Where they had found the flags, I don't know. And the cheering . . .'

'I know. There were at least a score of them sitting on my car at the time.'

'They blocked Downing Street, chanting my name, demanding to see me. I went to the window . . . I waved . . . the cheering was deafening. They wanted me to say something. I thought to open the window . . . But there was nothing I could say to them. My mind went back to August 1914.'

'The ultimatum to Germany? That's a day I'll never forget.'

'There were multitudes in the streets then, too – cheering, waving their flags, urging us on to war. Perhaps if they had known the horrors that lay before us . . .'

'But they have borne every one of them,' Churchill said, 'and they have emerged victorious. Bloodied, but unbowed. Their courage didn't fail them. And they know we didn't fail them.'

They were in the State Dining Room, Lloyd George sitting close to Andrew Bonar Law, the Unionist Party leader who had been responsible for the formation of the wartime coalition government, and who had done more than anyone to press Lloyd George into becoming prime minister in the dark days of 1916, when defeat had seemed a distinct possibility. For him, Lloyd George reflected, this was a day of particular poignancy, with two sons dead on the Western Front. But they spoke little of the war itself as they dined, only of the armistice.

'It seems hardly possible that something which went on for so long should have ended so suddenly,' one of the wives said.

'The French didn't believe it would,' said Lloyd George. 'But I could see what was happening almost as soon as the Germans sent their first note to Wilson in October.'

Clemenceau, the French Prime Minister, Lloyd George went on, had been afraid that the American President – who had not consulted the Allies until after he had replied to the first German note – would be most concerned with pursuing his idea of peace without victory and would therefore be inclined to resist demands from the British and the French that he considered inappropriate.

The French had wanted to allow matters to take their course, believing that if the rest of the Allies interfered at that early stage, laying down their own conditions for an armistice, they would provoke a rift with the Americans and thereby play into the Germans' hands. Lloyd George, however, with his intuitive grasp of political realities, had understood that Germany must have realized she could not win the war, and he had been anxious to exploit the initiative that Prince Max's note offered to the Allies. The Prime Minister had also immediately seen through the ploy with which the Germans had hoped to win President Wilson's support. Of course they would agree to evacuation – Lloyd George would have done the same himself in their situation – because that would actually have placed them at an advantage. Secure behind their own frontiers, they would have been justified in saying they had acted in accordance with Wilson's Fourteen Points, and, from the point of view of the Allies, four terrible years of war would have been wasted.

'That's why,' Lloyd George concluded, 'we had to lay down our own conditions for a ceasefire right from the start, whether the Americans liked them or not.'

Bonar Law said: 'We can't deny, though, that the eventual armistice terms were severe. Much more severe than the Germans would have expected from their exchanges with President Wilson.'

'That was the point, surely,' Lloyd George replied. 'We had to drive home a lesson to the Germans, and we had to make sure they were in no position to resume the conflict.'

'Well,' Bonar Law mused, 'I'm sure we were perfectly justified in demanding that they surrender their fleet, as well as their war material on land. But I can't say I was particularly happy with the French insistence that they occupy part of the Rhineland, or with their claim for financial reparations. Foch was most particular about the Rhineland business. I thought we were running a risk that the Germans wouldn't sign.'

Lloyd George shook his head. 'With Austria and Turkey

gone, they had no choice. But in any case, as soon as they made the appeal to Wilson, it was clear to me that they couldn't go on.'

'Nevertheless,' Churchill put in, 'they fought to the bitter end.'

'Defeat,' Lloyd George said, 'always comes as a surprise to the defeated.'

The meal over, Margaret Lloyd George rose and led the women into the drawing room. The men turned to their brandy and cigars.

'You know,' Churchill said, 'the awful thing is that we have ended the war more or less where we started it, militarily speaking.'

There was silence for a moment while they contemplated this thought.

'Four and a half years,' Churchill went on. 'Four and a half years of stalemate. Four and a half years of the Germans resisting everything the rest of the world could muster against them.'

'It hardly bears thinking about,' said Law, remembering his dead sons.

'And we kept saying, back in 'Fourteen, that it would all be over by Christmas.' It was the Lord Chancellor, the celebrated lawyer F. E. Smith, who voiced the thought.

'And so it might have been,' Churchill said in his characteristically ponderous way. 'If we had seized the opportunity that was presented to us, it would have been over in six weeks.'

They looked at him quizzically. It was, he explained, the

battle of the Marne, north of Paris, in September 1914 that had really decided the outcome of the war. After that battle, which had involved French troops being sent from the capital in taxis, there had no longer been any prospect of a German victory – and the Germans had known it. Their commander, General Moltke, had told the Kaiser on 10 September that the war was lost, and from that moment on the only question had been which side could support the stalemate longest.

'Four years of senseless slaughter,' Churchill said distantly. 'The question that will puzzle posterity is "Why?"'

'Today, however,' Law broke in, somewhat impatiently, 'there are more pressing questions. The general election, for one.'

That was another reason for Lloyd George's low spirits. Not that he would normally have been worried about the prospect of an election. Since his arrival in Parliament as the improbably young Liberal Party Member for the North Wales constituency of Caernarvon Boroughs more than twenty-five years earlier, his career had followed an unbroken upward path. But the manner of his arrival at the summit, the apparent betrayal of the leader of the Liberal Party, whom he had replaced as Prime Minister, had left him dangerously exposed in Parliament, if not among his constituents. The gossips in the House of Commons had been quite correct: his survival in Downing Street was by no means assured. His hour of triumph might well turn out to be the eve of his downfall – and Lloyd George's uncanny knack of taking the political temperature made him well aware of that.

He said: 'The armistice makes it more problematical than it

was even a week ago, when we last spoke about it.'

'Not at all,' countered Law. 'We have just won the war, after all. The popularity of the government could hardly be greater.'

'Along with the diversity of its political opinions,' Churchill observed wryly. 'Conservatives, Unionists, Labour, a sizeable slice of the Liberal Party . . .'

'It is a coalition,' Law said sharply. 'It is a government of national unity.'

Churchill smiled mischievously. 'Let us hope the electorate is similarly united in its view. Though I somehow doubt it will be. Nobody has had the opportunity to vote since 1910. It will be a happy release. And voters are nothing if not fickle.'

'There are many Conservatives who say that about you, Winston,' Lloyd George said. 'I had the devil's own job getting them to agree to your taking over the Ministry of Munitions. Tories have long memories.'

'So, no doubt, do Liberals, Prime Minister,' Churchill replied. 'It will be interesting to note the attitude of the members of our party who have set themselves up in opposition since Mr Asquith was removed.'

'I don't think,' Law said, 'that is a matter we need trouble ourselves about. The important thing is that national unity must be preserved. It has seen us through the war. It has brought us to victory. Our message to the electorate will be that it is the best means, the only means, of guaranteeing the peace and undertaking the reconstruction that everyone will agree is necessary. Those who wish to oppose us must accept the electoral risk.'

'I agree with you that we must have a mandate to do those things,' Lloyd George said. 'And since we have been responsible for formulating the aims of the struggle against Germany, it's only right and proper that we should be trusted to ensure that they are fully achieved. But I don't quite see how we're going to fight an election on that basis. You and I can agree a programme, but the people want to know who they're voting for. They have party loyalties. We can't just put up candidates with a label that says "Coalition" round their necks.'

'The British voter won't react well to some sort of popular front,' said Churchill. 'It smacks too much of socialism.'

'And talking of socialism,' Lloyd George added, 'what's to be done about the Labour Party? I can't see them agreeing to any programme the coalition might put forward, so I suppose we'll be fighting them at the election. That means the coalition can no longer present itself as a government of national unity.'

It had been important to bring the Labour Party into the wartime coalition government, even though it was a new political grouping and its representation in the House of Commons was small. The war effort depended on the workers as much as on the troops, and Labour was establishing itself as the workers' party, supplanting the much older and now considerably less radical Liberal Party. Labour's co-operation had been somewhat grudging – the party had a strong pacifist element – and Lloyd George had been more comfortable with the Tories he had once denounced and opposed so vehemently. The result was that neither side completely trusted him, and the feeling was mutual. He now had some delicate political calculations to make.

Bonar Law said he had no doubt that Labour would go its own way, and that would actually make it easier for the other coalition parties to unite in their appeal to the electorate. Their candidates could still present themselves as representatives of their own parties, but it must be made clear that what they stood for was a continuation of the government of national unity that had successfully steered the country through the war. That obviously meant Lloyd George would continue as prime minister.

'I don't know that I like that idea very much,' Lloyd George said. 'You would have the spectacle of Liberal standing against Liberal, those who have supported the coalition and me, and the others supporting Asquith. I don't want to go down in history as the man who split the Liberal Party.'

'Do you think a reconciliation is possible?'

Lloyd George shrugged.

'Well,' said Law, 'it may be rather unfair on Asquith and his supporters that we should fight the election on a "We Won the War" platform, but as you know only too well, they have spent the past two years doing their best to embarrass, undermine and discredit the government. I have no doubt that they would continue to do so. If you want to win the peace, I can't see that you have any choice but to oppose them.

'After all, if people really want Asquith back as prime minister, they'll have the opportunity to vote for him . . .'

But how, asked Lloyd George, were the voters to distinguish between Liberals who supported the coalition and those who wanted to bring it down?

The candidates approved by the coalition, Liberal,

Conservative and Unionist, would receive an endorsement, Law said – a letter signed by Lloyd George and himself that would identify them as standing officially on behalf of the government. All the parties would agree that they would not put forward other candidates of their own to oppose those endorsed. In that way, the government parties would be clearly distinguished from the opposition parties.

In effect, thought Lloyd George, the government candidates would indeed be wearing a label saying 'Coalition'.

He said: 'Do you think your party would accept that arrangement?'

'I think,' Law replied, 'that I can persuade them – with your help. Can you say the same for your supporters in the Liberal Party?'

Later that evening, Churchill seemed deep in thought, as he and his wife travelled home in their car.

'Is it settled about the election?' Clementine Churchill asked.

'It will certainly happen next month,' Churchill said. 'And, you know, whoever wins, I have the feeling that it won't be Lloyd George. Even if it turns out that we do have him back as prime minister. Oh, he'll blow this way and that, as he always does, but I don't think he'll be able to escape the trap that is being set for him.'

On 11 November 1918, the day Matthias Erzberger reluctantly signed the armistice, Germany had no government worth the name. Erzberger took his instructions from a Council of People's Representatives hastily cobbled together by Friedrich Ebert, the Social Democratic Party leader, who had suddenly found himself apparently in charge of a republic with no head of state, no constitution and no recognized executive or legislative authorities.

Three days earlier, Prince Max of Baden had called Ebert to see him at the Chancellery. Gustav Noske had settled the naval mutiny in Kiel partly by legitimizing the sailors' attempt at self-government, and as a result, workers' and soldiers' councils had sprung up all over the country. But not all were subject to military discipline, and many began to make plans to combine themselves into a provisional national government. One of the most militant councils was in Berlin, and the city was frequently paralysed by mass protests against the old regime that was now seen to have disastrously let down the German people.

'I'm resigning as Chancellor,' Prince Max told Ebert. 'There's nothing else I can do. The country is on the verge of revolution, and I will inevitably be associated with the Kaiser's government. It's up to you now, as majority leader in the Reichstag. The people demand to be heard, and you are their representative.'

'You mean . . . ?' Ebert began.

'I'm handing over to you the office of Chancellor,' Prince Max said. 'You must accept it so that there is an obvious and orderly transfer of power from the authority that is now discredited. Germany is relying on you to prevent this present slide towards revolution and anarchy.'

'But what about the Kaiser?' Ebert asked.

*The Kaiser is a scoundrel! Down with the Kaiser!* roared the mob in the streets outside.

Prince Max pointed towards the window of his office.

'There's your answer,' he said. 'The people no longer want the Kaiser. You must take control of the country before the revolutionary elements have a chance to do so. Once order has been re-established, you must take steps to determine the constitution of the state, including the position of the monarchy. For the moment, it must be made clear that the Kaiser is no longer head of state – but at the same time, there must be no appearance of a breakdown of government authority. Do you agree?'

Ebert did agree, and the next morning, 9 November, Prince Max handed him the seals of office.

'The new Chancellor,' he announced, 'will form a provisional administration to govern the country until elections can be arranged and a constituent assembly called to consider the future constitution of the Reich. In that regard, I wish to make it clear that the Kaiser and the Crown Prince intend to renounce their rights to the throne of Germany.'

In fact the Kaiser, at that stage, intended no such thing. He was still conferring with his generals at Spa, asking whether the army remained loyal.

'The army,' one of the staff officers told him, 'remains loyal to Germany. The army might be willing to continue to fight for Germany. What is not certain, Your Majesty, is that the army is willing to fight for the Kaiser.'

*Republic!* shouted the crowds outside the Reichstag building in Berlin. *We want a republic! Down with the Kaiser!*

Inside the Reichstag, the now Chancellor Friedrich Ebert was conferring with the members of his Cabinet.

'We must move quickly,' said one of the leaders of the moderate Socialist Party in Ebert's coalition, Philipp Scheidemann. 'Bavaria has already declared independence from the Reich, and the Berlin council of soldiers and workers is trying to organize elections across the country tomorrow. If they go ahead, we'll have lost control. We must make some sign to the people that we can give them what they want – and what they want is a republic.'

'But we can't just declare a republic,' Ebert protested. 'Without elections we'd have no mandate to govern, and if we throw over the old constitution we'll have no legitimate claim to be the government.'

'We're the people's representatives, duly elected,' said Scheidemann, 'and that's what gives us legitimacy. It's the banner under which we can form a provisional government.'

An hour later, Scheidemann was addressing the vast, noisy throng in the Reichstagplatz. Germany was entering a new era, he said, a time in which the people would truly have their say in government. If they would support the new Council of People's Representatives, they could hold the country together and protect it from the threat of a Bolshevik coup.

Then, above the clamour, he shouted dramatically, if inaccurately: 'The Kaiser has abdicated. Long live the great German republic!'

In Spa, the news was brought to Kaiser Wilhelm that same evening. Relieved of responsibility for the decision, he seemed ready to accept his fate.

'Have my train made ready for tomorrow morning,' he ordered. 'I must return to Berlin.'

His generals turned out to see him off at the little station in Spa – but it was not towards Berlin that the Kaiser was making his way. He had secretly issued other orders, and at a deserted railway halt in the Belgian countryside, he left the train and got into a car, which took him by the shortest route to the Dutch border. The officials at the frontier post were stunned to find the German emperor seeking entry in this clandestine way, and there was a delay of several hours while they consulted their government. Finally, word came back from The Hague that Holland was prepared to offer sanctuary, and Kaiser Wilhelm II disappeared into the obscurity of exile.

It was 10 November, and Matthias Erzberger had been at Rethondes, in the forest of Compiègne, for two days, desperately trying to persuade the enemies of his country to make some concessions in the punitive document they had presented to him. The seventy-two hours he had been given in which to accept the armistice were fast running out, and he had received precious little help from Berlin.

'I've managed to gain some small reductions in the armaments they expect us to hand over,' he reported, 'but on the main question of the blockade, they won't move. The most they will say is that they will try to ensure us adequate supplies of food for the winter.'

But this new provisional government in Germany seemed curiously uninterested in the details of the surrender that was now facing it. The message came back: *Just sign it. We have no alternative.*

So, at five o'clock on the morning of 11 November, Matthias Erzberger signed his name on the armistice dictated by the victors who had never actually achieved victory to the vanquished who had never actually been defeated.

'A nation of seventy million people is suffering,' he said when the fateful deed had been done. 'But it will not die.'

Marshal Foch, the Allies' supreme commander, regarded him coolly.

'*Très bien*,' he said.

*II*

—

General Sir Douglas Haig was becoming ever more irritated with the French. The commander-in-chief of the British armies on the Western Front had abandoned the railway carriage that had served as his operational command post and was now installed at the Château Beaurepaire, the army's general headquarters in the broad valley of the River Oise, a few miles west of the Forest of Compiègne, where the armistice had been signed. The war was over, but now it was beginning to seem as if in some ways the fighting had been the easy part. The politics in which the dour, uncommunicative Scottish general now found himself embroiled was significantly harder to come to grips with.

'Marshal Foch now wants to forbid the German postal service to function,' one of Haig's staff officers reported, after a visit to French headquarters to discuss Foch's plan for an Allied army of occupation in the Rhineland.

Haig clapped a hand to his forehead in a gesture of exasperation.

'Why can't they understand that it's in our interest to return to peacetime conditions at once?' he demanded. 'They seem determined to make Germany our enemy for years to come.'

'I believe you're right, Sir,' another officer said. 'Looking at these regulations the French have drawn up for the occupied zone, it seems that the only possible way for a German to avoid contravening one or other of the new laws will be to stay in bed. And even then he'll only escape provided he doesn't snore.'

Typical of Foch, thought Haig. He had never liked the Frenchman's manner, especially since he had been made the Allies' supreme commander. One had to admire him as a soldier, of course, but as a man ... the unwarranted arrogance, the insufferable self-confidence, the absolutely firm conviction that he was always right, and everyone else wrong. And, like all Frenchmen, he had to make such a big production out of everything. Haig knew that, with the fighting over, the conscripts among his vast army were already growing restless and wanting to go home as soon as possible – yet, if Foch had his way, large numbers of them would have to be sent off to Germany to act as policemen for this ridiculous French scheme.

The general stood up and went to look out of the window. The heavy frosts of recent days had broken and the weather had turned much milder, almost unseasonably so. There was even some weak sunshine filtering through the bare trees in the grounds of the château. This would cheer up the men somewhat, but it would do nothing to quell a disturbing mood that some officers had noticed in the ranks. It was his artillery commander who first drew it to his attention.

'I've seen a lot of it among the wounded men in particular. Frankly, it's the sort of talk I can only describe as republicanism. Even Bolshevist, perhaps. I suppose a lot of it has to do with the fact that our victory seems to have got rid of the monarchies in Germany and Austria. Some of the men are saying things like, "Well, why should *we* still have a king, then?" – and complaining about how costly it is to maintain a monarchy.'

The field officers were doing their best to keep the troops busy in this period of strange half-life, but hundreds of thousands of soldiers with no fighting to do – and so many of them civilians, in reality – presented serious problems of discipline. Haig had already been told of what amounted to a local mutiny back home, at the embarkation port of Shoreham in Sussex, and reports from the big camps in the Pas de Calais spoke of growing resistance to the ordinary business of army life.

'Perhaps it would be a good idea,' Haig suggested to his private secretary, 'if I were to publish the correspondence I have had with the King since the armistice. Some signs of real appreciation from on high might help to knock this revolutionary chit–chat on the head, before it goes too far.'

The King had indeed been a rock throughout it all, unlike most of the confounded politicians who thought they knew better than the soldiers how to fight a war. In contrast to them, George V had shown unwavering confidence in his generals and their troops. 'I'll support you through thick and thin,' he had told Haig during the anxious days of 1917, when it seemed that everything the general tried ended in costly failure and there had been a serious conspiracy against him among the War Cabinet. Lloyd George had even favoured a damned Frenchman over his own commander-in-chief.

It was particularly gratifying for Haig, then, in the hour of his triumph, to hear directly from the King.

'I wish to express to you personally my grateful thanks,' the telegram said. 'It is through your military knowledge and ability, combined with patient resolve, that you have led the British armies to victory.'

The general had responded as elegantly as a man might who was not much given to self-expression. He had, he said, been supported wholeheartedly by his troops in a way no commander had ever enjoyed before. But 'the confidence which Your Majesty has been so graciously pleased to place in me during so many trying years of war did much to strengthen and inspire me to do my duty so that I have been able to endure unto this victorious end'.

Making this exchange public, Haig told the secretary, would encourage the troops to feel proud of themselves for the way in which they had served king and country.

'But I suppose you'd better check with the Palace first, to make sure it's all right.'

It was some time before the reply came back. 'Colonel Wigram has just telephoned me from the Palace, Sir,' the secretary told Haig. 'He apologizes for the delay, but he thought it better to take up the matter with the King's private secretary before giving an answer. It seems the view is that it would be better not to publish. Lord Stamfordham thinks the Prime Minister might think it unconstitutional for the King to have wired his commander-in-chief in such terms entirely on his own behalf.'

'Unconstitutional!' Haig exclaimed. 'What the devil do they mean, unconstitutional?'

'Well, Sir, the King is bound to act only on the advice of his ministers. And, er, there is a feeling that in present circumstances it might be rather unwise to emphasize the King's support for *you* in so public a fashion.'

'Oh, what a cur the man is!'

'I beg your pardon, Sir?'

'Lloyd George, of course. He's behind this. Grubbing for votes, no doubt. I hear they're to have an election any day now. You know, every time I'm with that damned fellow I find myself unable to resist a feeling of distrust. Bonar Law always struck me as being a straightforward, honourable man, completely honest. But Lloyd George! Oh, yes, always anxious to be agreeable and pleasant, but underneath it all cunning, shifty and utterly unreliable.'

The antipathy was mutual. In London, Lloyd George had also received a missive from the King, and it had sent him into a fury.

'An earldom!' he roared. 'The King wants me to offer the damn fool an earldom!'

Perhaps fortunately, the only person within earshot was the Prime Minister's personal secretary. She was an attractive, intelligent ash blonde, not especially pretty, but with gentle grey eyes and a kind mouth that looked always as if it were about to break into a smile. Frances Stevenson was also utterly reliable, even fanatically loyal to Lloyd George. He had made sure of that when he had seduced her.

Frances had given herself to him as if in marriage. To her, the magical date of their first coupling, 21 January 1913 – she was just twenty-four years old – represented a sort of wedding ceremony, and as such the beginning of a lifelong commitment. Infatuated with Lloyd George since he had first employed her as a tutor for one of his daughters, she believed him when he told her that his real marriage was effectively over. That was, of course, not true. The relationship between David and Margaret Lloyd George was deep and enduring, in spite of the series of mistresses he had enjoyed during their long periods of separation. But Frances was content to be closer to him than his wife, to bask in reflected glory that made little impression on Margaret, and to supply all the admiration and support that Lloyd George craved.

Now, as he ranted about Haig, she asked: 'What are you getting so excited about?'

She was well aware that one of her roles was to soothe him. He had left her in no doubt about that. To him – he was quite open about it – women were to be used not just for the sexual satisfaction of men, but also to relieve their stresses and tensions, and to bathe their wounds, in what he saw as the male destiny of a life of continuous conflict.

'It's Haig, Pussy,' Lloyd George said. 'The King has sent me a message saying he wants me to make him an earl.'

'I suppose it's only right that the commander-in-chief should receive an appropriate reward.'

'But the man's been a disaster,' Lloyd George hissed. 'He's a second-rate commander, temperamentally and intellectually unfitted to lead an army of millions fighting battles on fields that none of the commanders can possibly see. No British general in history has been given such a gigantic undertaking, but it was completely beyond Haig's mental equipment. He couldn't plan the vast campaigns that were required, and he certainly lacked any sort of personal magnetism to inspire the troops. His name never sent a thrill through the ranks on the eve of a battle.'

'But he is the commander-in-chief,' Frances insisted, 'and in the end he did beat the Germans.'

'It wasn't Haig, Pussy. It was Foch. He's the one who beat the Germans. All Haig did was hang on until he was in a position to claim the credit for the victory. You can't fault his tenacity. This *honour* the King wants to give him is just a reward for stickability.'

He sat down at his desk and seized paper and pen.

'But he isn't going to get an earldom, I'm determined about that. I haven't forgotten the way he conspired against me with some of the Tory diehards, always relying on his friendship with the King to get his own way. Who knows what would have happened if I hadn't outflanked him and got Foch into the top job.'

He finished writing and handed the paper to Frances.

'Will you have that typed and encoded and wired to GHQ for Haig's personal attention.'

Frances read the message: 'I have the honour to inform you that His Majesty, on my recommendation' – that made her smile – 'has been pleased to approve that the dignity of a Viscountcy of the United Kingdom be conferred upon you in recognition of the signal services which you have rendered to the Empire as Commander-in-Chief of the British Armies in France and Flanders.'

'You won't get away with it,' Frances warned him. 'The King won't settle for a viscountcy. General Haig will have his earldom in the end.'

'No doubt you're right. But at least I'll have made my point.'

Frances rose to deal with the cable.

'You're due in the Cabinet Room in ten minutes,' she reminded Lloyd George. 'Some of the MPs are here already.'

Lloyd George groaned. 'This isn't going to be easy, Pussy. I have to convince my supporters that we're doing the right thing in joining up with the Tories to fight the election.'

'And *are* you doing the right thing?'

'I wish I could be sure. The Tories haven't been elected to office for fifteen years. This is a golden opportunity for them. They won't risk going to the country on their own terms, but they're quite happy to do it on our coat-tails.'

'On your coat-tails,' Frances said. 'The people are solidly behind *you*. You're the man who won the war.'

'It's not the voters that worry me. It's the people they're going to elect. Some of the candidates who are coming forward, and whom the Tories want to endorse, are really bent on our destruction, but because the coalition is so popular they aren't going to show their true colours. They want to be elected.'

'What about Mr Asquith?'

'That's personal, I'm afraid. He's always been convinced I was at the heart of the plot to remove him. I don't think anything I do will change his mind. But in a way, the Asquith Liberals might be my best hope. If they would join with us, I could endorse some of them and that would give me a stronger hand against the Tories. If not . . .'

'What are you going to say to your MPs today?'

'Well, somebody will have to go to the peace conference with authority from the people to speak in their name. That somebody should obviously be me, and I'm sure they'll agree with that. They've always supported me so far. I just have to convince them that we need the Tories to get the right result. I'll just have to be open with them ... Well, perhaps not completely open. They wouldn't like some of the Tory policies I'm going to have to present in the end, and I need time to find a way round that. As you well know, I don't favour frontal attacks, in war or in politics, if there's a way round.'

As Frances moved towards the door of the private office, with the cable in her hand, Lloyd George said quietly:

'It's a new game now, Pussy, darling. I'm not a free agent any more, now that peace has broken out.'

There would have to be some changes, said Bonar Law. The political landscape was quite different from what it had been before the war.

The small, slight figure of the party leader – the dark hair and moustache belying his sixty years – stood before some six hundred members of the National Unionist Association in the banqueting hall of the Connaught Rooms. It was the day after the signing of the armistice, the day following Bonar Law's dinner with Lloyd George at 10 Downing Street.

'Remember,' he told the assembled Conservative and Unionist Members of Parliament, would-be MPs who hoped to win seats at the forthcoming election, and old-fashioned Tory peers looking forward to a return to the way things had been, 'remember that this election will be like no other we have seen. For the first time, every working man in this country over the age of twenty-one will have the opportunity to cast his vote. We cannot tell whether those men will be swayed by the promises of the Labour Party, with its programme of wholesale social reform.'

There were mutterings in the room, with several among the gathering almost spitting out the word 'Bolshevists!'.

'They're calling it a "bosses' war",' said one prosperous-looking younger man, 'and they're accusing us of profiteering at the expense of our soldiers. Damned cheek!'

'Have you read that pamphlet they put out, *Labour and the New Social Order*?' asked his neighbour. 'That's not a programme for reform, it's a blasted socialist revolution.'

'They were never a hundred per cent behind the coalition anyway,' said a Conservative MP sitting nearby. 'Very nearly pulled out back in the spring – and at the very worst time, when the government needed all the support it could get.'

Bonar Law went on: 'There are also some six million women on the electoral register for the first time, and we cannot form an estimate as to how their votes might influence the result.'

'They should damn' well vote as their husbands tell 'em to,' shouted a voice from somewhere near the back of the room.

Bonar Law stilled the laughter with a gesture.

'The point is,' he said, 'that the government – the government which we created, of which we have formed a vital part, and for which we have provided unstinting support in the House – that government remains the most popular political force in the country today. Its popularity will be of incalculable value to our party at the election, and we must capitalize on it.'

'What?' someone called out. 'You mean we're sticking with the coalition?'

'Precisely,' Law said. 'It is our best hope of ensuring that the changes I think we all believe will be necessary for the reconstruction of our country after this terrible war, will be carried out in a manner that accords with the principles and policies that we hold dear. In my judgement, only a government that is secure in the support not of one of the two main parties, but of both, will have the chance to defeat the Labour challenge comprehensively and to implement essential reforms in a way as little revolutionary as possible.'

He paused for a moment before coming to his point.

'I am therefore proposing that we fight the election on a joint appeal with those members of the Liberal Party who have been loyal to the coalition in our conduct of the war and the achievement of victory.'

There was a gasp from his hearers, then a shout of, 'But what about Lloyd George?'

'The Prime Minister,' Law said, 'is the most popular politician in the land. You hear what people are saying – he's the man who won the war. But for two years or more, as we well know, he has been a prime minister without a party. We are, in effect, his party now.'

'But can we trust the little beggar?' demanded a Tory peer. 'After all, he was no friend to us before the war, with his new taxes and his attacks on landowning and his impudent restrictions on the powers and privileges of the Lords. The fellow's a damned radical, if you ask me.'

'And don't forget that he was a disarmer,' put in an MP. 'Why, even in 1914 he was criticizing our military budget. Fine mess we'd have been in if he'd had his way.'

'He's against the Empire, too,' someone added. 'I haven't forgotten that he stuck up for the Boers in the South African war.'

Bonar Law held up his hands to quieten them.

'I don't think you can fault Mr Lloyd George for the energy and commitment with which he prosecuted the war,' he said. 'He was our choice, and no one can so much as suggest that he has let us down. I should hardly have to remind you of what took place yesterday. Victory is ours, victory is complete. The country knows it. Mr Lloyd George could be prime minister for life if he so wished.'

He reached into the inside pocket of his morning coat and withdrew some folded papers.

'I have here a series of undertakings from the Prime Minister which I believe mean that the policies the coalition will pursue, when the government is re-elected, will be indistinguishable from those we should follow ourselves, were we in a position to form a majority government. And I must point out, gentlemen, that I see no prospect whatever, in present circumstances, of our being able to obtain an outright majority at the polls. The temper of the nation would not favour us if we were to fight the election in opposition to Mr Lloyd George and the Liberal Party, with Labour waiting in the wings.'

Lloyd George, he said, reading from the Prime Minister's

letter, had agreed to a programme designed to retain to the greatest possible extent the support of the Conservatives and Unionists. There was no need, at this stage, to discuss in detail how such a programme might actually be carried out, but the non-Liberal supporters of the coalition could rest assured that the Prime Minister's fundamental object was to promote the unity and development of the British Empire.

This declaration stirred the patriotic hearts of the assembled company.

Lloyd George, Bonar Law read, was committed to meeting *the imperative need of improving the physical conditions of the citizens of this country through better housing, better wages and better working conditions.* The last two objectives might provoke a flutter of concern among some of the Tory ranks, who placed the demands of their businesses well above the aspirations of their workers, but the Prime Minister only emphasized such matters *because the well-being of all the people is the foundation upon which alone can be built the prosperity, the security, and the greatness of the United Kingdom and of the Empire.* Well, yes, there might be merit in that: one did not, after all, want to provide any ammunition to the Bolshevist agitators, who seemed to be everywhere nowadays.

'What about the landowners?' asked a Tory member of the House of Lords. 'Can we trust him?'

The Prime Minister, replied Law, had clearly learned lessons from the war and was firmly of the opinion that government aid for farming – such as the subsidies paid to landowners under the Corn Production Act – would be maintained even in peacetime. Indeed, it would be a matter of policy to make sure that the improved position of agriculture brought about by wartime legislation would continue. That would no doubt please rural voters as much as it satisfied those who employed them.

Industrial interests need have no fear, either, Law assured his audience. The Prime Minister believed that *the key industries on which the life of the nation depends must be preserved and given security against the unfair competition to which they have been subject in the past by the dumping of foreign goods below the cost of production*. But trade protection would, of course, give preference to goods from the countries of the Empire when it came to imposing tariffs.

And what was Lloyd George's position, someone wanted to know, on Ireland? That was a subject which aroused like no other the passions of Unionists, who wished to see the United Kingdom preserved intact. The Liberals were Home Rulers, had been for thirty years, and they had even passed an Act of Parliament in 1914 designed to end rule from Westminster.

True enough, Bonar Law admitted, but the Prime Minister had indicated that the Act, which had not been carried through, was open to revision. The behaviour of the Irish during the war – their treacherous contacts with the Germans, who had supplied money and arms for nationalist revolutionaries – placed a question mark over the policy of Home Rule. But, whatever the outcome, the Prime Minister had promised not to countenance any settlement involving the forcible coercion of Protestant and Unionist Ulster.

That brought a murmur of surprise, and when it turned out to be the leader of the Ulstermen, Sir Edward Carson, a diehard Unionist and trade protectionist, who proposed *that this meeting approves Bonar Law's statement of policy and expresses its perfect confidence in his leadership*, the approval was unanimous.

'I wonder,' said a Conservative MP as the throng made its way out of the Connaught Rooms, 'whether Lloyd George really is a Liberal any more?'

A couple of miles away, in Downing Street, the Prime Minister was busy reassuring his supporters that his Liberal principles were as firm as ever – *Liberal from start to finish*.

'The way to prevent the spread of the revolutionary spirit we see all about us now is to embark at once on large schemes of sound social progress,' he declared.

What could be more Liberal than that? However, it must not be forgotten that the Unionists had demonstrated exemplary patriotism throughout the war – *they have given us constant support during the past two years*. When one embarked on a task such as the wholesale reconstruction that lay before them, *you must get the inspiration which comes from the knowledge that you have got the people behind you in the business which you have undertaken*.

'I have never witnessed before the new comradeship of classes such as we see now, and I'm glad, as an old political fighter who has been hit hard and has been able to return the blows, that we are approaching the new problems in a spirit of comradeship. Let us keep it as long as we can. I have no doubt human nature will prevail, but for the moment let us finish the task together, and when we have finished it, only then let us play political football.'

There was nothing to fear and everything to gain from renewing the mandate of the coalition, Lloyd George explained to the two hundred or so Liberals gathered in the Cabinet Room. The remarkable spirit of co-operation that had sustained him during the last, painful years of the war had resulted in the final victory, and if the peace, as well as the war, was to be won, it was essential that such a spirit continued. They should not forget that it was the supporters of his predecessor, Herbert Asquith, who had chosen to oppose the coalition, and to do their best to undermine it.

'They are men who were perfectly prepared at a critical moment to take advantage of temporary difficulties in order to overthrow the government when they were undoubtedly carrying through the work of the nation. What guarantee have we that they will not again take advantage of our difficulties when we are endeavouring to carry through a great social reconstruction policy? We cannot accept the support of men who come in on the promise of supporting the government and afterwards, when they are elected, begin to undermine and enfeeble us.'

The main thing, as any internationally-minded Liberal would appreciate, was to achieve a just and lasting peace, and if that meant relying on the support of men who, in ordinary times, would be their political foes, then so be it.

'Vigorous attempts will be made to hector and bully the government in the endeavour to make them depart from the strict principles of right, and to satisfy some base, sordid, squalid ideas of vengeance and of avarice. We must relentlessly set our faces against that. A mandate for this government at the forthcoming election will mean that the British delegation to the peace congress will be in favour of a just peace.'

It did not take a genius to work out that the spirit of vengeance and avarice would come from the right, from the old imperialists of the Tory backwoods. Better, then, to have their leaders in the government, so that their more rabid supporters could be kept in check.

The performance pleased Lloyd George, and seemed to satisfy his adherents.

'What happened?' Frances Stevenson inquired anxiously when Lloyd George returned to his private office.

'Unanimous. We join forces with Law.'

'Then we'll win the election.'

Lloyd George scratched his head. 'I don't know. I honestly don't know. Law is expecting a big majority, but I really can't begin to form an estimate. Still, I expect you're right. I suppose we'll win . . . Now, back to business.'

'There's a cable from the State Department in Washington. It seems President Wilson is coming to Europe.'

'What? You mean he's coming down from the clouds of rhetoric to save the heathen? I don't like the sound of that.'

'There's also a message from Mr Clemenceau.'

Lloyd George read the news from Washington. 'Hmm. Doesn't say precisely when the great man is planning to grace us with his presence, only that it will be immediately after the opening of the regular session of the Congress. When is that exactly? Some time this month, I'm sure. Ah, and he wants to take part in the discussion and settlement of the main features of the peace treaty before the conference begins.'

He picked up the message from the French prime minister. Clemenceau complained that Wilson's decision would disrupt arrangements for the peace conference: *It seems to me that we cannot begin the work before the President arrives. We ought all to agree in this respect. I propose that we should draw up some preliminary documents on the procedure to be followed, either in Paris or London, just as you wish.*

'Hello!' Lloyd George said suddenly. ' Did you read this? Clemenceau must have heard something. He seems to have got the impression that the President may be thinking about attending the conference himself, and he goes on to say that in his opinion that would be neither desirable nor possible. Well, well!'

'I wonder what President Wilson is like,' Frances said.

'I wonder if he's going to get in the way. Still, he can't be coming to London in the middle of an election campaign. Which reminds me – we must decide where the peace conference is actually going to be held. I don't favour London. I'd rather it was in a neutral country, probably Switzerland. We'd better cable Clemenceau with that suggestion.'

'I'll see to it. Oh, and there's a letter for you from Lord Curzon.'

'What's he got to say? You know I hate reading things.'

The hyperactive former Viceroy of India had mellowed little with age, and the pompous self-confidence that irritated so many people showed few signs of diminishing. Yet his brilliance was recognized by all, even if his constant stream of advice was often less than welcome and delivered in a way that made the recipient feel like a beetle in the presence of a god. Lloyd George had recruited him to his War Cabinet at an early stage. The Prime Minister appreciated Curzon's talents and, as a man not lacking in confidence himself, had no difficulty in countering the grand manner with plain speaking and the occasional outburst of temper. In short, Lloyd George found that he was one of the few people who could make Curzon do what he was told.

'He's concerned about the Kaiser,' Frances said.

Lloyd George looked puzzled. Wilhelm II was out of the picture now, rejected by his own people and fortunate to have found refuge in Holland. With the armistice signed and Germany in disarray, there appeared to be no prospect that the Kaiser would represent a threat to the peace. He would not have the stomach for it in any case. It was typical of him that, as his world collapsed about him, he should simply cut and run.

That was not the end of the matter for Curzon, however. He had been visiting Paris and had been persuaded by the French that the Kaiser was a war criminal who should be put on trial. Someone had to be held responsible for the horrors the world had just endured, and it was clear that the blame lay with the ambitions of the Kaiser. It was only right that he should face the judgement of the world for the unprecedented nature of his crimes, and history would not be kind to anyone prepared to let him escape retribution by means of a final act of cowardice.

There had been suggestions in Paris, and some in England, too, that the guilty Kaiser might be imprisoned or even executed. Lloyd George himself had heard shouts of 'Hang the Kaiser!' among the jubilation that had accompanied the news of the armistice. In Curzon's view, though, such severity might not be necessary to satisfy public opinion. A sentence of exile for life would surely signify mankind's abhorrence at the most colossal crime the world had ever known.

'Hmm,' said Lloyd George, 'typical Curzon. He always thinks on the grand scale. But, you know, there may be some merit in what he says. Mind you, I'm not sure what the legal position is. There's a meeting of the Imperial War Cabinet next week. We'd better tell Curzon to raise it then. A trial for the Kaiser would certainly be popular. A villain is always useful. I think we could probably even persuade President Wilson to go along with it.'

The Kaiser and President Wilson were both very much on the mind of Lord Northcliffe, as he sat brooding in his well-appointed office at the Ministry of Information. The proprietor of *The Times* and the *Daily Mail*, the two most influential newspapers in the country, had done his patriotic best – as he saw it, anyway – to support Lloyd George and the war effort. In fact, people were telling him that his contributions had done much to ensure victory, especially his direction of propaganda in enemy countries, which accounted for his presence at the Ministry.

'You have shortened the war by three years,' Northcliffe had been told by an American reporter in France as the Germans were preparing to sign the armistice. 'Germany is a long way from being beaten, and her armies are not destroyed. It is not her military situation that's so desperate – it's the internal upheaval caused by your propaganda.'

That was a source of intense satisfaction to the squat, Napoleonic figure seated in the large, green leather armchair – his likeness to the French emperor had often been remarked upon, and Northcliffe had cultivated it since his youth, even to the extent of mimicking the emperor's curl of hair across the forehead. But his pleasure in his achievements was tinged with anxiety as he contemplated the approach of what he regarded as a rigged general election, the impending descent on Europe of the American President, and the prospect of a peace conference at which both the punishment of the greatest crime in history and the vital interests of the British Empire risked being thrust aside in a welter of vague, internationalist do-gooding by politicians who had little idea of what the real world was like.

Northcliffe had never really trusted Lloyd George, and there were members of his government to whom he would not have given the time of day. Nor did he entirely trust the motives of President Wilson, whom he had actually met, unlike most of the European leaders now about to enter into negotiations with the President. Trust, indeed, was not a commodity much indulged in by the Napoleon of Fleet Street. Other people's judgement rarely seemed to be as sound as his own, and he knew from experience that most simply could not be relied upon to get on with their jobs unsupervised – they usually managed to get things wrong. There was always the need for a strong man in the background, and that applied to politicians as much as to his journalists. But where was the strong man in the government who would stand up for British rights, who would ensure that the fruits of victory and the lessons of defeat would be properly administered?

He had taken to heart the comment of an intelligence officer, writing confidentially to the foreign editor of *The Times* in the early summer of 1918: 'It seems we have no Englishman to lead us and express the mind of Englishmen ... However, there is still *The Times*!' There had been rumours that government had lost its nerve and, under pressure from a pacifist faction in the ranks of its supporters, was even considering some sort of peace agreement with Germany. Northcliffe had ordered an editorial, not in *The*

*Times* but in the more popular *Daily Mail*, warning 'weak and foolish ministers' that any such thought would be a shameful betrayal and would leave them at risk of being hanged by their indignant countrymen.

Now, as he prepared to leave the Ministry for the last time, having resigned his unpaid post, he suspected, even though the war had been won, there was still that weak-kneed tendency at work, especially among Lloyd George's Liberal entourage, and he feared that what he called 'Liberal sentimentality' would rob Britain of her just rewards for the sacrifices she had made and the famous victory she had won. There was a lot of talk in some quarters about a 'just' peace and about not being too harsh on Germany lest it lead to resentment and provoke a popular revolution along Bolshevik lines. Now President Wilson was coming to expound his airy-fairy, 'peace without victory' notions, which might serve to embolden those with what could only be described as pacifist leanings.

A few days later, Northcliffe discussed the matter with Thomas Marlowe, his editor at the *Daily Mail*, voicing his concern that the British people would be cheated out of their righteous claims against Germany and the criminal clique there that had started the war.

'The trouble with Lloyd George,' Marlowe said, 'is that he's operating on the assumption that Englishmen like to shake hands after a fight. They do, of course. But not this time.'

'Lloyd George is sometimes too timid to stand up for himself,' Northcliffe complained. 'I think it has a lot to do with his humble origins. He's afraid of criticizing the aristocracy, and he's surrounded by High Tory peers.'

'Then we'll have to do it for him, Chief.' Almost everyone called Northcliffe The Chief, after the habit he had developed early of describing himself as 'chief editor' of his newspapers. It was a very literal description.

'He's just so shifty,' Northcliffe said. 'It's an effort to make him run straight. You know, someone described him to me as like one of those toys people sell in the Strand, a little man who's always jumping out to the full extent of his elastic band, then coming back to the same place.'

The Chief thought for a moment, then, because Marlowe was becoming increasingly deaf, said loudly: 'Look here, once the election campaign is seriously under way, I want you to start a campaign in the *Mail* demanding that the Kaiser is put on trial for the war and that Germany is made to compensate us in full for what it's cost us.'

'Excellent,' Marlowe said. 'We'll really ram it down Lloyd George's throat.'

'And the other thing is, I want to give plenty of coverage to the Labour Party, now they've decided to break with the coalition. I was reading a speech one of them made in the House the other day, and I thought it was very interesting. He asked why it was that the government allowed a few thousand people to make millions of pounds during the war, while nearly a million ordinary men got only a soldier's grave for their service. That sort of thing will go down very well with the readers.'

Marlowe frowned, wondering if he had heard correctly.

There seemed to be a certain confusion in The Chief's mind. On the one hand he was always delivering homilies about the dangers of socialist revolution if the government did not pay heed to the aspirations of ordinary people, yet here he was offering a platform to people who seemed to be preaching the very revolution he feared. Did he want his papers to support the coalition or the Labour Party during the campaign?

'This government is tired,' Northcliffe went on, apparently unaware of the ambiguities he was dispensing, 'and some of its members are distinctly unsuitable. If the coalition is going to continue, Lloyd George has to throw out some of the old Tory reactionaries and replace them with men better fitted to tackle the difficulties we're going to face at home and abroad.'

Uppermost in The Chief's mind, though, were the Americans. He had developed a peculiar paranoia about the intentions of America, having spent much of 1917 involved in the work of a British mission sent to Washington for the purpose of increasing sympathy and co-operation with the war effort. He had been surprised by the lack of understanding of the British that he had found, the continuing resentment of the old colonial power, the distaste for the Empire and all it stood for, and the emotional support for Irish nationalism against what was seen as foreign occupation. It was not just American indifference to Britain's position that worried him, but rather a sense that many Americans would not be sorry if the war were to deliver a painful twist to the lion's tail.

On his return home to direct propaganda operations, Northcliffe had been equally dismayed by the lack of awareness in Britain about how differently the Americans saw the world and what that difference meant to future relations between the two countries. No one – apart from The Chief himself, of course – seemed to appreciate the power and the ambition of a mature and increasingly self-confident United States, of what effect there might be on the British Empire if that power and ambition were used to challenge it. He had discussed the matter with leading politicians in London, Lloyd George among them, but they appeared incapable of understanding that the Americans' view of Britain as old-fashioned and undemocratic might induce them to use their participation in the war, and especially the victory that such involvement made certain, as an opportunity to promote a refashioning of the world in the image of American notions of liberty, justice and democracy.

Naturally, Northcliffe had rejoiced at America's entry into the war, but he had harboured a nagging concern that President Wilson would be inclined to impose his will in the prosecution of it, to the detriment of Britain and the other European allies. Now, with victory achieved largely through European efforts, The Chief began to worry that an America barely touched by the horrors or scarred by sacrifice, would look to its own experience rather than that of the Europeans in the task of establishing and maintaining the peace. Americans might see only that it had been their president to whom the Germans had turned, and who had brokered the armistice. That would encourage them to pursue their own interests at the peace conference, believing in their moral superiority over the nations that had indulged in an orgy of bloodletting, unable or unwilling to bring it to an end themselves.

Northcliffe had warned the Prime Minister, he told Marlowe, that Britain must go to the peace conference armed with a policy that defended the interests of the Empire, and make it clear to the Americans that no concessions would be made. But he was far from sure that Lloyd George had really been listening to him. Of course, he would do what he could through his newspapers, but he could not help thinking that Britain was going to need someone with his insight and experience at the forthcoming negotiations if she was to benefit fully from the victory she had won.

Back at his country house, overlooking the sea near Broadstairs in Kent, Northcliffe heard the news that the peace conference was to be held in Paris – the French government had insisted that it was the only appropriate setting, and the British and Americans had, with some reluctance, agreed. Since the end of October, the Americans had had a mission in the French capital, headed by President Wilson's closest adviser, Colonel Edward House, a man Northcliffe knew well from his six months in Washington. He decided to go to Paris and consult Colonel House about whether he himself might perform some useful function at the peace conference.

The Colonel was well aware of the influence exercised by the Northcliffe newspapers and, ever mindful of the President's best interests, he thought they might be useful in smoothing Wilson's path through the treacherous undergrowth of European politics.

'Northcliffe is a kind of dictator in England, you know,' House told one of his staff as they waited for the press lord to arrive. 'The government are terribly afraid of him.'

He was at pains to flatter Northcliffe, complimenting him on the brilliant success of his propaganda campaign.

'I don't believe you've received the credit due to you for the winning of the war,' the Colonel said. 'You managed to stimulate the courage and energy of the Allies by making them realize the magnitude of the task they had on their hands. And, I must say, we were deeply impressed by the fact that you were one of the first to realize the significance of the distinction the President made between the German military autocracy and the German people. With your efforts in making sure the President's words circulated among Germans in their thousands, you did more than anyone, except the President himself, in breaking down the enemy's morale.'

The Napoleonic ego was duly massaged. In the course of a pleasant discussion, Northcliffe raised the subject of the peace conference and his own interest in it.

'Well,' House said diplomatically, 'I suppose you should be among those people who are going to have to work overtime to keep the conference on a straight course.'

Delighted with himself, and full of enthusiasm, Northcliffe wrote to Lloyd George, suggesting that, now he was no longer engaged on propaganda work, his services might be well employed in Paris during the course of the peace conference. The Prime Minister seemed taken with the idea. His reply appeared to suggest that if Northcliffe were to set himself up with an office in Paris, and take with him some of the staff he had used at the Ministry of Information, he could make himself available for consultation by the British delegation and might be particularly useful in determining how Britain was to present the negotiations to the press and the public of the world.

To Northcliffe, this sounded perfect: an official position that would allow him to exercise his considerable influence on behalf of his country. He set about finding suitable accommodation, settling finally on the Hôtel Majestic in the Avenue Kléber, almost in the shadow of the Arc de Triomphe. He had visions of himself staunchly promoting British interests by directing press relations and the entire official propaganda machinery surrounding the deliberations of the conference. He might have had a government position, of course – it had been offered to him in the past – but in his heart he cared little for politicians, and with the freedom his new post would give him, he could employ his talents to the full.

He rushed back to London and went to see Lloyd George at Downing Street. The Prime Minister was not in the best of moods, anxious about the election, which was to take place on 16 December, and worried by the sniping that was already beginning to appear in the newspapers, Northcliffe's among them. He had been particularly irritated by the constant barrage of advice and exhortation coming from *The Times* and the *Daily Mail* – how the new government should be constructed, how the Kaiser should be dealt with, how Germany should be forced to make financial reparation for the loss and damage caused by the war it had started. Grateful as Lloyd George had been for Northcliffe's support during the war, he now began to think that the power the man had enjoyed had gone to his head. Northcliffe seemed to have taken hold of the idea that he could run the country as well as his newspaper empire. He would have to be taken down a peg or two.

The Prime Minister also had a particular reason to be irritated with Northcliffe. One of The Chief's editors, the busybody Geoffrey Dawson of *The Times*, who liked to see himself as part of the political establishment, had contrived to give Lloyd George the impression that the real role Northcliffe was imagining for himself at the peace conference was that of an official delegate. It was a thought that filled Lloyd George with trepidation.

'I'm sorry,' he said, when he received Northcliffe in the Cabinet Room, 'but I cannot see my way to endorsing an official position for you in Paris.'

'But, Prime Minister,' Northcliffe protested, 'you gave me to understand that I could offer valuable service at the conference.'

Lloyd George was icy: 'Sir George Riddell will be in charge of the British publicity arrangements.'

'Riddell?' Northcliffe shouted. 'Are you serious?'

He was the chairman of the *News of the World*, one of Northcliffe's publishing rivals. He was also a firm friend of Lloyd George.

'The decision has been made,' Lloyd George said.

'This is an insult!' Northcliffe roared. 'I won't stand for this. After all the support I have given you, after my work in Washington, after nearly working myself to death on the propaganda campaign . . . I can't believe you could treat me like this.'

'You were always an unreliable helper,' Lloyd George

retorted, his temper rising. 'You're too used to subordinates who do what they're told. You can't deal with associates who work on agreed lines. I will not be dictated to. Rather than having you in a position of power at the peace conference, I will cease to be prime minister.'

'It might well come to that,' Northcliffe threatened. 'You have an election to fight, and you will do it against the opposition of the most widely read newspaper in the land and the most respected journal of opinion. You'll regret treating me like this. And whether you win the election or not, it won't end there. You can count on the implacable hostility of my newspapers.'

'Oh, go to hell!'

There was a moment of impenetrable silence as the two men faced each other. Then Northcliffe stamped out of the Cabinet Room, slamming the door behind him. His face contorted with rage, he marched out to the street and dived into his car. Lloyd George, for all that he understood about the power of the press, had carelessly made an implacable enemy. He could have adopted the attitude he had taken during the war and found something useful for Northcliffe to do. But, fearful that Northcliffe's presence, even on the periphery of the peace conference, would be a constant irritation, he had chosen confrontation. The Prime Minister had miscalculated. From now on he would have to fight a different kind of war – and one in which the heavy guns were all on the other side. Northcliffe's aim might be becoming wilder, but his shells would still cause damage.

'That man is intolerable,' Northcliffe told Thomas

Marlowe when he arrived at the offices of the *Daily Mail*. 'We're going to have to stop him before he leads us into disaster.'

He picked up the telephone: 'Get me Dawson at *The Times* . . . Dawson? My *Times* is supposed to be an independent newspaper. It is not displaying the independence that it should. It is not being hard enough on the government. I am determined to bring pressure to bear . . . We have to take a very firm line over this election, and especially over the peace conference . . . The Prime Minister is evading the main issues, as usual. He doesn't appear to understand that what is going to happen in Paris is nothing less than a struggle for world supremacy between Britain and the United States.'

# CHAPTER 3

# The Tiger's Eye

*I*

The shops in the Rue Caulaincourt, where it bends east away from the great cemetery of Montmartre, seemed as busy as they had been before the war. Not that there was a great deal to buy, of course. For the past four years, everything had been sacrificed to the war effort – and when even the heroic *poilus*, huddled in their trenches, had sometimes found themselves short of food, the civilians back home could hardly expect much. But, in these first few weeks after the armistice, the ritual of shopping was a comforting sign of returning normality, and the people in the Rue Caulaincourt that Saturday morning – mostly elderly, mostly women – seemed to find enough to buy to make it worth carrying their baskets.

There was one shop, though, that remained closed and shuttered, its paintwork faded and filthy, the name above its door rendered illegible by weather and long neglect. Rusting metal advertising panels indicated that it was, or had once been, a grocery store, but it was clearly many a year since anything had been sold there. The reason, for anyone interested enough to find it, was explained by a large piece of card, yellowed and curling at the edges, pinned to a wooden shutter. On this card was a message written in lead pencil. The words had almost disappeared by now, but if you looked very closely, you could just make them out:

*Fermé.*

*Le patron et le personnel sont sous les drapeaux.*

At the top of the card, on the left-hand side, was written a date: *3 août 1914.*

They had been called to the flag of France in the very first days of the war, the grocer and his shop assistants, no doubt sent north to meet the invading Germans as they swept through Belgium and towards the French border. They must have been army reservists, numbered among more than a million who reported for duty in early August and found themselves, first, without officers or weapons, and later – duly armed and properly led – sent into battle wearing the traditional red coats and blue breeches of French infantrymen, which made them outstanding targets for German machine-gunners.

'*Vive la France,*' they would cry passionately as they assembled for the charge. '*A la baïonette! . . . En avant!*'

And many of them would sing the *Marseillaise* as they advanced, in close formation, bayonets fixed, upon an enemy who outnumbered them by sometimes three to one and whom they could barely see, so well were the Germans dug in and so dense the smoke of their artillery fire.

Perhaps the *épicier* of the Rue Caulaincourt and his staff were part of the ill-fated Third Army, which lost four divisions to German shelling when they had hardly left their camp near Arlon, the Belgian city on the border with Luxembourg. Perhaps they were sent even farther north, to Charleroi, where the Germans were astonished to see French cavalrymen charging at them bedecked in the sort of armour Napoleon's *cuirassiers* had worn a century earlier.

But maybe the men from Montmartre were luckier and survived the battle of the frontiers, in which three hundred thousand of their comrades were killed, wounded or captured. They might have been part of General Lanrezac's inspired tactical retreat in the face of overwhelming odds along the River Sambre near Maubeuge, a decision that at least ensured France was left with an army to fight another day. If so, their luck ran out at some point as the disasters of August and September gave way to the false hope of the battle of the Marne and then to the years of murderous, pointless attacks, retreats and counter-attacks among the trenches of the Western Front.

Whatever their story, it ended tragically. Those men who had abandoned their ordinary lives in a spontaneous surge of pride and anger did not come back to the Rue Caulaincourt, and the sad shake of the head from some of their former neighbours, as they passed the shop now, indicated that they never would.

They and nearly one and a half million other Frenchmen, dead or missing, buried or left where they fell in the mud and the shellholes – 'so many mistakes, bringing so much misery', thought the Prime Minister, Georges Clemenceau, as he passed through Montmartre on one of the regular outings in his car that he enjoyed so much. Clemenceau had been mayor of the 18th Arrondissement, but that was long before *le patron et le personnel* of the sad, deserted little grocer's shop in the Rue Caulaincourt received their call to arms. His abiding memories belonged to an earlier moment of tragedy made all the more poignant by the position in which he now found himself.

The Prime Minister turned to his companion, a much younger man, and like Clemenceau a journalist turned politician. In some ways, André Tardieu reminded Clemenceau of himself when young. Tardieu's patrician upbringing and his education at the Ecole Normale Supérieure, the training school for the ruling classes, were very different from the background of the one-time country doctor from the Vendée, but like Clemenceau he was a radical, impatient with the corrupt and suffocating republic that had been built on the ruins of the last empire. Clemenceau had always been on the far left of politics, while Tardieu naturally inclined towards the libertarian right, but they shared a certain disgust at the weak, conventional, self-serving and insufferably bourgeois political class that had installed itself so firmly in power.

'I was twenty-nine when they made me mayor here,' Clemenceau recalled. 'September 1870. We were sitting practically under the Prussian siege guns.'

Tardieu smiled. 'I wasn't even born then.'

'We got elected, my supporters and I, by appealing to the fighting spirit of the citizens. I told them, I remember, that our breasts would be the country's last rampart against the Prussians. We were the children of the Revolution, I said, and if we followed the example of our forefathers, we would be victorious, as they had been. My grandparents used to tell me about the Revolution, you know. My grandmother Joubert watched the Vendée rebels capture Montaigu with just one old cannon.'

The chauffeur turned the car left into the Rue du Mont and headed north towards the Mairie of Montmartre.

'But we had no victory,' Clemenceau continued, gazing out at the familiar street. 'The government gave up. They'd moved to Bordeaux, out of harm's way, leaving Paris to face the Prussians alone. Well, they entered the city at the end of January 1871, and an armistice was signed. That was Thiers' doing. How I detested that man! Of course, it was mutual. I'd been elected to the National Assembly by then, and I went to Bordeaux to try to stop the peace treaty. I was in the Chamber when Favre, the Foreign Minister, came back from a personal interview with Bismarck and described the terms that the Prussians demanded. Lower Rhine lost, Upper Rhine, Moselle, Meurthe, Vosges. And all the rest. They had defeated us, humiliated us, and now they treated us with an insolence and an arrogance of which only Germans are capable.'

They were passing the Mairie, which Clemenceau pointed out with his gloved hand – he always wore suede gloves to hide the eczema that permanently troubled him.

'From there,' he said, 'in my office, I watched the Prussians burning the Château de Saint-Cloud. I stood there helpless as the smoke and flames rose from that beautiful building.' There was a break in his voice, and Tardieu thought he detected tears in the old man's tired brown eyes, a tremble of the lips below the white walrus moustache. 'But when they burnt it, it was burnt into my memory. That's my personal souvenir of the Germans.'

Tardieu sighed. Until 1916, when called to diplomatic duties, he had served with the light infantry on the Western Front.

'They've left us plenty more souvenirs now,' he said.

Clemenceau grimaced. 'That's the trouble with the Germans. They see the future only through the blood-red mists of a civilization grafted on to the survival of barbarism. And they operate on the assumption that victory excuses every crime.'

'Well, they haven't got away with it this time.'

The Prime Minister turned towards him. 'The funny thing is, I can't help feeling that they would eventually have got the better of us if they had stuck to peaceful means. But, no, they just had to indulge in that one mad act that forced us into military resistance.'

'And even then it was very close,' Tardieu admitted.

'Absolutely. When I was called upon in 'Seventeen, the German shells were falling on Paris again, just as they had been all those years before, when I was in Montmartre. There were mutinies in the army and the people at home were desperate. The government had no idea how to carry on the war. There was a smell of defeatism in the air. I'm very familiar with that smell.'

He fell silent, remembering the grim autumn of 1917, when all hope seemed to be evaporating after three ineffectual governments in six months. Clemenceau had been out of office for almost a decade, having destroyed the administration he himself led with the savage ruthlessness that had earned him the nickname of *le Tigre*. If you were not with The Tiger, you were against him, even when you might be nominally on the same side. Until 1914, he had contented himself with sniping at the political establishment from the columns of his newspaper, *L'Homme Libre*, but as disaster gave way to catastrophe and it began to look as if the humiliation of 1871 might be repeated, Clemenceau's attacks on a succession of inadequate governments and incompetent generals became ever more vituperative. They tried to stop him by censoring his editorials. His response was to change the masthead of his newspaper to *L'Homme Enchainé*.

There had come a day, in November – was it only a year ago? Clemenceau asked himself, as he stared blankly now from the car – when the realization dawned that President Raymond Poincaré, the dull, fussy little lawyer whom Clemenceau despised, and who seemed to have been awarded the presidency by default, had nowhere to turn. The latest administration was obviously doomed and no one had emerged who was likely to form a new government. Talk of appeasement was beginning to spread among the frightened members of the National Assembly, as much to prevent the army from throwing down its weapons as anything else. In some more robust quarters, however, the name of *le Tigre* had begun to be mentioned as the potential saviour of France.

Clemenceau could picture that November day. He had been at his apartment in the Rue Franklin, behind the Trocadéro Gardens, a short walk from the banks of the Seine. He was seated at his horseshoe desk, a little toque – like a gnome's cap, an observer would have thought – on his head, correcting galley proofs of articles for the next day's paper and dictating editorial instructions to the young man who had become his secretary, Jean Martet.

The loyal but by no means uncritical Martet had remarked on the intensity of the campaign Clemenceau was conducting against President Poincaré. He quoted back at the old man the editorial he had just been proof-reading: *Monsieur Poincaré is a man who does not want to know and does not know what he wants . . . So what is Monsieur Poincaré thinking about? He is thinking about himself.*

In his mind, Clemenceau replayed the conversation that had followed.

What about it? he had asked gruffly.

Martet had pointed out that by ceaselessly attacking Poincaré, Clemenceau was making it impossible for the President to call upon him to take power in this moment of national emergency – *The war will end without you, and I am afraid it will end very badly.*

The war, Clemenceau had responded sarcastically, would end as it had begun and as it was being fought.

That, said Martet, was precisely the problem. France needed *le Tigre* to put things right, and the young man was sure that Poincaré was only waiting for some sign from Clemenceau that would give him the opportunity to offer the premiership to the wily old fighter. For the love of God, make that sign, Martet pleaded.

Like everyone else, Clemenceau had heard the loose talk that presented him as the one man the President could call on to form a government and direct the war. But he waved away Martet's suggestion.

He would not make that sign, he said, for the simple reason that, while so many other worthy people were actively seeking power, he himself was terribly afraid of it and would give anything to avoid it. *You just have to look at me and see clearly that I'm a goner – seventy-six years old, rotten with diabetes. How do you expect me to pull it off? Anyway, I'm not even sure we could pull it off in our present state.*

Did that mean, Martet asked with an anxious frown, that Clemenceau did not believe the Germans could be defeated?

*I think it will be a difficult job*, Clemenceau heard himself saying. *Not because Germany is Germany. German strength has its limits – the Boche is stupid, narrow. But because France is France. My unhappy country frightens me. I look about and on all sides I see nothing. I see the parliament bewildered and enslaved, a preposterous press, public opinion unbalanced and distracted . . . and beyond that, just words. Never have such beautiful speeches been heard. Pity that isn't enough for victory.*

But Martet persisted. What would Clemenceau do if Poincaré did offer him the premiership? Surely he would not refuse at a time when his country needed him most?

Clemenceau smiled to himself as he remembered the exact words he had said to the importunate Martet: *I'll accept, of course. You can't refuse office. But I will not have sought it. There*

*will be nothing to reproach me with, not the wink of eye, not the
shuffle of a foot. Then the power that will be offered me will have
this new and special quality about it – that it will be real power.*

Poincaré had offered, Clemenceau had accepted. And now,
a year later, and with victory achieved, as he headed in his car
from Montmartre towards Saint-Dénis and the countryside
beyond, to where Parisians had liked to spend their summers
before the war, he said suddenly: 'It was on *my* terms.'

'What was that?' asked André Tardieu at this abrupt break
in his mentor's reverie.

'It was the only way,' said Clemenceau. 'I had to have
absolute power. They had to understand that the only course
was to wage war. Domestic policy? Wage war. Foreign policy?
Wage war. I told them straight: *All the time I wage war.* And
do you know what they said? They asked me what my war
aims were. What a question! There could be only one aim –
victory.'

He shook his head slowly. 'Even my own government
didn't really get the message. They're nice fellows, all right,
but they all share one fault: they're too decent. They weren't
made for war. Things are different when you're looking into
the jaws of the Boche.'

Tardieu grinned mischievously. 'From all I've heard, you
seemed to be making war on the National Assembly as well.'

Clemenceau shrugged. 'The soldier of the law made
common cause with the soldier of battle. I said so in my
declaration when I took office. The country had to know it was
being defended. People who refused to defend the country
had to be dealt with. I gave them fair warning.'

'Deputies arrested, collaborators shot . . .'

'It was war,' Clemenceau insisted. 'I told them – crimes against France will be punished. And, don't forget, after I came into office things got very much worse before they got better. By March the Germans were within a hundred kilometres of Paris. You should have heard the deputies squawking then. I had to be ruthless. There were too many people ready to give in. But, I'll tell you something, my friend, I had the support of the soldiers.'

'Because you promoted Foch, I presume.'

'Foch? I'll tell you about Foch. I've had less trouble with anarchists than I have with Foch. He only does what he wants to do. I make it a rule not to meddle in military operations, but in certain cases I say "to hell with the rules" – it's country before everything. With Foch, I had to proceed very warily. He played all sorts of shabby little tricks on me – still is playing them, I suppose. He's very thick with Poincaré these days. I don't actually like him. I soon realized that. I don't like people of his kind, in whose souls ability and courage live with . . . less attractive traits.'

'Nevertheless you did raise him up.'

'Who else was there? Oh, General Pétain was a loyal and trustworthy man, and he always behaved in an exemplary fashion. But as commander-in-chief? No, I could see he wasn't the man to finish the war. You know what Pétain's instructor said about him when he was at military college? He said if this young man ever rose above the rank of major, it would be a disaster for France. Well, the disaster was happening. So who else could I turn to? I saw no one but Foch. He has fire.'

Of course, Clemenceau explained to Tardieu, he could not

simply replace Pétain with Foch. Two commanders-in-chief had already been sacked, and Pétain had become a popular hero after beating back the Germans at Verdun in 1916 – though whether the credit should really have gone to him was doubtful.

Anyway, in March 1918 the German advance had looked unstoppable. There was a crisis meeting at General Pétain's headquarters in Compiègne, a few miles behind the crumbling front line. Pétain had flung twenty-four army divisions into the breach created by the German breakthrough, but the British commander, Sir Douglas Haig, was talking of falling back to the Channel ports and identifying embarkation points for retreating troops. Somebody had to take charge of the situation and co-ordinate the two armies to resist until American troops arrived to shift the balance to the Allies' favour. Clemenceau knew who that person should be, and had thoughtfully invited the British Secretary for War, Lord Milner, to the meeting in order to win his support.

Milner was well aware that his own prime minister's views were not so far from Clemenceau's. Lloyd George had already done his best to undermine Haig's obstinately defended independence and was quietly pressing for the appointment of a military overlord. Unfortunately, Lloyd George's judgement had been seriously called into question by his emphatic support for the French General Nivelle, whose wild and pointless aggression had sent Allied losses soaring, provoked mutiny among his own troops and led to his replacement as commander-in-chief by Pétain in 1917. Now Milner was happy to endorse Clemenceau's candidate for generalissimo.

He agreed to try to persuade Haig to accept a supreme commander.

Clemenceau proposed another meeting the next day in the town of Doullens, north of Amiens. President Poincaré would be there, as would Milner, of course, and Pétain – but the most important figure would be General Foch.

'Foch is only about ten years younger than I am, you know,' Clemenceau told Tardieu. 'And he also has vivid memories of 1871. He was a student in Metz then, and he remembers the Germans strutting about the city when they annexed it. Of course, he also has great military skill – he proved that on the Marne in 1914, at Yser and at Ypres. Then, naturally, the general staff became jealous of him, so he was tucked away in Army Group North for years, and starved of men and supplies so he couldn't have any more successes. They didn't notice him again until 'Seventeen, when they brought him to Paris as an adviser at the War Ministry – an adviser they didn't listen to. He knew perfectly well that the Germans were preparing a make-or-break attack, and he also told the minister that the Germans would have worked out that the Allies' greatest weakness was the lack of overall command among their forces. They couldn't co-ordinate their strategy properly. Well, as I said, they didn't listen. But I did.'

Clemenceau resumed his story. At Doullens on 27 March, Haig and Pétain discussed the military situation with their subordinates in the Hôtel Les Quatre Fils Aymong, while President Poincaré and Clemenceau had their own talks with Foch outside in the Place du Marché.

'Remember October 1914,' Foch said in his

characteristically forceful and staccato way. 'We must not indicate a line of retreat, or everyone will take it. We must hang on. We must hold fast. We must not give up another metre of ground. We will not withdraw. We will fight where we are.'

'*C'est un bougre!*' Clemenceau said – 'That's my boy!'

All depended on Milner's meeting with Haig, but the British minister had not arrived yet. Pétain emerged from his talks with the British commander and the group snacked on sandwiches the general had brought with him. At noon, Milner appeared and went straight into a private meeting with Haig. Twenty minutes later, the French party entered.

'If General Foch consents to give his advice, I shall be very glad to follow it,' Haig said. He was adept at shifting on to others the blame for his own inadequacies, and here was another opportunity to cover himself when things went wrong, as they seemed to do so often.

But Clemenceau was not going to let him get away with it.

'That's not what we're talking about,' he snapped, leaping to his feet. 'What Foch needs is an independent post from which he can exercise some control.'

Pétain intervened soothingly: 'Everything you decide will be carried out.'

Clemenceau resumed his seat and took up paper and pencil. He wrote: 'General Foch is charged by the British and French governments with co-ordinating the British and French operations at Amiens . . .'

'Better make that "on the Western Front",' Foch said.

'You're right, of course,' Clemenceau said, and made the

alteration. He continued writing: 'He will come to an understanding to this effect with the two commanders-in-chief, who are invited to furnish him with all necessary information.'

No one dissented and they all went into lunch together with as much good humour as they could muster, given the precarious state of their armies.

'Well, General,' one of the French party said to Foch, 'so you've got your piece of paper now.'

Foch laughed: 'Yes – and a fine time it is to give it to me.'

A fine time it was, too, all sarcasm apart. As Foch had predicted, the Germans were counting on the fragmentation of the Allied command for the success of their 'big push'. That, Clemenceau told Tardieu, was why he had determined to press for Foch as supreme commander.

'I told him he wasn't sufficiently in charge,' the Prime Minister recalled. 'I said he should go the whole hog and start giving orders. I knew the British would go along with it. Lloyd George was as worried as we were – and I knew he would take care of Haig.'

Orders were precisely what Foch wanted to give. Within a few days, the general was officially gazetted as assuming 'strategic *direction* of military operations on the Western Front', while the French, British and, by this time, American commanders-in-chief retained tactical control and could appeal to their own governments if they seriously disagreed with Foch's orders. By July 1918, Pétain had gone, retired and elevated to the honour of a Marshal of France. In August, Foch himself became a Marshal, having mobilized all the forces under his command to push back the Germans to their defensive line and make their eventual surrender inevitable.

'Yes,' Clemenceau concluded, 'Foch has fire all right. He has the fire of all the devils in hell.'

'He's not the only one,' Tardieu said. 'It's you they're calling *Père Victoire*.'

'Victory is one thing,' Clemenceau replied. 'Peace is quite another.'

Tardieu turned his face away and smiled at this expression of The Tiger's famous pessimism.

'We've won the war,' Clemenceau went on, 'but what we have to do now is mount a close guard over what have become the frontiers of freedom. We must be much more vigilant in the future than we have been in the past. We didn't learn the lessons of 1871. We have to take them to heart this time. We didn't go to war to protect our national rights only to end by giving them up in peace.'

The terms of the armistice, he conceded, were harsh, but severity was necessary because the Germans had to be prevented from regrouping and starting the war again. Yet even in drawing up those terms, the Allied leaders had taken no account of the devastation the Germans had wrought in France. It was Clemenceau himself who raised the subject of compensation, over the objections of the British that such a requirement was pointless because nothing could be done at that stage to enforce it. But Clemenceau insisted that the principle of reparation be included in the final document. It amounted to a public acknowledgement by the other leaders that France had suffered most during the war, and in his mind that acknowledgement must remain at the heart of the peace negotiations.

The Prime Minister was under no illusion that it would be an easy task. They would be confronted by an American President who seemed to look down upon them from a mountain-top of morality, who tended to ignore the practical realities in favour of the self-righteous waffle of his now famous Fourteen Points, which spoke of peace without victory, fairness and justice for all peoples, and unspecified new ways of managing international relations. That might be all very well, but what France required was a peace treaty ensuring that Germany could never again be a threat to her. She had been the victim in the Franco-Prussian war of 1870-71, and she had become the chief victim again this time. Now the power of Germany to make war must be removed – whatever idealistic aims the Americans might have, whatever agendas the British and the Italians might pursue.

But it was obvious, Clemenceau told Tardieu, that such a treaty could only be created with the willing participation of the other Allies. They had come to the aid of France in her moment of danger and France had to show that she was grateful. Without them, she might not have emerged victorious, no matter how strong her resolve and how great her sacrifices. France could not now simply set out her demands as if she had won the war all by herself, which seemed to be the attitude that President Poincaré and Marshal Foch, along with many others, were adopting. There could be no question of the wartime alliance breaking apart over the peace. That was the challenge: to place the vital interests of France first, which meant neutralizing Germany, but to do it in such a way that the Americans and the British and the Italians would not regard it as selfishness or vindictiveness.

'That's what we have to guard against,' Clemenceau concluded. 'We and our friends are going into this peace conference united. We've got to come out of it as brothers. At the same time, however, we have to consider the needs of France, her security, her future, and the expectations of the French people. The people won't understand if their sacrifices are not fully taken into account when it comes to the peace settlement. The Germans started this war. They're going to have to pay for it.'

He leaned closer to Tardieu and patted him paternally on the knee. He would, he said, be relying on the young politician to help him, to write the draft of a treaty that would ensure both the security of France – above all else – and the continuation of the alliances forged in war.

'I'm going into these discussions,' he said confidentially, 'not with the idea of walking out, or smashing the serving tables and the china, as Napoleon liked to do. I'm going with the idea of making myself *understood*. If you get my meaning.'

There was a heavy swell in the English Channel as the steamer made its way out of the shelter of Calais harbour and ploughed into the grey-green waves topped by the strips of white foam the French call *moutons*.

'At least there's no danger of Boche submarines any more,' said Georges Clemenceau.

The last time he and his retinue had made this journey – they could hardly believe it was no more than a few months earlier – their boat had been surrounded by a protective screen of warships, the lookouts anxiously scanning the sea for any sign of a periscope. Now all they had to worry about was keeping their footing as the boat rolled and pitched on the surging water. They were on their way to London for the conference of the European Allies suggested by Clemenceau in order to agree the outline of peace proposals that could be presented to the American President during discussions in which he apparently wished to take part himself before the formal peace conference. Clemenceau liked to be outside during the Channel crossing and had led the party on deck, undeterred by the stiff breeze.

'You know,' said the Prime Minister, 'I've been wondering about President Wilson and his Fourteen Points. How is it that *he* feels it necessary to deliver fourteen commandments when the Lord God Himself was content with ten? And, come to think of it, we don't take too much notice of the ten.'

He seemed in relaxed mood as he wandered about the deck,

protected from the elements by a heavy black overcoat and a little cap.

'I'm looking forward to being in England again,' he said. 'She's been a very great lady, England – aloof, ruthless, but still somehow with an engaging quality. I would say that, of all peoples, the English have the willpower that has held out longest. But I can't help wondering how long that willpower will survive. They've done so much, the English. Just look at their empire. But after a while, the satisfaction of conquest no longer serves to quicken the blood of the conqueror. I suppose it's only natural. The history of the English goes back such a long way.'

His discursive good humour surprised some members of his entourage, those who knew about the bitter row he had just had with President Poincaré and Marshal Foch. Clemenceau, as he had revealed to André Tardieu, had been well aware that the President and the pugnacious little soldier had spent a good deal of time together working on a series of demands they would want him to present at the peace conference.

'They're not consulting me about any of this,' he told Tardieu. 'They're not even keeping me informed. That's not a very constitutional way to do things, is it? But then Poincaré has never really wanted to conduct himself like a president of the republic, any more than Foch has been disposed to behave as a good soldier should.'

'What do you mean, exactly?' Tardieu asked.

'Well, Poincaré has no business holding private meetings with my subordinates. I'm the prime minister, after all, the head of the government. He's clearly not acting in the national interest – only in the interests of Raymond Poincaré. As for Foch, I remember him once saying to me he supposed that, in constitutional terms, he wasn't really obliged to take orders from me. Strange attitude for a soldier who's supposed to be a servant of the state, don't you think? Of course, I told him, in a very friendly way, that he'd better not try that game with me.'

Foch had been wise enough not to confront Clemenceau, but instead had endeavoured to place himself beyond the Prime Minister's reach by dealing with the President behind closed doors. The result had been a seemingly endless series of notes to Clemenceau from the Elysée Palace, suggestions about what should be included in the peace treaty and how it should be negotiated – all in the minutest detail from Poincaré's fussy, legalistic mind.

'Lord, how that man can write!' Clemenceau had complained to his secretary. 'Every time I see his dainty little handwriting, it sends me into a fury.'

But the news of President Wilson's determination to take part personally in discussions, and the obvious necessity for a conference of the European leaders before his arrival, had obliged Poincaré and Foch to show their hand to Clemenceau.

'What I'm most concerned about,' Foch said when the three men met at the Elysée before the departure for London, 'is the Rhineland.'

'What about it?' asked Clemenceau. 'It's clear that Alsace and Lorraine will be handed back to France. Everyone has accepted that. Even the Germans aren't arguing. The justice of our case is indisputable.'

Poincaré, even more diminutive than his prime minister,

stood up, his prim face flushed above its neat white beard.

'Yes, yes,' he said irritably, 'but that isn't the point. We're talking about the other provinces on the west bank of the Rhine.'

'I don't follow,' Clemenceau said. 'Those provinces are equally indisputably German.'

'But there is a French population there, especially in the Saarland.'

'What are you talking about? They can't be more than a handful.'

Foch broke in: 'Well, whatever the figures, the fact is that the German provinces on the west bank of the Rhine cannot be allowed to threaten the future security of France.'

Clemenceau looked at him in disbelief. 'You're talking about annexing them?'

'No, no, absolutely not. Annexation is not a word that would pass my lips.'

'Then what *are* you talking about? It's already agreed with the British that our joint forces will occupy the Rhine bridgeheads, even on the east bank, for the time being. How long that continues is a matter for negotiation, and it depends on the demilitarization of Germany. As you know, it is my intention that the Germans should not be in a position where they can attack us again.'

'But we haven't thought about how we can guarantee that,' Foch said. 'We've seen to our cost that it's no good relying on neutral states to provide security against a German invasion. Look what happened in 'Fourteen. They just marched straight through Belgium and Luxembourg. And next time they'll do it better. They'll head straight for the Channel ports to deny us help from the British. We owe it to ourselves to build some kind of permanent barrier against them. Who knows what might happen in fifty years' time?'

Poincaré said: 'We certainly know what's happened in the last hundred. Three times the Germans have crossed the Rhine to invade us. Twice they've got as far as Paris . . .'

'I know that,' Clemenceau interrupted him. 'I was there last time, remember.'

'And I was in Lorraine,' Poincaré snapped. 'Yes, I was only a boy – but a boy who had to grow up surrounded by swaggering German soldiers in those damned spiked helmets. I'm going to make sure, if it's the last thing I do, that no Frenchman has to endure that sort of experience again.'

Clemenceau saw the connection between the President and the Marshal: Foch the student in Metz, Poincaré the schoolboy in Bar-le-Duc. He recalled that one of Foch's first actions after the armistice had been to travel to Metz to watch the Germans withdrawing.

'What I propose,' Foch said, 'is that Germany should be restricted to the right bank of the Rhine. The German provinces on the left bank should enter into an association with us – and Belgium and Luxembourg, of course – to provide armed forces sufficient to deter any possible invasion in the future.'

'So you *are* talking about annexing them,' Clemenceau said.

'I'm *not* talking about annexation,' Foch hissed. 'Those provinces could all be independent if they wanted to be, or else they could form a single state of their own. All I'm saying is that they should belong to our military and economic systems.'

'You're out of your mind,' Clemenceau said sharply. 'What do you think the British are going to do if we turn round to them and say, "Right, we've won the war, thanks for your help, and now we're going to seize this and that for the greater glory of France"? And what's President Wilson, with his Fourteen Points talking about freedom for oppressed peoples, going to say about this crazy scheme? Whom do you think he would see as being oppressed under this crazy scheme?'

Poincaré and Foch exchanged glances. The President said: 'I'm sure it would have solid support in the National Assembly.'

Clemenceau snorted. 'No doubt!'

Foch said: 'And I think we can bring the others round to our point of view. They don't trust Germany any more than we do. I've prepared a memorandum we can present to Lloyd George when we go to London. He would help us to convince Wilson.'

'There's no *we* about it,' Clemenceau retorted. 'I'm not putting my name to anything like that. It's a thoroughly bad policy.'

'Really, Prime Minister,' said Poincaré, 'I think you ought to remember your position. I, as head of state, am persuaded that Marshal Foch's strategy is the correct one, and, as I said, I believe it would be supported by a majority of the National Assembly.'

'Fine. Then Marshal Foch can present it to the British. I'm certainly not going to.'

And at that the matter had been left. Poincaré had no desire for an open breach with *Père Victoire* at this stage. As Clemenceau and his party crossed the Channel, Foch had his memorandum in his document case. The Prime Minister was quite comfortable that it should be there, hence his good humour. He knew Lloyd George well enough to be able to predict what his reaction would be, and since the hare-brained scheme would not be presented with Clemenceau's imprimatur, its inevitable rejection would not compromise his negotiating position – rather, it would strengthen his hand, if anything, because it would serve to inhibit further interference from the Elysée. He might even be able to use this ridiculous Rhineland proposal, since it was not his own, as a bargaining counter, a means of obtaining a less risky form of security. The peace treaty he would take to the French people would be his own, but forged in co-operation with the friends of France. He would obtain guarantees of protection against Germany, but he would do it in a manner that would not antagonize the Americans and the British. Let Poincaré see what he could make of that. There was a presidential election due in 1920.

Foch, in spite of Clemenceau's opposition to his plan for the Rhineland, was equally cheerful as the boat docked at Dover. Poincaré was on his side and the Prime Minister had not dared to go so far as to oppose outright the presentation of the idea to the Allies. In fact, the Marshal calculated, it would do him no harm to be seen as the promoter of an eminently sensible proposal to confine Germany behind her natural frontier in the west. He felt sure the Allies would favour an idea that would help to guarantee the future peace and security of Europe. Foch was very much enjoying the experience of being celebrated as a military hero, and his plan for the Rhineland would merely set the seal on his acknowledged strategical brilliance.

He had every reason to feel confirmed in his opinion when the group emerged from the boat train at Charing Cross Station in London. As they walked through the great arches of this railway cathedral, a deafening chorus of cheers rose from streets packed with people. The King himself was there to greet them, and Foch swelled with pride as he exchanged salutes, then the King led him to an open carriage for a triumphal drive to Buckingham Palace.

'I've never seen anything like it,' Lloyd George said to Clemenceau. 'So many people, and so much enthusiasm.'

The two prime ministers travelled together by car to the French embassy, Clemenceau almost overwhelmed by the wild cheers he also received. It took them several minutes to cross Trafalgar Square, so dense was it with people. The crowds extended along The Mall to the gates of the Palace and beyond, up Constitution Hill to Hyde Park Corner and Knightsbridge.

'This is incredible,' Clemenceau said, moist-eyed, as the waves of cheering followed their stately progress. 'I didn't know the English had it in them. And for a foreigner, too. Incredible.'

When they finally reached the embassy in Knightsbridge, Lloyd George said: 'We'll meet this evening, then, at Downing Street.'

'Ah,' said Clemenceau, 'I won't be there, unfortunately.'

'What? But it was you who asked for this meeting.'

'Not *this* meeting,' Clemenceau said evasively. 'No, no, the important thing is that we sit down with the Italians tomorrow and agree the terms we're going to put to President Wilson. *That's* the meeting I was wanting. I think you'll find that this evening Marshal Foch merely wants to talk about the Rhineland.'

'Oh, the arrangements for deploying our troops at the bridgeheads?'

'Yes, yes, technical stuff. Foch will deal with that. I, er, I have a pressing social engagement with the ambassador this evening. We'll get down to the politics tomorrow.'

Still, it was odd, Lloyd George told Bonar Law that afternoon.

'Do you think he's up to something?' Law asked. 'He's a cunning old bird.'

'I expect we'll find out this evening.'

Foch was in bullish mood, brisk and businesslike as always, never wasting a word.

'We think,' he said confidently, 'that military necessity demands that we take full control of the left bank of the Rhine.'

Lloyd George and Bonar Law looked at each other in surprise.

'You mean German territory?' Law asked.

'Well, what is German territory at the moment.'

'What exactly do you have in mind?' Lloyd George inquired.

Foch outlined the reasons for the plan he had discussed at

the Elysée a few days earlier, though he did not mention Poincaré or Clemenceau.

'Even if the Germans are restricted to their territory east of the Rhine, there will still be sixty-five or seventy million of them – and we don't know what sort of government might eventually emerge there. It could be one that would wish to repeat the experience of 1914, and then where would we be? Now, I've worked out that, with the return to France of Alsace-Lorraine, and taking into account Belgium and Luxembourg, we would have an opposing population of forty-nine million. Add to that the German provinces on the left bank, and you get to nearly fifty-five million. So far so good. That, I think, would be adequate to hold the line of the Rhine in the event of an attack – unless, of course, it was a surprise attack, which would leave us back where we were in 'Fourteen.'

'So you're assuming,' Lloyd George said, 'that even if the Rhine provinces were separated from Germany in some way, there would have to be some sort of additional guarantees against attack?'

'Precisely. What I am proposing is that we prepare an alliance – that is France, Belgium, Luxembourg and Britain, and including the Rhenish provinces – that would be organized for the defence of the Western Front. Of course, it would be controlled by you, us and Belgium.'

'But these Rhenish provinces,' Lloyd George wondered, 'how do you imagine they would be organized politically? Do you expect them to be independent, or how else would they be governed?'

'Oh, I don't think we need discuss that in too much detail,' Foch replied crisply. 'I imagine they would probably be independent, either as a single state or several different ones. I'm not talking about *annexation*, you understand. I'm merely looking for a way of providing a proper defence along the Rhine, learning from our recent experience.'

The Prime Minister was not convinced. 'But you must see that what you are suggesting doesn't exactly accord with President Wilson's Fourteen Points, on which we're supposed to be negotiating a treaty. I mean, the whole idea is that we don't act as oppressors.'

'I think we can get round that,' Foch said. 'We would justify what I have in mind by pointing out that Germany can't be trusted to abide by international treaties, conventions or anything else. No amount of signatures on pieces of paper prevented her from starting this tremendous war. So we have to take precautions, and a military barrier along the Rhine is the most obvious one.'

'But I come back to the Fourteen Points, to which we've all agreed in principle. How do you intend to manage self-determination for the Rhine provinces? What if, for example, you held a plebiscite and the inhabitants decided they would prefer to remain with Germany?'

Foch was dismissive. 'They probably wouldn't. For one thing, they would be attracted by the economic structure we have and, for another, I'm sure they'd prefer to be on the side of the victors rather than the conquered.'

'But,' Lloyd George persisted, 'it's hardly likely to be unanimous. These people are Germans, after all. You'd simply be creating an Alsace-Lorraine in reverse.'

'Well, of course, we'd have to do everything possible to conciliate the feelings and interests of the people.'

'That's not so easy,' Bonar Law said. 'Look at the trouble we've had for years trying to conciliate the Irish.'

'Anyway,' Foch concluded, 'I've put the whole thing down in this memorandum, and I'd appreciate your studying it with some care.'

Lloyd George smiled. 'That goes without saying, Marshal. Anything that comes from you we're bound to consider very seriously – and, I may say, with a favourable disposition.'

His mission accomplished, Foch took his leave.

'Well,' Bonar Law said, 'what do you make of that?'

Lloyd George reached for a cigar. 'They've kept very quiet about it up to now, which must mean something. But for Foch to come here with the specific intention of raising the issue, and that alone, means they must attach a lot of importance to it.'

'But then why didn't Clemenceau take part?'

'I've been thinking about that.' Lloyd George lit his cigar and watched the heavy smoke rise slowly towards the ceiling. 'Obviously this social engagement that was suddenly so vital doesn't wash. He didn't want to be here when the bombshell was dropped. Which means either that he doesn't really support the idea, or, more likely, he thought it would be better coming from Foch because of the debt of gratitude we owe him.'

'But do you think Clemenceau would really believe we would go along with something like this?'

'Whether he does or not, he's shrewd enough to see that the suggestion of it would give him something strong to bargain with. Who knows what else he has up his sleeve.'

'Perhaps we'll learn something at the conference tomorrow.'

'I rather think,' Lloyd George said, 'that Monsieur Clemenceau is saving his real demands for the peace conference itself. He'll be on home ground, after all. And I think he wants to see the whites of President Wilson's eyes.'

'I always remember Bismarck's comment about the Italians,' Clemenceau remarked as he and Foch made their way by car to Downing Street. 'He said they had large appetites, but it was a pity they had such poor teeth.'

Foch laughed. 'Do you think they're going to be pressing their ridiculous territorial claims at the meeting today?'

'Well, it's the only thing they're interested in. I mean, the sole reason why Italy came into the war was the promise of gaining a little empire for itself.'

'That was pretty obvious,' Foch said. 'Heavens, the trouble we had getting them to take any interest in military operations that weren't directly connected with their own concerns! I began to wonder whether we were fighting the same war.'

'And then, at the negotiations over the armistice terms,' said Clemenceau, 'they had the gall to accuse me of being obsessed with what we could get out of Germany and not giving a fig for what they might gain from the old Austrian and Turkish empires.'

Foch laughed again. 'I saw something amusing in the

newspaper the other day. It seems the Italians are calling Piave the battle that decided the course of the whole war.'

'They are rather prone to exaggeration.'

'Exaggeration? Pure fantasy, I call it. As I remember, we had to put in six divisions to stiffen their backbone after the disaster at Caporetto. And for all their refusal to look beyond their own theatre, it was the British and us who smashed the Bulgarians at Salonika, which according to the Italians is right in their own backyard. Now, to hear them talk, you'd think they had won the war all by themselves.'

'Caporetto was a terrible shock to them,' said Clemenceau. 'What was it, more than half a million men they lost in that one battle?'

'Depends what you mean by lost. Two-thirds of them either surrendered or deserted, if my memory serves.'

The defeat at Caporetto had been a bitter blow from which the Italians' self-esteem had still not recovered. The army had reorganized itself and regained its nerve sufficiently to take the field again, and successfully – no mean achievement in the circumstances – but there remained a sneaking feeling among the other Allied commanders, and it was shared to some extent by their political masters, that Italy had done rather less than its fair share of the fighting. It was that feeling which inclined Clemenceau and Lloyd George to reconsider the rewards for Italy promised in the treaty that had brought her into the war, especially when the Italians began to trumpet their lately discovered military prowess and, as some saw it, exaggerate their contribution to the victory.

In 1914, Italy had been bound by treaty to Austria-

Hungary, its powerful neighbour to the north and overlord of the Slav peoples on the eastern shore of the Adriatic. The Italians had chosen not to fight alongside the Central Powers, seeing little or no advantage to be gained for themselves from the war. But in the spring of 1915, when the war that was to have been over by Christmas had settled into bloody stalemate, and there was even the prospect that the Entente forces might actually be defeated, Britain and France set out to persuade Italy to revoke its Austrian treaty and throw in its lot with them. Naturally, there had to be a significant incentive. The British and French promised that if Italy joined the Entente, and the Central Powers were defeated, the peace settlement would transfer to her the Austrian Tyrol, the bulk of the Istrian peninsula at the northern end of the Adriatic, and a large swathe of territory on the Dalmatian coast, all part of the Austrian empire.

For the government in Rome, it was a tempting prospect. Italy was suffering serious political and economic difficulties, and since its unification had developed into nothing more than a second-rate power. The offer from the Entente suggested that Britain and France were finally taking Italy seriously – and the territorial gains that were being promised could form the beginnings of an empire that would give her the important role in the world that history suggested was her destiny. People remembered the glory of ancient Rome, and saw that here was an opportunity to rebuild it in the modern age.

With high hopes, the proposal was accepted, and confirmed in a secret treaty signed in London. Italy played her part in the war – perhaps less gloriously than her newly confident people had expected – and now looked for her rewards from the victory. The situation in November 1918, however, was very different from the dire circumstances of 1915. Not only had the Austro-Hungarian Empire unexpectedly collapsed, so that there was no question of negotiating new frontiers for it to Italy's benefit, but there was also a new power to be taken into account – America. And the American President had made it clear in his fourteen-point proposal for peace that peoples liberated from the old central European empires should decide their future for themselves. That clear and strongly held view, which the Allies had appeared to accept in responding to President Wilson's armistice negotiations with Germany, was in direct conflict with the Treaty of London, and it presented Clemenceau and Lloyd George with a dilemma.

The question was: Should a treaty signed in good faith be honoured whether or not the position it had envisaged no longer existed, or could it be set aside on account of the changes that had occurred since its signature? Lloyd George and Clemenceau sympathized with Italy's conviction that a promise was a promise, even though they themselves had not personally been parties to the treaty. More important, however, was the fact that America had not been a party to the treaty, either – had not even known about it, and would not have agreed to its terms if it had known. To Clemenceau and Lloyd George, there seemed little chance of the Treaty of London being incorporated in any peace settlement involving the Americans, and they were both thinking about how they might talk their way out of it. Sensing this, the Italians had embarked on a determined and noisy campaign to ensure that they would receive what they persisted in believing was their due.

'I hope,' Clemenceau said to Foch as their car approached Downing Street, 'that we aren't in for another diatribe on the merits of Italy's claims to the Tyrol and Croatia and Albania and whatever else it is – they're demanding so much for their new empire, I forget the details.'

He need not have worried. When he and Foch were met by Lloyd George, they found that the Prime Minister had more urgent matters of his own on the agenda. With the election campaign in its first week, Lord Northcliffe's newspapers had been earnestly pursuing The Chief's now personal vendetta against Lloyd George, hounding the Prime Minister about the prospect of putting the Kaiser on trial for war crimes, and about how much Britain would be claiming from Germany as compensation for the costs of the war. For days, the *Daily Mail* had been carrying on its front page a banner proclaiming 'HE HAS NOT SAID IT YET' – a reference to the fact that the Prime Minister had made no public statement about the financial reparations which, according to Northcliffe, the British people had every right to expect. It was getting on Lloyd George's nerves. He had already compromised with the Tories in order to fight the election. He had no wish to win it on the basis of policies advanced by Northcliffe.

'We must settle the business with Germany first,' Lloyd George said in answer to Clemenceau's question about the Italians, whose prime minister and foreign minister had not yet arrived. 'Wilson will be here in a week or two, and it was he who forced the Germans to accept the Fourteen Points as the foundation of peace. Now, you and I know that the Wilson doctrine is too vague to be workable, so it's essential that we have *our* key points clearly established. It's a pity Colonel House's illness has kept him in Paris. His presence might have saved us a lot of time.'

'Haven't the Americans sent anyone else?' asked Foch.

Lloyd George shook his head. 'The President doesn't seem to trust anyone to represent him but House.'

There was an exchange of pleasantries when the Italians were ushered in – Vittorio Emanuele Orlando, the Prime Minister, and Baron Sidney Sonnino, the man who had done more than anyone to encourage Italy's entry into the war and who, in consequence, was determined to pursue to the limit the rewards that had been offered. Then, with everyone seated, Lloyd George came straight to the point.

'The first subject we have to discuss,' he said, 'is war reparations. Now, as we all know, public opinion is demanding that we obtain as much from Germany in the way of compensation as we possibly can. What public opinion doesn't understand, however, is that the question of assessing and collecting reparations is no easy matter. People seem to be under some illusion as to the size of the sums that might be involved. The fact is that Germany possesses only about a hundred and fifty million pounds' worth of gold, and very little in the way of foreign securities. We must guard against inflated expectations, so I propose that we establish a commission of experts who will identify what the true position is.'

Orlando, an animated and amiable-looking Sicilian, and the

shortest man in the room, said with some force that Italy assumed Germany and Austria would be jointly responsible for all reparation settlements with Allied governments.

'The Austro-Hungarian state has disappeared,' he said, 'so who will be responsible for the bill? As a lawyer, it seems to me that it's a question of international law rather than politics – just as if you went to court with a claim for damages. Anyway, although we were fighting mainly against Austria, there were German troops opposing us, and our shipping was sunk by German submarines, so clearly Germany has collective responsibility for the payment of compensation in our case.'

Clemenceau sighed. They were thinking only of themselves, the Italians, as usual.

'I don't think there's any matter of principle to be argued about here,' he said. 'It's simply a question of having the commission set up sub-committees to examine the financial, legal and other aspects of the problem, and to carry out a detailed investigation into the resources Germany has – railways, mines and so on.'

'You're right,' Lloyd George agreed. 'To my mind, the greatest difficulty will lie in discovering precisely where any compensation might come from.'

Sonnino, beetle-browed and intense, with the dark skin tones of his Jewish father, spoke for the first time, punctuating his words with the strange motion of the right hand towards his chest that had become his habit for imparting emphasis. There had to be some common principle on which claims for reparations were based, he said. Both the justice and the amount of any claim would have to be properly assessed.

Clemenceau, sensing that the Italian was concerned lest his country should be short-changed, said it was up to each government to formulate its own claims, and these could then be examined by an expert committee representing all the Allies.

'I don't think there can be any sort of general principle,' he added. 'I mean, I don't think I'm competent to judge what Italy should claim, any more than Baron Sonnino could say what France ought to ask.'

But the British Foreign Secretary, Arthur Balfour, supported Sonnino. 'We can't have each government working out its claim on a different basis.'

'Exactly,' Sonnino said. 'There has to be a common denominator. I mean, suppose a place that was famous for bathing put in claims on the ground that it had lost all its patrons because of enemy action. Would that be a justifiable claim?'

This time the others ignored him. They were well used to his unfortunate penchant for lapsing into homely metaphors that did not add a great deal to the point under discussion.

'We're agreed, then?' said Clemenceau. 'Each government will work out in detail its own claim for compensation, and they'll all be examined by a commission nominated by us.'

They were agreed, it seemed. During a short break, Lloyd George turned to Clemenceau and said: 'We're going to have the devil's own job with this reparations business, you know. The sort of sums that are being bandied about here are sheer fantasy. I'm very much afraid that expectations are being raised that we haven't a hope of meeting.'

'We all have public opinion to contend with,' said Clemenceau. 'And I don't think you can argue there's anything wrong with the principle of reparations. That's why I had it inserted in the armistice terms.'

'It's not the principle I'm worried about. It's where the money is actually going to come from. And your people don't help, with your finance minister going about saying that we'll be able to recover the entire costs of the war.'

'Klotz?' Clemenceau said. 'Oh, take no notice of what he says. He's the only Jew I've ever met who knows nothing about finance. But the fact is that we're all going to face serious budgetary problems as a result of the war, and the taxpayers won't put up with footing the bill.'

Lloyd George turned away. 'Oh, well,' he said, 'let's go and talk about what we're going to do with the Kaiser. I'm going to have to say something about that before the election, too.'

'At least it will mean we aren't talking about the new Roman empire,' said Clemenceau.

Lloyd George smiled. 'There's a feeling among some members of my Cabinet that we should leave the Americans to deal with that subject. I'm half inclined to let them.'

# CHAPTER 4

# *Pax Americana*

## I

The twenty-eighth President of the United States of America was looking forward to the prospect of making history. Thomas Woodrow Wilson was to become the first holder of his exalted office to quit his native shores while still lodged at the White House. President McKinley had wanted to visit Europe at the turn of the century, but had doubted his legal right to leave his country. Theodore Roosevelt had actually set foot in Panama in 1906, but that did not count, since it was virtually an American possession. Most recently, William Howard Taft had gone so far as to give up his customary annual holiday in Canada, no doubt fearing disaster if he strayed into old colonial territory – though he had stepped very briefly across the border into Mexico. But it was to be Woodrow Wilson, the Democrat who had soundly beaten the Republican Taft in the 1912 election, who would take the presidency almost literally into uncharted waters.

Technically, he had already done so, and with some style. At Hoboken harbour in New Jersey, the President boarded the great ocean liner *George Washington* and, to the accompaniment of hundreds of ships' sirens and whistles, sailed majestically past Manhattan, where a populace thrilled to participate in the historic moment waved him on his way with handkerchiefs and ticker tape. At the entrance to the bay, a naval airship escorted the liner to a rendezvous with the battleship *Pennsylvania* and the ten destroyers that completed the presidential flotilla for the wintry cruise into posterity.

Now, far out in the north Atlantic beyond American territorial waters, with a blueprint for world peace in his luggage, Wilson contemplated the triumph to come as he healed the wounds of war-scarred Europe with the balm of American ideals of liberty, justice and democracy. It had been President McKinley who had established the United States as a world power in the Spanish-American war, but it would be President Wilson who would lay claim to his country's leadership of the world – and do it in person, at that.

Not that the last element had really been part of the plan. Throughout the course of the war, the tall, bespectacled, lantern-jawed Wilson had conducted himself with the professorial aloofness that came naturally from the years he had spent at the university of Princeton, before his somewhat unexpected success at the summit of politics. At first, while Americans watched with fascinated horror as the great armies clashed in 1914, their President's attitude had manifested itself in a self-righteous sense of Olympian detachment from the fray.

'There is such a thing as a man being too proud to fight,' the President had announced loftily. 'There is such a thing as a nation being so right that it does not need to convince others by force.'

America had, and had wanted, no part in this sordid conflict. As Wilson's closest confidant and adviser, Colonel House, told him in the early days of the war, there would be no good outcome to look forward to.

'If the Allies win, it means largely the domination of Russia on the continent of Europe, and if Germany wins, it means the unspeakable tyranny of militarism for generations to come.'

'We must remain neutral,' Wilson said, 'in fact as well as in name. We have to be impartial in thought as well as in action.'

It was with this in mind that he wrote to each of the emperors and kings of the belligerent nations within a few days of the outbreak of hostilities:

> *I feel it to be my privilege and my duty to say to Your Majesty, in a spirit of most earnest friendship, that I should welcome an opportunity to act in the interest of European peace, either now or at any time that might be thought more suitable as an occasion to serve Your Majesty and all concerned in a way that would afford me lasting cause for gratitude and happiness.*

It caused the crowned heads to be scratched in some perplexity. The American ambassador in Rome cabled, prophetically as it turned out, to his boss, while the Germans swept towards Paris in the autumn of 1914, that 'it seems to be considered that the war will not end until one or other party is absolutely discouraged and that no tenders of friendly offices will avail before that crisis'.

Later, Colonel House, dispatched on a tour of European capitals to counsel restraint, had to report an even dustier response from the German Kaiser.

'The Kaiser told our ambassador in Berlin that he and his cousins, George in England and Nicholas in Russia, would make peace when the time came,' he informed the President. 'He made it clear that mere democracies like France and the United States could never take part in such a settlement. His whole attitude seemed to be that war was a royal sport.'

Wilson was disgusted. 'The only way to put a stop to this sort of thing in the future is to go for disarmament and at the same time to form some kind of association of nations with the power to punish those who break the peace.'

'But in the meantime,' House said, 'there is the question of what our stance should be now.'

'I suppose the best solution would be a deadlock in Europe,' said Wilson, 'without triumph or punishment. So far as I can see, the war aims of the two sides are virtually the same – though I must say, my sympathies lie on the side of the British and French. I've never liked the way the German mind works, and I've never been fond of the German character.'

'In that case, Mr President, I suggest you offer to call a conference to discuss the terms on which the war can be ended, with the proviso that if Germany refuses to accept conditions you and the Entente powers find acceptable, we would go in on their side to compel German agreement.'

'You can try it,' Wilson replied, 'but we are not concerned

with the causes and objectives of this war. We ought to keep out of it. Look, I'm heart and soul for the Allies. No decent man could be anything else. But that's only my own, personal opinion and there are many others in this country who think differently. In places like the West and the Middle West, there's probably no opinion at all. I can't force my opinion on the people of the United States and bring them into a war they don't understand.'

Colonel House thought he understood the situation. The tall, languid Texan banker – the 'colonel' was not a military rank, but a courtesy title in the old Southern manner, bestowed on a member of the plantation aristocracy – was a student of psychology, and he flattered himself that he was familiar with the way the President's mind worked. He knew that Wilson saw himself as a political philosopher in the mould of the Founding Fathers. His heroes were Jefferson, Madison, Webster and Hamilton, and to him their high ideals were an essential part of the American birthright. House had followed him along the campaign trail, and the voters had taken this unlikely academic to their hearts because he seemed to remind them of what 'The American Idea' was all about – *a government of all the people, by all the people, for all the people; a government after the principles of eternal justice, the unchanging law of God.* But above all a government of the head more than the heart.

The test of a nation, Wilson had asserted after the outbreak of war, was its capacity for self-possession, its ability to resist excitement and think calmly. House reassured the President that a policy of 'benevolent neutrality' was the only sensible course.

And so it had remained, even when the loss of American shipping and American lives to German submarines meant that physical neutrality was no longer a credible policy, and the United States reluctantly entered the war on the Allies' side in April 1917. By that time, Wilson had convinced himself – with the help of Colonel House, whose motives were more political than philosophical – that 'The American Idea' must be exported to the world in order to save it from itself. The philosopher and the politician in Wilson had reached an accommodation with each other, the one demanding a cause, the other seeking action and results.

'The tragical events of the last thirty months,' Wilson declared after winning a second presidential term in the autumn of 1916, 'have made us citizens of the world. There can be no turning back. Our own fortunes as a nation are involved, whether we would have it so or not.'

That was the politician speaking. Colonel House had helped to persuade him that the Allies were so weakened and demoralized as to be on the point of seeking terms from Germany.

'But that would be a disaster,' the horrified President had exclaimed. 'It would mean a victory for militarism.'

The Colonel, more openly anti-German from the outset, had quietly raised hopes in London and Paris that American power might soon tip the balance, and though Wilson had disavowed his remarks, the President had conceded privately that America's involvement in the war was beginning to look inevitable if she were to protect her own vital interests. Apart from anything else, there were billions of dollars of outstanding American loans to the Allies, much channelled into the purchase of American goods – an Allied defeat or an unsatisfactory peace would have had disastrous consequences for the economy. Action was required to produce the right result.

Yet whatever the political necessities, the philosopher would not be silenced, as Wilson made clear when, preceded by a squadron of cavalry befitting any militaristic European monarch, he made his way up Capitol Hill on the dark, damp evening of 2 April 1917, to ask the Congress to vote for war.

'It is a fearful thing to lead this great peaceful people into war,' he intoned, rather in the manner of the Presbyterian preachers he remembered from his boyhood in Virginia, 'the most terrible and disastrous of all wars, civilization itself seeming to be in the balance. But the right is more important than the peace. The world must be made safe for democracy. America will fight for her greatest values, for democracy and freedom, for the principles that gave her birth and happiness and peace which she has treasured.'

He concluded with a sentence cribbed directly from Martin Luther: 'God helping her, she can do no other.'

But still, somehow, she would remain above the conflict into which she was sending her young men to die – or at least the President would.

'We must fight without rancour and uphold with proud punctilio the principles of right and fair play we profess to be fighting for.'

It was not a war so much as a crusade, and Wilson lost no

time in letting his new allies know where he stood. To begin with, he made it clear that America was not really an ally at all, merely an associated power fighting on the Allied side for the sole purpose of ending the war and establishing a just peace.

'We are glad, now that we see the facts with no veil of false pretence about them, to fight for the ultimate peace of the world and for the liberation of its peoples, the German peoples included; for the rights of nations, great and small, and the privilege of men everywhere to choose their way of life and of obedience. Peace must be planted upon the tested foundations of political liberty.'

'Good God!' King George V exclaimed when he heard. 'Have we got a co-belligerent or a damned umpire?'

It was left to the ubiquitous Colonel House to descend from Olympus and tell the Allies what they really wanted to hear. He sent a cable to Lloyd George that cut through the rhetoric:

> *Tell your people we are with you to the finish of our resources in supplies, money and men. We are prepared to go the whole hog. They have no idea how soon we can raise a big army; many thousands of young men already have the necessary training – cadets in our military schools and state institutions. Texas alone has 200,000 men who can ride and shoot. They are men of the calibre of your Canadians and Australians.*

Meanwhile, the politician and the philosopher in Wilson continued to wrestle with each other. The first, with his desire for quick results, insisted on conscription rather than conviction and gave orders for the establishment of a military draft that compulsorily raised an army of nearly two million men in a matter of months. To the philosopher, though, the details of war-making could be left to lesser mortals while he concerned himself with preparations for imposing the peace. It became an obsession with him, and by January 1918 he was ready to deliver his Pax Americana to a world obviously in sore need of it.

'We entered this war because violations of right had occurred which touched us to the quick and made the life of our own people impossible unless they were corrected and the world secured once for all against their recurrence. What we demand in this war, therefore, is nothing peculiar to ourselves. It is that the world be made fit and safe to live in; and particularly that it be made safe for every peace-loving nation which, like our own, wishes to live its own life, determine its own institutions, be assured of justice and fair dealing by the other peoples of the world as against force and selfish aggression. All the peoples of the world are in effect partners in this interest, and for our own part we see very clearly that unless justice be done to others it will not be done to us. The programme of the world's peace, therefore, is our programme, the only possible programme, as we see it . . .'

It was his finest hour, as he went on to enumerate what became known as the Fourteen Points:

> Open diplomacy to replace secret negotiations and treaties;
> Absolute freedom of navigation on the seas in peace and war;

The removal of economic barriers and the establishment of equal trading arrangements;

Reduction in armaments to minimal levels guaranteeing
security;

Settlement of colonial claims, taking into account the
wishes of the local populations;

Comprehensive settlement with Russia in the wake of
the Bolshevik Revolution;

Evacuation by Germany of Belgium;

Withdrawal by Germany from invaded French territory
and the restoration to France of Alsace and Lorraine;

Choice of new systems of government by the peoples of
Austria and Hungary;

Readjustment of Italy's frontiers with former Austrian
territory;

Establishment of independent states in the formerly
occupied Balkans;

Creation of independent states in regions formerly
occupied by Turkey;

Establishment of an independent state of Poland, free
from German or Russian domination;

Formation of a general association of nations under
specific covenants for the purpose of affording mutual
guarantees of political independence and territorial
integrity to great and small states alike.

Woodrow Wilson basked in the knowledge that he had
outdone even the Founding Fathers. In the future, the star-
spangled banner would wave benignly not merely over the

home of liberty, but over the entire world – and it had been achieved not by conquest, not by secret diplomacy, but by the triumph of The American Idea. If a certain amount of force had been necessary in expressing the idea, that was unfortunate, but it could be justified. In the face of evil, there was sometimes no alternative to force, 'force to the utmost, force without stint or limit, the righteous and triumphant force which shall make right the law of the world and cast every selfish dominion down in the dust', as the President put it, sounding ever more like an Old Testament prophet.

As he looked back on it now, making his stately progress across the Atlantic, it had all been remarkably easy, a tribute, surely, to the power of reason and goodness. The Germans, having previously resisted all attempts at making peace, had recognized the Olympian disinterest of the Fourteen Points and placed their faith in the American Way. They had needed a certain amount of encouragement, of course, as was only to be expected with an old-fashioned autocracy, but it was particularly gratifying that their transition to a democratic system of government had been accomplished so readily. It was clear proof that, given freedom, fairness and justice, men could be trusted to behave sensibly.

The President's only regret was that the British, the French and the Italians had conducted themselves with rather less grace than he might have hoped. All those notes from Lloyd George, for instance, asking what certain passages in the Fourteen Points meant in practice, and niggling about the restoration of territory or the freedom of the seas; France refusing to see the difference between what Clemenceau called the balance of power and what Wilson referred to as the 'concert of power' under the aegis of a league of nations; Italy interpreting its territorial concessions as an excuse to grab whatever Orlando and Sonnino could get their hands on. It was disappointing to see their apparent inability, or more likely unwillingness, to look beyond the short-term gains of the victory that had been delivered to them and fix their gaze on the greater prizes to be won in the creation of a better world.

That, indeed, had been part of Wilson's reason for abandoning the philosophical heights and taking his message in person into the political lowlands.

'Look,' he told Colonel House, after persuading the Germans to accept his terms, 'we must try hard to prevent the Allies from achieving too much success and security under the military conditions of the armistice. If they end up in too strong a position, that will make a genuine peace settlement exceedingly difficult, if not impossible.'

He had sent the Colonel to Paris towards the end of October, since it seemed to be the French who were demanding that Germany be left defenceless and, apparently, bankrupt, which was entirely against the spirit of the Fourteen Points. There had also been disturbing reports from the American embassy in London that Lloyd George had been less than enthusiastic about having his war aims determined by a man who had been a college professor until only a few years ago.

'Tell them,' Wilson instructed House grimly, 'that if they

will not accept the Fourteen Points as the basis of an agreement, we would be obliged to pass on that information to the enemy, and we might then have to consider opening direct negotiations with Germany and Austria ourselves.'

It was something of an empty threat, perhaps, given that American soldiers were now deeply committed on the Western Front, but it was one the British and French could not afford to ignore. America had resisted complete integration of its forces into the Allies' overall military command under Marshal Foch, and it had remained clear about its position as merely an associated power. It would not have been impossible, had President Wilson chosen to do so, for the Americans to make peace on their own terms, leaving Britain, France and Italy the choice of either continuing to fight without American support or, more likely, accepting peace terms that took no account of their interests.

The Colonel delivered the President's message at a meeting with the Allied leaders on 29 October, cabling the White House afterwards: *It had a very exciting effect on those present.* Lloyd George had blustered about continuing the war, Clemenceau had been sarcastic, but *We had the whip hand, and I pushed our position to the limit.*

Nevertheless, when the harsh terms drawn up by Marshal Foch were revealed, Wilson saw just how little attention had been paid to his idea of peace without victory, and when he heard that his own army commander in France, General Pershing, had tried to undermine the President's position by pressing for unconditional surrender, the man of action rose up. Within a week of the signing of the armistice, House received a cable in Paris:

> I am issuing the following announcement: The President expects to sail for France immediately after the opening of the regular session of the Congress, for the purpose of taking part in the discussion and settlement of the main features of the treaty of peace. It is not likely that it will be possible for him to remain throughout the sessions of the formal peace conference, but his presence at the outset is necessary in order to obviate the manifest disadvantages of discussion by cable in determining the greater outlines of the final treaty, about which he must necessarily be consulted.

They tried to dissuade him, of course, both Colonel House and the Secretary of State, Robert Lansing, the international lawyer from New York who had stepped into the job in 1915 when the then secretary had objected to the President's intention to take a harder line against Germany.

House counselled that, by appearing in person, the President would make himself the focus for all manner of discontent among European radicals opposed to governments that were less democratic than America's.

'That may be no bad thing,' Wilson reflected. 'If the politicians won't see reason, I can appeal directly to their people.'

Lansing, schooled in a somewhat old-fashioned manner of diplomacy, preferred that the details of the peace treaty should be left to professionals.

Wilson snapped: 'I do not intend to allow this treaty to be drawn up by lawyers.'

Even the President's doctor, Rear Admiral Grayson, joined in. The chronic indigestion that troubled Wilson had been brought under control by Grayson's prescription of a bland diet and regular habits, but his health had never been robust. Although he appeared to have recovered fully from a stroke he had suffered twelve years earlier, Grayson was ever-watchful for signs of a recurrence. Wilson was now sixty-two, and the risk increased with each passing year. In Washington, the President's workload was strictly controlled, with frequent periods of rest, and the doctor was afraid that the effort and excitement of a trip to Europe would be too much for him.

Those objections, too, had been waved aside. Wilson was thinking not of his health, but of history, and in this the politician and the philosopher were at one. From the political point of view, his second presidential term had not been marked by the popularity, bordering on adulation, that had accompanied his first. The American people had not lived up to his expectations of their appetite for social reform and idealistic government. His victory in 1916 had been narrow, and since then the number of his critics had grown steadily, not only among Republicans but also in certain parts of the Democrat ranks. Some thought him too radical, others not radical enough. And since he had been, though unwittingly, re-elected as 'the man who kept America out of the war', the reversal of policy in the spring of 1917, a couple of months after his inauguration, had aroused further discontent in some quarters. That was reflected in the Democrats' indifferent performance at the congressional elections of 1918, a week before the signing of the armistice, when they lost their majorities in both the House of Representatives and the Senate.

If he was not to finish his term as a lame duck president, Wilson needed a popular success, and with domestic policy in disarray because of the war effort, foreign affairs seemed to offer the best opportunity.

The Fourteen Points and their role in achieving the armistice had brought public acclaim for the President. A triumphant conclusion of the peace conference, showing America firmly established at the head of a new world order based on freedom, democracy and disarmament, would ensure that his last years in the White House would take the form of a golden sunset. He knew he could achieve that by maintaining his air of muscular detachment, but if you were going to have a triumph, why not enjoy it to the full?

'I don't think personal prestige is worth anything unless it rubs shoulders with the world,' he said as he canvassed support in the Senate for his historic trip. 'If it's so sensitive a plant that it can't be exhibited in public, it will wither anyhow.'

Colonel House had told him of the reverence with which his name was spoken in France, and the prospect of an outpouring of foreign gratitude, relayed in graphic detail back to the American press, was impossible to resist.

Similarly, the philosopher was excited by the opportunity to deliver his tablets directly to men he had up to now known only on paper. He imagined himself appearing at the peace conference, standing before Lloyd George and Clemenceau and an assembled throng of bit-players on the world stage, and declaiming: 'Gentlemen, I am here to say for the United States that I don't want anything out of this. And I'm here to see that *you* don't get anything out of it.'

He had fobbed off House and Lansing with the idea that he would bestride Europe for a brief moment, describe the outline of the peace treaty he wished to see adopted, and return to Olympus to await in lonely splendour the conclusion of his marvellous work. But, as the *George Washington* spread her massive wake under dark Atlantic skies, he was coming to the conclusion that the only man capable of constructing the peace after the most destructive war in history was Woodrow Wilson. He owed it to himself. He owed it to America. He owed it to the world. And, as his grandfather, his father and his uncle – Presbyterian ministers all – would have said back in Virginia, he owed it to God.

'You know, dear,' Wilson said, turning towards his handsome wife, Edith, as they sat in their stateroom, 'the future of civilization may depend on this moment, and I can't help feeling that I'm more than equal to the challenge. I doubt if any statesman has ever had such an opportunity before.'

She smiled at him. 'And I'm right beside you, dearest.'

'You know how much that means to me. Being here reminds me of what I said to you, oh, it seems a long time ago now. I said the ship of state had sailed into dangerous waters with the war in Europe and I felt like a pilot who had to pay attention every moment so it wouldn't strike a reef.'

'And you said you must have me in the pilot house.'

He frowned. 'I can't trust them, you know, the others. Oh, House has great powers of observation and a wonderful ability to give clear, cool reports . . .'

Edith said: 'Well, I certainly wouldn't trust *him* with great affairs of state. He's so, so . . . *ingratiating*. And I'm not sure he always tells the truth.'

'And Lansing,' Wilson continued, 'well, he's just stupid. I have a constant fear that he'll make some really serious blunder. He's a figurehead at the State Department, nothing more. I suppose he'll have to be in the delegation, but if this thing is to reach the proper conclusion, I have no choice but to take charge of it myself.'

'I wonder what they're like,' Edith mused, 'Mr Clemenceau and Mr Lloyd George.'

'From what House tells me, I don't think I'm going to get on with them very well. But no matter. They depend on us now. They kept on urging us to come in on their side, and we did, and we brought it to an end. We have, as House put it, the whip hand. They accepted my Fourteen Points and now they're going to have to live with them, especially the league of nations. They're going to have to get used to the fact that the world has changed, that the bad old ways won't work any more.'

'Well, it won't be long now.'

'Day after tomorrow, dear. Friday the Thirteenth, just as I planned.' Wilson grinned at his wife. He had always regarded thirteen as his lucky number.

## 11

—

At ten o'clock in the morning, the boom of a great cannon split the air over Paris and reverberated all along the Champs Elysées from the Arc de Triomphe to the Place de la Concorde. As the noise died away, an excited crowd lining the boulevard, and swarms of spectators on the fringing rooftops, heard the clattering hooves of many horses, then strained with anticipation when a detachment of cavalry, bedecked in Napoleonic splendour, trotted under the Arc and into the wide avenue. The riders were followed by a swelling roar of voices as hundreds of thousands of people caught their first glimpse of the man they had all come to see – 'Voodro' Veelson! Voodro' Veelson! Voodro' Veelson! . . .'

The President, seated in an open carriage alongside Raymond Poincaré, smiled and waved his hat almost wildly to the cheering multitude that made up the most enthusiastic welcome Paris had ever bestowed on a visiting foreign dignitary. Since his arrival in the port of Brest the previous day, Wilson's reception had resembled nothing so much as the triumphant progress of a Roman emperor returning from conquest. Indeed, a special edition of the newspaper *L'Humanité* compared the President to Marcus Aurelius Antoninus, the sainted ruler of second-century Rome.

Poincaré, never much of an orator, surpassed himself when he began his speech of welcome in the gilded grandeur of the Elysée Palace, where the flower of France had gathered for a luncheon in Wilson's honour:

'Paris, indeed the whole of France, has awaited your arrival with impatience, eager to acclaim the illustrious democrat whose words and deeds have been inspired by exalted thought, the philosopher delighting in the solution of universal laws from particular events, the eminent statesman who has found a way to express the highest political and moral truths in formulas which bear the stamp of immortality. We have a passionate desire to offer, through you personally, our thanks to the United States for its invaluable assistance to the defenders of right and liberty. France knows the friendship of America. She knows your rectitude and elevation of spirit. It is in the fullest confidence that she is ready to work with you.'

That, however, was the full extent of Monsieur le Président's purple prose. It was also – at least so far as official France was concerned – the limit of the welcome. They might flatter the philosopher, almost deify the great democrat, but the French were not about to allow the high-flown ideals of a political parvenu interfere with the pursuit of their just retribution for the crimes committed against France in her heroic and costly defence of freedom. The pleasantries over, Poincaré outlined what was really expected from the new champion of Western civilization. The assembled dignitaries – members of the Cabinet, former presidents, prime ministers, foreign ministers, presidents and vice-presidents of the Senate and Chamber of Deputies, high commissioners, Marshals of France, foreign ambassadors and ministers, and a goodly number of high-ranking Americans – were treated to a comprehensive list of German war crimes, a catalogue of 'deliberate savagery' and of what Poincaré called a cynical programme of pillage and industrial annihilation. President Wilson would see with his own eyes the evidence of these atrocities and would be in a position to deliver a verdict on the culpability of the Germans. That verdict, of course, would be 'Guilty'.

'Should this guilt remain unpunished,' Poincaré said pointedly, 'the most splendid victories would be in vain. France has not struggled, endured and suffered for four long years only to see those responsible go unpunished and to face the possibility of being some day again exposed to aggression. The country is yearning for a peace of justice and security.'

And as if that were not clear enough, the diminutive, neatly bearded President laboured the message in his peroration: 'Peace must make amends for the misery and sadness of yesterday, and it must be a guarantee against the dangers of tomorrow. We must introduce into the peace we are going to build all the conditions of justice and all the safeguards of civilization that we can embody in it.'

He was not a philosopher, Poincaré, not by any means, and many people harboured doubts about his abilities as a statesman. His was a deviously legalistic mind, bearing witness to the profession that had occupied most of his attention before his sudden elevation to the premiership in 1912 and thence to the presidency a year later. He dealt in what he saw as facts, always provided they suited his prejudices – and with those he was well-endowed. Chief among them were his dislike of the hierarchy of the Roman Catholic Church and his passionate hatred of Germans. It was that loathing which informed his political career, which had prompted him to invent the alliances that had made a general European war inevitable once Serbia was attacked by Austria in 1914.

He was a man without humour, with little imagination, without flexibility of thought. An opinion once formed was never changed. That was part of his appeal to the conservative French bourgeoisie. You knew where you stood with Raymond Poincaré. He lived up to his name, according to the unfriendly assessment of Georges Clemenceau – *caré* being related to the word that means 'square'.

Lloyd George was learning to share Clemenceau's distaste for the French President, but for Woodrow Wilson, now in only his second day in France, that was something which would come later. He had been well briefed, of course: Colonel House had set up what amounted to an overseas branch of the State Department at the Hôtel Crillon, in the Place de la Concorde, and he had made himself more than familiar with the character of Monsieur Poincaré. Wilson knew what he was up against, but House had assured him that, in general, relations with France were steadily improving. Responding to that long, boring speech at lunch in the Elysée, Wilson was blandly diplomatic.

'I am sure,' he told Poincaré, 'that I shall look upon the ruin wrought by the armies of the Central Empires with the same repulsion and deep indignation that it stirs in the hearts of the men of France and Belgium. I appreciate the necessity of such action in the final settlement of the issues of the war as will not only rebuke such acts of terror and spoliation, but make men everywhere aware that they cannot be ventured upon without the certainty of just punishment.'

But of course there was a bigger picture, and Wilson's attitude from the outset had been that in any war there are two sides, each necessarily engaged in acts of terror and spoliation. It was necessary to remind these belligerent, barely democratic Europeans that America's support of the Allied cause had been far from a foregone conclusion.

'I feel that what I have said and what I have tried to do,' Wilson declared, 'have been said and done only in an attempt to speak the thought of the people of the United States truly and to carry that thought out in action. From the first, the thought of the people of the United States turned toward something more than the mere winning of this war. It turned to the establishment of eternal principles of right and justice. It realized that merely to win the war was not enough; that it must be won in such a way, and the questions raised by it settled in such a way, as to insure the future peace of the world and lay the foundation for the freedom and happiness of its many peoples and nations.'

The message was not lost on the French President. His government had managed to avoid actually adopting Wilson's Fourteen Points as the basis of a peace settlement, and had ignored them altogether in formulating the terms of the armistice Germany had been forced to sign. The Points had done their job in persuading the Germans to give up, but there had always been the assumption that, when it came to serious negotiations, the harsh light of reality would expose Wilson's philosophical aspirations for the laudable flim-flam they really were. Now, though, it was beginning to look as if the American President was taking them seriously.

'I know,' Wilson said, 'with what ardour and enthusiasm the soldiers and sailors of the United States have given the best that was in them to this war of redemption. They have expressed the true spirit of America. They believe their ideals to be acceptable to free peoples everywhere.'

Poincaré did not particularly like what he was hearing. 'War of redemption'? What on earth did that mean? In French eyes, this had been a war fought to victory, won by great sacrifice and indomitable courage. Yet Wilson had uttered the word 'victory' only once, and then almost in passing. Who was being redeemed here? France had redeemed herself. Germany was beyond redemption. Conquest and oppression, that was the German way, and it had to be stopped for good. All this claptrap about ideals and the principles of right and justice would not stop a new wave of grey uniforms and spiked helmets crashing upon France if the Germans were allowed to get away with their crimes for the sake of American ideals.

The more conservative sections of the press had seen the danger, too, pointing out that the Fourteen Points were not exactly Holy Writ and that the Allies had better build on the military superiority they had achieved over Germany as a result of the armistice, just in case Mr Wilson's brave new world of friendly co-operation turned out to be less appealing than the President made it sound. *Le Figaro* went so far as to state openly that, grateful as they might be to Wilson, Frenchmen should not permit themselves to be persuaded by him that their own interests should be subordinated to some vague notion of internationalism – which in any case had about it the rank smell of socialism.

Such support reassured Poincaré, as he listened impassively to Wilson's speech, that his policy of 'France First' was what the mass of the people really wanted. The euphoria would die down and, sooner or later, the Americans would go away and all their nonsense would be forgotten. It would probably be unwise to show his hand openly at this stage – Wilson had, after all, just drawn a crowd of some two million – but there would be plenty of opportunity to set matters on the right course when the details of the peace treaty began to be worked out. Marshal Foch knew exactly what had to be done. The only difficulty was Clemenceau. The Prime Minister's resistance to the Rhineland plan had deeply irritated Poincaré and made him wonder just how much Clemenceau could be relied upon to protect French interests to the full. He seemed much too concerned about maintaining good relations with the Allies, and, of course, not only did he have strong socialistic instincts, but he also fancied himself as something of a philosopher. It would, Poincaré reflected, have to be managed with great care.

Clemenceau himself, sitting a few feet away, had not been greatly interested in what his President had had to say. He was in no doubt about Poincaré's intentions for the peace treaty, and he could not deny that, in many respects, they matched his own. The difference between them was that Poincaré was prepared to risk a breach with the Allies for the greater glory of France, while Clemenceau – anxious as he was to punish and contain the Germans, and to strengthen the French position – wanted the new balance of power in Europe to be supported by the Americans and the British. Listening to

President Wilson, though, he could sense that his aims would not be easily reconciled.

'They live in a different world, these Americans, don't they?' he said quietly, when the speeches had ended, to his Foreign Minister, Stéphan Pichon, an old journalistic colleague from the days when Clemenceau had edited *La Justice* in the 1880s.

'Of course, you were over there, weren't you?' Pichon recalled. 'And your wife . . .'

'Well, the least said about that . . .' Clemenceau replied. 'We were very young. I'm not sure I learned a great deal about America from Mary.'

In his radical youth, he had taken himself off to the United States to see at first hand how things worked in the cradle of liberty. To support himself, he had become a teacher at a girls' school in Stamford, Connecticut, where he had met and eventually married one of his students, Mary Plummer. She had not settled in France, and had returned to America with the couple's three children.

'No,' Clemenceau went on, 'I was thinking that, when I was there – 'Sixty-six or 'Sixty-seven – I was impressed by the freedom of speech, guaranteed by the constitution, and the serious way they went about the processes of democracy. And yet I found there were serious flaws in the way they conducted themselves. I mean, I had very nice and apparently intelligent Americans explaining to me how they were compelled to defend themselves against the Negroes because they were afraid of degenerating if they allowed the races to mingle. I didn't understand it then, but now I think that sort of attitude arises from the fact that the Americans are still too near their beginnings. They need a bit of a past so they can overcome their innocence and see the world for what it is. It takes a country a thousand years to reach the point of understanding that a man is a man. You can sense the same lack of history in what we've just heard from President Wilson. All this business of outlawing war is just a colossal piece of buffoonery.'

'You don't think much of American ideology, then?' said Pichon.

'I think it's a wonderful little article for export.'

The Prime Minister had been both impressed and repelled by the enthusiasm his fellow-countrymen had shown for their illustrious visitor, because he knew that, in part at least, it had been stage-managed by the more extreme socialist parties and the labour unions, whose collectivist ideology he despised. They had been prevented from organizing an official reception, but they had been highly successful at persuading their supporters to fill the streets, and Clemenceau had learned that the Socialist Party would be sending a delegation to see Wilson later this very afternoon, for the purpose of offering support to his internationalist policy.

'The socialists will make as much capital as they can out of Wilson,' he told Pichon. 'They're obviously trying to turn him into some sort of left-wing cult figure on which to pin their hopes of a worldwide workers' revolution.'

The Foreign Minister shrugged. 'Well, we saw them off in the Assembly last week. If we remain firm and continue to block their demands for a foreign policy debate, we should be able to bury this fashion for Wilsonism when the peace conference starts.'

'Just so long as we can bury expansionism as well,' Clemenceau said, glancing across at Poincaré. 'But, if we play our hand cleverly, I think Mr Wilson might well turn out to be our trump card there.'

It was the prospect of just that sort of manipulation that worried some of Wilson's own staff at the Hôtel Crillon, as taken aback as Clemenceau had been by the intensity of feeling displayed by the ordinary people of France.

'This wasn't just an abandon of joy,' the State Department's press spokesman, Ray Stannard Baker, told Robert Lansing as they compared notes on what Colonel House had called *a glorious day, in some ways*. 'There was no organized demonstration, but the labour leaders must have put their millions on the streets. There were an enormous number of workmen and socialists out there.'

Baker knew a socialist when he saw one. The mild-mannered reporter had made his name as a campaigner against the old conservative forces in America and had become associated with an overtly socialist tendency in the press that spent its time exposing political corruption, sharp practice in business and cases of the repression or exploitation of the working classes. 'Muckrakers,' they had been dubbed by the hero of libertarian conservatism, Theodore Roosevelt, the former President whose splitting of the Republican Party had allowed Wilson to win his first presidential election.

'These people,' Roosevelt had said, 'with their sensationalist and politically motivated revelations, are helping to provoke an unhealthy condition of excitement and irritation in the popular mind.'

Baker, now middle-aged and more moderate, and anyway never a committed socialist himself, had jumped aboard Wilson's bandwagon – even affecting pince-nez similar to those worn by the President – because they seemed to share an intellectual, principled, objective and vaguely do-gooding approach to liberty and social justice. But the fearless investigations of his firebrand years, and the hostility they had aroused in some quarters, had given Baker an idea of the risk Wilson was running in Paris.

'The socialists here are going to use Wilson as a stick to beat Clemenceau with,' he said. 'They're out to improve their own political condition.'

Lansing fiddled with his neatly clipped moustache. 'It's not going to go down very well back home. The last thing we need is for the President to be associated with some kind of socialist movement. Teddy Roosevelt is already going about saying the Fourteen Points are nothing more than socialistic mischief-making. And we do have a Republican majority in the Congress to deal with.'

'The trouble is,' said Baker, 'the socialist groupings seem to be the only ones that really believe in the President. I mean, it's obvious that the masses are with him to a man.'

The Secretary of State sighed. 'No, the trouble is that the masses aren't going to write the peace treaty.'

'And that's another problem,' Baker said. 'I'm afraid he's going to have the struggle of his life with the ugly old forces of reaction we have around us here. I don't know if he realizes how powerful they are – or how sly and greedy and cunning.'

None of this, however, was troubling the President. He was much more concerned about the activities of his Secretary of State, and in no very good mood when Colonel House arrived, late in the afternoon, to see him at the eighteenth-century mansion, adjoining the Parc Monceau, placed at Wilson's disposal by Prince Murat, descendant of the famous Napoleonic marshal.

'I can't trust Lansing to do anything right,' Wilson thundered. 'He has no imagination, no constructive ability – in fact, I doubt whether he has any real ability of any kind. I seem to have to do everything myself if I want it done properly.'

Lansing had appointed three career diplomats to lead the President's staff at the peace conference, but, in his customary way, he had failed to consult the President first. Wilson, whose mind was too lofty to concern itself with details, had assumed that House was creating an organization in Paris that would be headed by men they would choose together – men Wilson could trust. He knew nothing of Lansing's appointments until his ship was crossing the Atlantic, and he had fumed about it ever since.

Named secretary to the American delegation was Joseph Grew, a young, handsome Bostonian who had served with some distinction at the embassies in Berlin and Vienna before America's declaration of war, and had lately become acting head of the Western European Affairs division of the State Department. He was intelligent, able and, like Lansing, a realist in foreign policy questions. Unfortunately, he was also a Republican by inclination, and that – along with his similarities to Lansing – was unacceptable to Wilson. Grew's assistants were, naturally enough, two more State Department professionals, Leland Harrison and Philip Patchin.

'I'll put them all out,' Wilson snarled. 'We'll start again and do the thing as it should have been done in the first instance. Do you have anyone in mind?'

The Colonel argued that, although Grew's political leanings and connections with Lansing might not make him the ideal choice, he was qualified for the post and at least he was a gentleman, who would know how to behave honourably.

'Then I'll send Harrison and Patchin home,' the President countered.

'Let's talk to Grew,' House suggested.

He sent for the young man, an impressive figure, endowed with great charm and exemplary manners. With great respect, he begged the President to let him keep his assistants, men he could rely upon to do their work honestly and impartially. Reluctantly, with the persuasion of House, Wilson agreed.

'But I'm not going to let these clerks make a mess of things,' he warned House.

The Colonel soothed him as he always did, recalling the remarkable upsurge of warmth he had inspired in the French people.

'I really think your visit is changing the political climate here,' House said. 'The government is realizing that it can't afford to ignore the feelings of the people, and that's bound to make our task a great deal easier. I was thinking that it might be no bad thing if you were to get a similar kind of endorsement in England.'

'What did you have in mind?' Wilson asked.

'Well, we've been rather concerned about the tone of the election campaign over there, which seems to have been less about peace and more about punishing the Germans. Of course, the Labour Party has always been solidly behind the principles of the Fourteen Points, but now it has broken with the Lloyd George coalition, it looks very much as if it will come out of the election rather badly. The ambassador is suggesting that the Conservatives who are running with Lloyd George will win hands down.'

The campaign for punishment and retribution had been led, of course, by Lord Northcliffe, but, as Colonel House had said, it was now threatening to produce the opposite of the election result that The Chief wanted to see. While doing his best to support left-wing candidates in his newspapers – because of his vendetta against Lloyd George and the overwhelmingly Tory coalition – Northcliffe's attempts to force the Prime Minister into demanding financial reparation from Germany had encouraged a chorus of support among the right-wingers whose re-election he was seeking to prevent. One hard-liner, indeed, had been provoked into promising that Britain was going to 'get everything out of Germany that you can squeeze out of a lemon, and a bit more . . . to squeeze her until you can hear the pips squeak'.

Far from persuading Lloyd George to return to his radical roots, the constant sniping from *The Times* and the *Daily Mail* on the subject of reparations had served to convince him that it was the people who would vote for the Tory candidates under the coalition banner to whom he must appeal if he was to win the election. That worried him, and especially their demand that Germany should repay to Britain the full cost of the war. It was not that he had any philosophical objection to the concept of reparations – there were, after all, historical precedents, such as the settlement at the end of the Napoleonic wars. But he was afraid that a heavy financial penalty imposed on Germany by the triumphant Allies would make the peace treaty unworkable. If the Germans were to pay compensation, it must be fair and reasonable, and an amount that they could afford.

Conscious of the wild expectations whipped up by Northcliffe and his supporters, the Prime Minister appointed an expert commission of finance ministers, businessmen and financiers to consider the practical possibilities of extracting reparations from the Germans, and to estimate how much Germany might be in a position to pay. Unfortunately, this group, which included the governor of the Bank of England, proved to have been tainted by the hysteria that raged all about it. The commission's report, delivered just before the December election, read:

> The total costs of the war to the Allies is the measure of the indemnity which the enemy powers should in justice pay. Although it is not yet possible to estimate what the total cost of the war will be, the figures available indicate that so far the direct costs of the war to the Allies have been £24,000,000,000; and the committee have certainly no reason to suppose that the enemy powers could not provide £1,200,000,000 per

annum as interest on the above amount when normal
conditions are restored. The indemnity should be paid
in cash, kind, securities, and by means of a funding loan.

Lloyd George and Bonar Law, who read the report
together, were thunderstruck.

'It's sheer madness,' the Prime Minister gasped. 'It's
incredible that men of such position, experience and
responsibility should have put their names to a report like this.
We can't possibly publish it. It would just excite foolish hopes
that the enemy could shoulder the whole, or even a substantial
part of our war burdens.'

Bonar Law, who inclined towards Lloyd George's view
about reparations, agreed: 'It would be far too dangerous.
Those figures would depend on making slaves of German
workers for generations to come, and world markets would be
thrown into chaos when they were flooded with German
goods that had to be bought so the Germans could meet their
financial obligations to the Allies.'

Both men knew that the re-election of the coalition
government would depend at least to some extent on the
votes of extremists. They were aware of the risk involved in
giving credence to the wild, fantastic aspirations that were
appearing daily in the press. If such expectations were
encouraged but not met, the effect on a government elected
on the basis of them would be fatal. At the same time,
however, they could not afford to dash completely public
hopes of obtaining compensation from the beaten enemy if
they were to win the election. To cover the gap, they

concocted the phrase 'up to the limit of capacity', which the Prime Minister would introduce in a campaign speech he was due to deliver.

'Germany should pay to the utmost limit of her capacity,' Lloyd George told a noisy election audience in Bristol. 'Why have I always said "up to the limit of capacity"? Well, if I were to say to you, "Not merely ought Germany to pay, but we can expect every penny", I should be doing so without giving you the whole of the facts. Let me give you the facts. Before the war, it was estimated that the wealth of Germany was between fifteen and twenty thousand million pounds. The bill is twenty-four thousand millions, so if that estimate of the total assets of Germany was correct – that is, our estimate before the war – it is quite clear that, even if you take the whole of this wealth away – and you cannot do that because there are seventy million people who have got to work in order to make that wealth available – there would not be enough.'

He carefully avoided suggesting any figure that might meet the case, but, as the cheers rolled round the hall, the excitement of the occasion overcame him, and he declared: 'We propose to demand the whole cost of the war.'

It was a careless promise that would return to haunt him after the election.

President Wilson asked Colonel House: 'When will we know the result of the British election?'

'Almost certainly on Monday.'

'And you think that if Lloyd George and the coalition are re-elected, it will cause difficulties for us?'

House grimaced. 'It looks as if Lloyd George will be in the grip of the old-fashioned imperialist Conservatives even more than he has been up to now. Remember all the problems over the armistice. Lloyd George picked over almost every word of your notes to the Germans. And then there was the business over the freedom of navigation. They said your proposal was against the interests of their empire. I had to get pretty tough with them. I think there may be a similar fight over the league of nations.'

'I'm standing absolutely firm on that,' Wilson said. 'Without the league of nations, nothing else gets done.'

House pointed out that the greatest support for the idea of a league of nations, and international co-operation in general, was to be found among the working classes, who also admired American ideals of democracy and sought reform on that basis in their own countries. That, he was sure, would be as true in Britain as it obviously had been in France, where the President had seen ordinary working people turn out in their thousands to welcome him. If, as seemed likely, the old ruling class was returned to power in the election, it might be a good idea for the President to visit Britain and appeal directly to his natural supporters there. He would certainly have time to do it, since all the indications were that the peace conference would not begin until about the middle of January.

Wilson liked the idea. He had been impressed by the enthusiastic reception of the French people, and it would be greatly to his credit – not least among the voters back home – if he was seen to provoke such public acclamation in Britain, too. There would be no difficulty about arranging a state visit at short notice. The King had already issued an invitation, to which the President had not fully replied.

In that case, House said, it would do no harm to prepare public opinion in Britain for the President's arrival. He had heard from Lord Northcliffe, who was extremely anxious to conduct a personal interview with the President. Northcliffe had generally been very sympathetic towards the American view of the world, and there had been extremely favourable coverage in *The Times* of Wilson's visit to Paris. Granting Northcliffe an interview might serve to reassure the British that they had nothing to fear from the President's policies.

Accordingly, a few days later, the Napoleon of Fleet Street arrived at the Napoleonic mansion in the Rue Monceau, generously offering President Wilson the opportunity to speak through what he called the democratic megaphone of the press. In truth, however, Northcliffe was more interested in using the opportunity to further his own curious causes than in broadcasting any message Wilson wanted to deliver.

The results of the election had been declared, and The Chief had been dismayed to see that, in spite of his best efforts, Lloyd George and his coalition supporters had won by a landslide. All but fourteen of the candidates who had received the Bonar Law–Lloyd George endorsement – 'the coupon', as it had become known – had been returned to Parliament, and they were overwhelmingly Tories. The Prime Minister still had no more than the hundred or so Liberal supporters at his back, while the official Liberal Party had been almost wiped out, and Labour had failed to achieve the breakthrough it had sought by appealing directly to the country. The ugly old forces of reaction, as Ray Baker had characterized them, were firmly in control.

'It's turned out much worse even than I predicted,' Northcliffe had muttered darkly to one of his executives at the *Daily Mail*. 'I'm afraid this government of Tory reactionaries is going to be a direct incentive to dangerous discontent.'

It was with the fear of a workers' revolution in mind – quite apart from his disgust at Lloyd George – that he had ordered his editors to give prominence to what he had described as 'the sane and intellectual Labour line' during the election campaign, emphasizing the socialists' appeal to idealism and internationalism and using Wilson as its touchstone.

'We are all idealists now in international affairs,' he had trumpeted in *The Times*, 'and we look to Wilson to help us realize these ideals and to reconstruct out of this welter a better and fairer world.'

But the appeal had failed, as well it might, given that at the same time Northcliffe's newspapers had been supporting the extremist Tories' demands for severe financial penalties for Germany and for the arrest and trial of the Kaiser as a war criminal. The contradiction made no impression on Northcliffe's mind as it slid into megalomania. And now, having been signally unsuccessful in his attempts to influence the composition of the new government, The Chief had fallen prey once more to his paranoid suspicion of Lloyd George, and had set himself the task of ensuring that the Prime Minister did not bow before American power and allow President Wilson to dictate peace terms that might be to the disadvantage of Britain.

At the Villa Murat, as he admired the ornate First Empire furniture, the overcrowded bronzes, the Aubusson carpet and the David paintings, Northcliffe carefully steered his interview with Wilson in the direction he desired. He was keen to make the President acknowledge that he would take account of British interests, and his first step was to try to identify what the Americans' objectives at the peace conference might be. He asked why the President had chosen to come to Paris, rather than leaving the peace negotiations to his State Department.

'The issues which must be determined,' Wilson replied, 'will be of such overwhelming importance that the United States cannot refuse to share with the Allies their great responsibility to civilization, and it is only by the frankest personal counsel with the statesmen of the Allied countries that I can in some measure assist in the solution of these problems.'

That was too vague for Northcliffe. What did the President think the peace conference was meant to achieve?

'I think the plain man on the street could answer that question as well as I can,' said Wilson, bearing in mind his own purpose in giving the interview, which was to appeal to the European public over the heads of the politicians. 'The plain people of all nations, I am sure, are asking themselves this one question: *Will there be found enough of wisdom and purpose among the great statesmen to safeguard against future wars?*'

Northcliffe then led the President to discuss his immediate plans. Wilson said he hoped to visit all the Allied countries in order to judge for himself their problems and aspirations. He would also like to spend time with the American forces in Europe and with 'some of our comrades in arms in their own countries'.

In that case, Northcliffe said innocently, might the President find time to visit the British fleet?

Wilson was guarded. 'I am afraid I shall not have time to do that now,' he said, wondering about the thrust of the question. 'I have so fully realized from the beginning that behind the great armies there was the strong, silent, and watchful support of the British navy. There has been a very happy comradeship and loyal co-operation between the navy of Great Britain and the navy of the United States, and I am sure that all of our people at home are keenly appreciative of it and know its full significance in the winning of the war.'

That was the cue for Northcliffe to ask the real question which happened to be occupying his mind at that moment. The President, he said, made much in his Fourteen Points of the idea of freedom of navigation for all nations on the high seas. It was a noble aim, no doubt, but there were certain difficulties with it. If the vessels of any nation, friendly or otherwise, were allowed by international agreement to go wherever they pleased without interference, that would seriously affect the position of powers such as Britain, which depended on her naval strength to defend herself and her empire. In fact, during the war, it had been the exercise of that naval might that had actually preserved the freedom of the seas for the free peoples of the world.

Wilson knew there had been rumblings in London about his wish to prevent strong nations from intimidating weaker ones by the use of naval power. His first reaction had been to insist that his Fourteen Points were accepted in their entirety as the basis for the forthcoming peace treaty, but now he seemed prepared to compromise a little.

'We comprehend and appreciate, I believe,' he told Northcliffe, 'the grave problems which the war has brought to the British people, and fully understand the special international questions which arise from the fact of your peculiar position as an island empire.'

It was by no means a guarantee, but it was a hostage to fortune, and Northcliffe was satisfied with that. 'He convinced me that he is a believer in the decency and honesty of the Anglo-Saxon race,' The Chief noted.

'I'm hoping to visit England very shortly,' Wilson said, returning to his own agenda. 'It is essential to the future peace of the world that there should be the frankest possible co-operation and the most generous understanding between the two English-speaking democracies.'

He felt he had assured himself of a warm welcome in London and given strength to his natural supporters there after their electoral disappointment. If he could not rely on the new government to see things his way, then he could appeal directly to the people.

Northcliffe, for his part, went away convinced that he had made a dent in the Fourteen Points that would allow Britain to protect her own interests. 'I left the President,' he wrote, 'with assurance ringing in my ears that he desired to co-operate with the British, and with all the Allies, in ordering with their counsel a new state of affairs throughout the world.' He had let the Americans know they should not expect to have things all their own way.

When the interview was published in *The Times* a few days later, Lloyd George read it with interest. He had just received a cable from Clemenceau saying that the French Prime Minister had raised the question of the freedom of the seas in a discussion he had just had with Wilson.

'I mentioned the crucial role of the blockade by the British fleet in defeating Germany,' Clemenceau wrote. 'The President replied that he had nothing to demand in regard to freedom of navigation which could displease either of us.'

But there was more. *Le Tigre* was beginning to believe that he had taken the measure of Wilson, and his confidence was growing that he and Lloyd George could turn to their advantage the President's woolly idealism and obvious lack of experience in foreign affairs. That suggested a change of tactics.

'After talking to Wilson,' Clemenceau told Lloyd George, 'I've changed my mind about his attendance at the peace conference. I have urged him to attend as the chief American delegate.' Disingenuously, he added: 'If it became known that the President had expressed the wish to be present and had been refused, the effect would be very bad, at any rate in France.'

To Stéphan Pichon, he remarked: 'Wilson is naïve, an innocent. He's nothing more than a sheep!'

*III*
———

'Well, what did you think of him?' asked Frances Stevenson. Lloyd George had just returned to Downing Street from Buckingham Palace, where Woodrow Wilson was staying. The King had been less than happy about the timing of the President's visit – 'Damn it all! That means I'll have to break my Christmas holiday at Sandringham!' – but George V was nothing if not dutiful, and Wilson's arrival on 26 December, Boxing Day, had been a model of the awesome pomp at which the British monarchy was so skilled. There had been the ceremonial drive from Charing Cross railway station to the Palace, followed by a royal banquet of such magnificence that Wilson looked almost out of place in his plain dress suit among all the Court uniforms with their rich colours, their medals and ribbons and jewelled insignia of merit or nobility.

'He's a bit of an odd fish,' Lloyd George told Frances after his first business meeting with the President the following day. 'Rather cold, I'd say. I noticed it straight away when I shook hands with him at the station.'

'But did you like him?' Frances wanted to know.

'Oh, he was friendly enough. Very pleasant, really. I'd had the impression from Clemenceau and Orlando, after their meetings with him in Paris, that he was inclined to lecture you as if you were a young student, but he certainly didn't show any sign of that with us. He was quite charming. A good talker, very clear and to the point, and he seemed to be a very good listener, too. But definitely lacking in real warmth, I think.'

The Prime Minister had thought it strangely insensitive that, in his speech at the Palace banquet, Wilson had made no reference to the tremendous war effort of Britain and the Empire, or expressed any sympathy for the great loss of young life they had suffered. Several people had remarked afterwards on an omission they considered ill-mannered and even insulting.

'You would have thought he could have at least shown some appreciation for the fact that we did so much to bring his troops safely across the Atlantic, German submarines and all,' a high-ranking naval officer grumbled. 'Pretty poor show, I call it. You'd almost think the Americans had fought the war all by themselves.'

The same lack of real engagement had been evident to Lloyd George at their meeting. It was not just a natural coolness, but a sense that Wilson's emotions, whatever they might be, were detached from his actions and even from his intellectual processes – that and a rather worrying impression that on the grand scale of the President's thoughts, other people's feelings did not matter very much either.

'Since you ask,' Lloyd George went on, 'I couldn't help liking him. But I don't think that you'd ever get to know him. I have no doubts about his sincerity or that he's acting with the best of intentions, or that he's an extremely intelligent and thoughtful man. But he hasn't got the human touch. He might be a great president, but he's no Abraham Lincoln.'

'I suppose,' Frances said, 'the important thing is whether you'll be able to work with him.'

That was another question entirely, and one that Lloyd George tested a day or two later when he reported on his meeting with Wilson to the Imperial War Cabinet, which brought together the senior members of the British government, the prime ministers of the overseas Dominions – Australia, Canada, New Zealand and South Africa – and representatives who spoke on behalf of India. President Wilson was visiting Manchester, receiving the same homage from the Labour Party, the trades unions and ordinary working people that he had enjoyed from French socialists and their supporters. In terms of a direct appeal to the public, Colonel House's initiative seemed to be achieving its objectives. People listened with reverence and responded with passion as Wilson delivered moving but largely inconsequential speeches that many thought had the qualities of church sermons. But the politicians on whom House had hoped the public would bring pro-Wilson pressure to bear were made of sterner stuff, as Ray Baker had warned his Secretary of State in Paris.

'The only thing he seems to care about is his league of nations idea,' Lloyd George told the War Cabinet, 'but apparently he has no actual scheme in mind for setting it up. What he's most concerned about is that it should be the first subject for discussion at the peace conference. Now, frankly, I don't think that's a bad idea, because once the league of nations is out of the way, it will be easier to deal with matters such as the freedom of the seas and what we do with the former German colonies. On the freedom of the seas, for instance, Wilson is very vague, and perhaps the best way of approaching it is to refer it to the league of nations once it has been set up.'

The President favoured an early settlement of the question of international disarmament, Lloyd George said, and it had seemed to him that if limitations of the kind being considered were to be placed on Germany, it might be necessary for France to reduce the size of its armed forces. On the matter of what should happen to the former German colonies, Wilson agreed that they should not be returned to Germany but he appeared to have very much his own views on what should happen to them.

'We tried to impress upon him the distinction between those neighbouring colonies conquered by the British Dominions and those which the forces of the whole Empire had had a share in capturing. German East Africa, for example, might be placed under the protection of the league of nations by means of a British mandate, but it was clear that German South West Africa should go to South Africa, since it was practically the same country.'

That might well be the case, the President had agreed, but it was hardly an argument to be used in favour of Australia, which was claiming the old German colonies in the Pacific. When it had been pointed out to him that formerly German-held islands in the north Pacific had been promised to Japan, Wilson said he was not necessarily prepared to abide by that treaty, and doubted whether Japan could even be given a league of nations mandate.

'And,' added Bonar Law, who had been at the meeting with Wilson, 'he went so far as to remark that he regarded it as part of his function to prevent disagreeable things happening, such as the retention of those islands by Japan.'

'Hold on a minute.'

The voice was that of Billy Hughes, the eccentric and combative Welshman who had emigrated to Australia in his twenties and had eventually become its prime minister. Now in his fifties, and with his adopted country solidly behind him, Hughes was not known for mincing his words, and his natural aggression had enlivened many an imperial conference.

'I think,' he said, 'that if we're not very careful we're going to find ourselves being dragged along behind President Wilson's chariot here. I mean, we all appreciate the part America has played in the war, but that doesn't entitle Wilson to be the god in the machine at the peace conference and to tell the world how it's going to have to live in the future. The Americans came in pretty late, after all, and I don't suppose they even spent the profits they made in the first two and a half years, when they were keeping out of it.'

These were not the sort of sentiments calculated to appeal to the Canadian Prime Minister, the cool and moderate former barrister Sir Robert Borden. In his customary measured tones, he said it would be a matter of regret if Britain went to the peace conference with a feeling of antagonism towards the President of the United States.

'I've said before,' he went on, 'that good relations with the United States would be one of the most desirable results of this war. My own discussions with Mr Wilson have left a very favourable impression.'

'That's one thing,' Hughes retorted, waving his arms about.

'I'm not saying we shouldn't give America all the respect that's due to a great nation for what it did in the war. But it would be intolerable for President Wilson to dictate to us how the world is going to be governed. If the saving of civilization had been left to the United States, we'd have been in tears and chains today. It's Britain and France who made the great sacrifices, and I think it's up to Mr Lloyd George and Mr Clemenceau to settle the peace of the world. The Americans didn't even lose as many men as Australia did.'

Sir Robert placed his hands flat on the table before him. 'I absolutely agree that we should stand up strongly for our own interests,' he said calmly. 'But I have to say that if the future policy of the Empire means working in co-operation with some European nation as against the United States, we in Canada would not be able to support that policy. Our view is that, so far as is possible, the Empire should avoid becoming entangled in European complications and alliances. I should have thought that was obvious, after the war we've just endured and which we were drawn into by agreements and promises and understandings that we in the Dominions were not even aware of.'

'I hope you're not suggesting . . .' Lloyd George cut in.

'No, no,' Sir Robert said patiently. 'I'm not criticizing the behaviour of the imperial government in the past, and I will admit that, since this Cabinet was established, we have been fully consulted. I merely wish to emphasize the importance of our relationship with the United States and to point out that, so far as the President is concerned, we have not yet been made aware of his final point of view.'

Hughes grunted. 'Well I hope his attitude towards this league of nations is not an indicator of what's to come. He doesn't seem to have any practical idea of it at all. It's like a toy to a child – he won't be happy until he's got it. He just wants to go back to America and say "Look what I've achieved", and leave everything else to the league. Well I don't think the peace of the world can be settled that way. And in any case, the idea that it should be discussed first is wrong. The league of nations should be the gilded dome on top of the cathedral, not its foundation stone.'

Lord Curzon said: 'I rather agree with Mr Hughes.'

The two men could hardly have been more different, but they had a shared interest in building on imperial power. The earl had long nursed an ambition to be foreign secretary, and believed he might achieve it in the new government, dominated as it was by Conservatives.

'President Wilson shouldn't be regarded as the sole arbiter,' Curzon added. 'He is, after all, only one member of the group that will be round the conference table. I think our Prime Minister should be fully aware of the power conferred upon him, not merely by the result of the election but by the sacrifices made by the British Empire and the interests it represents all over the world.'

'Whereas,' Hughes said, 'Wilson doesn't even speak for America, if the results of the election there are anything to go by.'

Curzon continued: 'I can quite see that the future does depend largely on co-operation between England and America, but it seems to me there might well be some issues on which our work at the conference might be best served by an alliance with Clemenceau.'

This irritated Lord Reading, one of the Liberals who had supported Lloyd George in 1917 and who had been rewarded with the post of ambassador to the United States.

'Look here,' Reading said, 'I think it would be a great pity if we all got the idea that there were serious divisions between us and the Americans. Of course, we must put up a fight for what we believe in, but I do hope we can remember that one of our main objectives now is to bring about close co-operation between the United States and ourselves.'

Curzon retorted: 'That is as may be, and I quite accept your point. I am merely trying to point out that when our Prime Minister goes to the peace conference, he does so with an authority that is equal, and indeed superior, to that of President Wilson.'

Lloyd George leaned forward in his seat. 'I think we should all realize,' he said, 'that I am merely reporting the views President Wilson expressed at our meeting. In no sense is any of this to be regarded as final. On the colonies, for example, I made it clear to him that the question would have to be fought out at the conference and that the Dominions would be entitled to put their own case.'

'Well,' Curzon remarked spiritedly, 'all I can say is that unless the President can go beyond what seems to have been this very loose discussion with the British government, the peace conference is going to be nothing more than a dreary fiasco.'

*

Robert Lansing was finding it difficult to escape the feeling that things were already beginning to go wrong. President Wilson had been in Europe for a little more than two weeks – he was now on his way back to Paris from England – and, while he had been fêted on the streets as a popular hero, his effect where it really mattered, among the politicians he would have to face at the peace conference, seemed to have been the reverse of his intention to convert them to the cause of international understanding, peace, fairness and justice. If anything, his presence appeared to be hardening the very old-world attitudes the President believed his visit would serve to melt.

In his room at the Hôtel Crillon, the Secretary of State had just read reports of a speech made by Georges Clemenceau in the National Assembly. The Prime Minister's words filled him with foreboding.

Faced with a challenge from the Socialists to embrace what they called Wilsonian principles – 'as of the day America entered this war, and President Wilson began to speak, the methods of the old diplomacy simply had to change . . . the diplomacy of the people is taking over from cabinet diplomacy' – Clemenceau had responded with the first flash of his tigerish claws.

> *The old system may have its detractors and it may not be exciting, but I remain faithful to it, at least in part. Nations arrange their security by establishing their frontiers, by having armies, by maintaining the balance of power. The system of alliances that had operated in the past could have*

*prevented the war if in 1914 it had been more firmly*
*established. But out of the war has come a web of alliances*
*which I am determined to preserve in this post-war era –*
*and for that I shall make whatever sacrifices are necessary.*
*I intend to pursue certain claims, but I will not say what*
*they are, because I may have to sacrifice some of them*
*during the course of the negotiations with our allies.*

In his peroration, the old man turned directly to the subject of Wilson, and the burden of his message could hardly have been clearer:

'I have had many meetings with the President and there is much common ground between us. Mr Wilson is a man who inspires respect with the simplicity of his words and the noble frankness of his spirit. But America is a long way from Germany's borders, and it is hardly surprising that the President's preoccupations are not the same as mine.'

And he berated the Socialists for perverting Wilson's exalted aims to their own narrow, partisan ends: 'They ascribe designs to Wilson which may not be his at all. Wouldn't it be better if, instead of concerning themselves with bringing a new spirit to international affairs, they displayed a new spirit in domestic affairs?'

Colonel House had seen the reports, too, and the huge majority Clemenceau had obtained among the deputies in a debate he had turned into a motion of confidence in his government. The Colonel was equally pessimistic.

'This is about as bad a blow for progressive principles at the peace conference as we could have had,' he said. 'What with the result of the English elections, coming on top of our own, we're in a very bad position strategically. The only ray of hope is that we succeeded in having the Fourteen Points made the basis of the armistice.'

Lansing was not entirely surprised at the turn events seemed to be taking. What depressed him was that it was happening so soon. As was his habit, he kept his own counsel, but in his thoughts he could only blame the President. The Secretary of State, as an experienced international lawyer, was well aware of the traps that could lie in the negotiation of treaties, where lip service might be paid to the spirit of co-operation, but in reality the nations involved were most anxious to protect their own interests. It was for that reason that he did not share Colonel House's faith in the Fourteen Points. They were too vague, too much open to interpretation, too vulnerable to subversion by politicians whose objectives were very different from Wilson's. It had already happened with the armistice, which seemed to make a mockery of the President's notions of peace without victory. Lansing had not been particularly worried by that: he had always believed that the military defeat of Germany was necessary. Now, though, the triumphalism of the British, the French and the Italians threatened to waste the opportunity that victory offered. All that seemed likely to happen was that the old, dangerous balance of power in Europe would simply be replaced by a new one. That was certainly the import of Clemenceau's speech.

America should have taken the lead by coming to Paris with concrete proposals to present to the Europeans. It was all very well talking about the Fourteen Points, but they were no more than a guide to what the shape of a treaty might be. The President had not done any work on them, had not even sketched an outline of the actual, practical terms the conference should consider. All he had was his draft covenant for a league of nations, but it was in a crude and undigested form that would permit the British and the French, still clinging to their imperial power, to adapt it for their own benefit. In fact, Lansing feared, unless the American delegation moved quickly and decisively, it would be the Europeans who would write the entire treaty.

Yet it was just such decisive action that Wilson's presence in Paris was inhibiting. Lansing had tried to impress upon the President the necessity for professional diplomacy and the establishment of a proper legal basis for the treaty, but Wilson seemed to prefer the advice of Colonel House, whose main consideration was apparently to tell the President what he wanted to hear. The enthusiasm with which Wilson had been greeted in France – now in England too – had served to confirm his conviction that his idealism resonated with the people of Europe. Lansing could not deny it. What troubled him was that the President seemed not to understand that his popularity would count for nothing among the more hard-headed European politicians unless he could convert the principles so admired by public opinion into definite policies for which he could fight.

Well, thought Lansing, if the President was unable or unprepared to build on his prestige, then he would have to do it for him. He resolved to speak to the American delegation with a view to converting the principles of the Fourteen Points into the draft of a workable treaty that would enshrine vague objectives in a legal framework. The initiative given by public acclaim must not be wasted.

Wilson arrived back in Paris later that day, New Year's Eve, but, as usual, it was to Colonel House rather than to the Secretary of State that he turned for an assessment of Clemenceau's unrepentant speech in the National Assembly.

'I think he's made a great diplomatic blunder,' House said. 'He doesn't seem to realize that his attitude could cost France millions of dollars we might otherwise have given her. But what it tells us is that we might be well-advised to work more closely with the English. It could be that Clemenceau has given us a great opportunity here. It's a straight choice between the league of nations and the balance of power, and I think you'll find the British more supportive of the league.'

Wilson nodded. 'After the reception I had in England – and here, for that matter – we might consider that a direct appeal to the people would be the best way of making their governments see sense. There's too much of an inclination to grab whatever they can, and it may be that we have to make that publicly known.'

The President had been particularly irritated by the insistence of the Italians that, whatever acceptance of the Fourteen Points might imply, it could not set aside the territorial rewards offered to them by the Treaty of London. But the reaction of ordinary people in France and now in Britain had convinced him that, when he visited Italy in a few days' time, he would be able to influence public opinion to set aside such outmoded, imperialistic claims. Ray Stannard

Baker had been there to prepare the ground, and had reported that, while the attitude in government circles and in sections of the press was discouraging, he had been impressed by the support for the Wilsonian vision he had found among socialists and working people. That had inspired in the President a determination to curtail the official programme the Italian government had set out for him and to reach out directly into the streets, especially in the big industrial centres of Milan and Turin.

When Wilson arrived in Italy on 3 January 1919, he found that Colonel House and the American ambassador in Rome had succeeded in circumventing only some of the restrictions on his movements the Italian government had tried to impose for fear that he would excite too much enthusiasm among its political opponents. He did appear in Milan and Turin, but a ceaseless round of official receptions had the effect of preventing him from addressing a public meeting in Rome, as he had planned. Nevertheless, people turned out in their thousands just to see him, and if anything their adulation exceeded that of the crowds in England and France. Banners proclaimed him as a saviour, a god of peace, an American Moses, a knight of humanity – and one excited provincial official, in his speech of welcome, even compared the visit to the Second Coming.

In the little time he had to himself, Wilson made a point of meeting popular political leaders sympathetic to the Fourteen Points and the league of nations, and opposed to the government's expansionist policy.

'That,' he told Colonel House later, 'will put them on notice that I can always go over the heads of the government and appeal directly to the people.'

But both the President and those who travelled with him were misled by the cheers that followed him everywhere. The socialists and their supporters were in the minority. Too many Italians had read Georges Clemenceau's speech and approved of its sentiments. Many more were convinced by the promises the British and French had made in the Treaty of London. Italians had fought and died in the war, and they would not be told that their sacrifice had been for nothing. Italy was ready to take its place among the strong nations of the world. For once, it would carry weight in the balance of power.

When the President had left, one of the opposition leaders he had met, Leonida Bissolati, addressed a public meeting at La Scala in Milan. Bissolati had resigned from Orlando's coalition government in order to support the Fourteen Points and the league of nations, and his intention was to present a vision of Italy's future quite different from the one the government had in mind.

But within minutes of the beginning of his speech, a howling mob had made Bissolati inaudible and scuffles had broken out in many parts of the theatre. Bissolati tried to carry on, but his message was completely overwhelmed by the uproar. Looking on helplessly from the stage, Bissolati saw a face he recognized. It belonged to a thirty-five-year-old journalist and agitator, a man with a history of violence who seemed to have an uncanny ability to rouse a mob.

His name was Benito Mussolini, and he had just founded a political movement with the compelling slogan of '*Viva l'Italia!*. The name of the new party was *Fascio di combattimento*, but its members were called simply 'Fascisti'.

# The Wounds of Peace

*The Wound of peace is surety,*
*Surety secure.*

WILLIAM SHAKESPEARE
*Troilus and Cressida*

# CHAPTER 1

# *Winter of Discontent*

*I*

A group of soldiers in the uniform of the Horseguards Rifle Division burst out through the doors of the Eden Hotel, in the quiet, middle-class Charlottenburg district of central Berlin. Guns at the ready, the men glanced up and down the street, then took up positions on either side of the hotel entrance, forming short lines towards two parked cars with more soldiers inside them. The hotel doors opened again and two officers emerged, pushing before them a dishevelled-looking man and woman, both in middle age. The couple were Karl Liebknecht and Rosa Luxemburg, leaders of the Spartacus League, named after the legendary rebel of ancient Rome and, like him, dedicated to violent revolution.

As Liebknecht and Luxemburg drew level with the sentries outside the hotel, one of the soldiers raised his rifle and, with its butt, struck each of them across the back of the head. They slumped to the ground.

'Get them into the cars,' ordered Captain Pflug-Hartung.

In their semi-conscious state, Liebknecht and Luxemburg

were dragged across the pavement and bundled separately into the two cars. The Captain got in after Liebknecht, motioning Lieutenant Vogel to go with Luxemburg.

'You know what to do,' Pflug-Hartung told his junior officer.

The military drivers started their engines and the cars accelerated away in the direction of the Tiergarten. There were few people about in the zoological gardens on this cold January day. Suddenly, Pflug-Hartung's car slowed down. A door was flung open and Karl Liebknecht fell into the road. The Captain drew his revolver and shot him.

'He was trying to escape,' Pflug-Hartung told his soldiers. 'Let's get him to the mortuary. But take all identification off him first.'

Lieutenant Vogel's car had turned off towards the Landwehr Canal, where it stopped. A shot rang out. Two soldiers got out of the car and hurriedly manhandled the body of Rosa Luxemburg into the murky water.

Soldiers were running amok in Berlin and in other cities across Germany. The outbreak of rioting and general disorder that had panicked the government into signing armistice terms far harsher than they had ever imagined had, since November, begun to look like the beginning of a revolution. The attempt by Prince Max of Baden, now retired to private life, to maintain a semblance of stability by handing over the responsibilities of government to Friedrich Ebert, the one-time jobbing saddler from Heidelberg, had been less than successful. The workers' and soldiers' councils continued to hold sway in many cities, having assumed effective control of their regions and still threatening to band together to form a loose Marxist state on the lines of the soviet the Bolsheviks were constructing in Russia.

German soil was fertile enough ground for revolution to grow in. People weakened by years of worsening food shortages were dying in their tens of thousands as that winter's virulent strain of influenza swept the country. For those who did not succumb, there was still little enough to eat: the British naval blockade remained in place and American promises of emergency supplies to relieve the widespread hunger – near starvation in some places – never seemed to amount to anything.

Allied 'experts' had determined that Germany had the ability to feed itself until the spring, but they did not have to dig rotting potatoes from frozen fields, or drink coffee made from acorns, or queue for hours for half a loaf of mouldy bread. And they had failed to take account of the return home of millions of soldiers, who would no longer be fed by the army. British troops moving in to occupy part of the Rhineland under the terms of the armistice were so moved by the sight of emaciated women and children that they began to distribute their own rations. Nor was it easy to keep warm as the first snows fell. Coal was almost impossible to obtain and even the woody, smoky lignite used to replace it could hardly be found. Money was worthless. There was precious little to buy even if you could earn, which was difficult in itself now that war work had abruptly ceased.

Worse still was the pervading sense of hopelessness. The severity of the armistice terms had come as a terrible shock to a people who had been persuaded to put their faith in the dream of peace proclaimed by the American President. Adding to it was the bewilderment: until the autumn of 1918, Germans had believed that their years of sacrifice would ultimately prove to be worthwhile, that Europe would some day lie at their feet. Now they themselves lay prostrate before a vengeful conqueror, and who could tell what new horrors were to come?

'Approaching Invasion of Germany', screamed the Social Democrats' own newspaper *Vorwärts*:

> It is almost certain that the Entente is preparing a new ultimatum to enforce the re-establishment of legitimate peace and order in Germany. At the forthcoming Paris conference, the Allies will consider a note about the immediate disbanding of the workers' and soldiers' councils. This note sets a four-week time limit for the restoration of the legitimate authorities. There are further reports from London which support the credibility of this threat. *The Times* writes that a Spartacist victory would be a summons to the Allies to invade Germany.

As the days passed, the chaos deepened, and the government's authority withered away, Chancellor Ebert feared a leftist coup might overtake him at any moment. In an attempt to placate the workers' leaders, Ebert's so-called Council of People's Representatives might have hastily announced that Germany was now a republic, but, without a constitution and with time needed to organize parliamentary elections, all the change meant was that the various revolutionary groups redoubled their efforts to seize control. Ebert, for whom organization came before everything, turned for help to the Supreme Command of the army, just as the Kaiser would have done.

General Ludendorff had gone into exile in Sweden after his dismissal, but Field Marshal Hindenburg and his new commander-in-chief, General Wilhelm Groener, were no less prepared than Ludendorff would have been to defend the state by whatever means necessary. They had little to work with. Millions of men were being demobilized following the armistice, and those units that did remain were so demoralized as to be unreliable. Hindenburg and Groener appealed to the officer class to take personal responsibility for civil security by setting up their own volunteer forces of soldiers they could trust. Soon, posters began to appear calling on former junior officers and other ranks to renew their commitment to the Fatherland:

> Our new government needs strength for the struggle on our borders and the struggle within them. Russian Bolsheviks, the Poles and the Czechs stand at Germany's frontiers and threaten them. Inside the Reich, chaos is growing. Disorder and looting are everywhere. Nowhere is there respect for law and justice, for personal or government property. WE MUST INTERVENE!

The new units were to be called the Freikorps. Some men volunteered and put on their old uniforms out of patriotism, others because they could recapture the comradeship of their old regiments, many because they were hungry and without work. Soon the Freikorps were roaming the streets of the big cities, breaking up workers' demonstrations, guarding public buildings and attacking 'Bolshevist sympathizers' wherever they could find them. From the point of view of Chancellor Ebert, they had been created in the nick of time. Early in January 1919, the professional revolutionaries Karl Liebknecht and Rosa Luxemburg unleashed their Spartacist forces in an armed uprising, beginning in the very centre of Berlin.

It was a poor affair, badly planned and carried out, and with much less popular support than the authorities cared to admit – they preferred to present it as the showdown with Bolshevism. The Freikorps men moved against the rebels with all the ruthless efficiency they had shown in their regular units on the Western Front, and armed to the teeth. Heavy machine-guns, flame-throwers and even small artillery pieces were brought into action as the Spartacists were methodically dislodged from the buildings they had seized and the districts they had occupied. By 15 January, it was all over in Berlin, and Liebknecht and Luxemburg were dead. There had been no popular uprising. In some places, people had even cheered when the Freikorps marched in.

Still, it seemed there were would-be Red revolutionaries everywhere – Dresden, Wilhelmshaven, Düsseldorf, Bremen, Magdeburg, Leipzig, and in the 'independent Soviet Republic of Bavaria'. The Freikorps killing machine prepared to move on. The Fatherland would be saved at any price.

'Germany,' said Georges Clemenceau, 'could turn out to be just as dangerous now that it is a republic as it was under the Kaiser.'

He was meeting privately with President Wilson, who had moved from the Villa Murat to a less palatial residence in the Place des Etats-Unis, close to the American Embassy. It was more convenient, now that the peace conference was about to go into session. Clemenceau's apartment in the Rue Franklin was just a short distance away and Lloyd George had taken a pleasant flat in the Rue Nitot, round the corner from the Place.

'We take the view,' Clemenceau went on, 'as you will have seen from Marshal Foch's memorandum, that Germany ought to be deprived of all territorial sovereignty on the left bank of the Rhine. That will remove the facility for sudden invasion, as happened in 1914, and we regard it as an indispensable guarantee of peace.'

Wilson sighed and gazed out of the window at the dark sky. It was early evening, and he was tired.

'I rather think,' he said deliberately, 'that what you are proposing would make peace less likely, not guarantee it.'

'That is not our opinion,' said Clemenceau. 'And we, after all, are the ones who suffered when the Germans used the springboard of the Rhine provinces to outflank our natural defences and sweep south almost to Paris.'

'But under the terms we have outlined, Alsace and Lorraine are returned to France, which is as it should be. The remaining provinces on the left bank are indisputably German. What you are talking about is annexation.'

Clemenceau stroked his drooping moustache with thumb and forefinger, recalling the conversation he had had with Poincaré and Foch. He had still not raised the matter of the Rhineland in open meetings, though he knew Foch had done so and that André Tardieu had been instructed by Poincaré to include it in the draft treaty he was composing. He had not inquired what Tardieu's personal view might be. The Prime Minister was merely gauging the opinions of the other leaders, though he already had a good idea of what those would be. He was testing how far he could go. He would decide later whether to press the point or to keep it in reserve as a concession he might be only too willing to make, whatever Poincaré and Foch thought.

He said: 'Let me make it clear that France is not seeking either territory or sovereign rights over those provinces. That would be against our interests and our ideals. We are merely saying that strategical considerations must be an important part of the peace treaty and that, along with the disarmament of Germany, her western frontiers must be fixed at the Rhine.'

'So you want to see Germany absolutely helpless,' Wilson said.

'We simply do not want to be threatened by Germany again.'

'But the league of nations will be there to make sure you aren't threatened and to resolve any disputes that might arise in the future between France and Germany. All you will be doing, if you persist in the course you propose, is building up animosities that will work against you at the league of nations. You would have little sympathy among other countries if these provinces did prove to be the cause of disputes.'

'If sympathy depends on our being attacked again,' Clemenceau said tartly, 'then it's something we'll be better off without. The idea is to prevent attack in the first place.'

Wilson stood up. 'Well, it's getting rather late, and we have a long meeting ahead of us tomorrow. Obviously this is a matter for further discussion. I'd be obliged if you would have your staff prepare a memorandum setting out in detail the practical aspects of your proposition and your reasons for it. As you know, we're going to discuss the league of nations before we reach the detailed terms of the peace treaty and I think your proposal might be best considered in that context.'

Clemenceau took his leave. Wilson wandered disconsolately into the drawing room, where he found his doctor, Rear-Admiral Grayson.

'I don't know what we're going to do with the French,' Wilson said. 'I just can't reconcile their demands against Germany with what we're trying to achieve with this peace treaty. They want a buffer state in the Rhineland that goes completely against the principles everyone accepted with the Fourteen Points.'

'What do the British think about it?' Grayson asked.

'Lloyd George is as concerned as I am. But he's in a difficult position. The French are saying that their claim is a security matter no different than the British insistence that the German fleet should be handed over as part of the armistice terms. We're going back to the old idea of what they call the balance of power, which is completely contrary to what we're trying to achieve with the league of nations.'

'You need some rest,' Grayson said. 'These constant long meetings are a terrible strain.'

Wilson smiled. 'They go on so long because they keep being interrupted. You know, we were meeting the other day in the conference room at the Foreign Ministry, and we were discussing a very important point, when suddenly a whole crowd of servants came into the room and started clearing the tables for afternoon tea. I ask you! The future of the world is to be settled and we're breaking off for a tea party! I had great difficulty in stopping myself saying something about it.'

'They don't do things in Europe the way we do,' Grayson said.

'They certainly do not. I've been here a month now, and we're still arguing about how to organize the conference.'

That, indeed, was still the subject of the meeting of the four leading Allies the following morning, at the Foreign Ministry on the Quai d'Orsay by the River Seine. Lloyd George, however, had other things on his mind, too. Lord Northcliffe's unrelenting campaign against him had made the Prime Minister more than usually sensitive to the power of the press, especially its ability to create in the public mind an impression that was not one Lloyd George wished to see there. Since his arrival in Paris, he had been concerned to note that the newspapers appeared to be concentrating on the differences between the leading powers that might arise at the peace conference, rather than – as he would have preferred – emphasizing the points on which they were likely to agree.

He was acutely aware of the delicacy of his own position, thanks partly to Northcliffe, but also because the more rabid Tories whose election had helped to maintain him in office would be keeping a very close eye on him during the negotiations. Any sign of weakness on his part, any hint that the French or the Americans might be gaining the upper hand, could be seriously damaging to him. He wanted the freedom to negotiate as he saw fit, shifting his ground as he always did according to the political runes he was so adept at reading. He would rely on the agreements obtained by these means to obscure any sudden, and perhaps hard to explain, changes of policy that might have been necessary to achieve them.

'We know that our discussions usually end in agreement,' he told the meeting at the Quai d'Orsay, 'but if the press jump in before agreement is reached, the differences between us might become stereotyped, and that would have a bad effect on the public. We have to put a stop to the press's discussing controversial matters.'

The journalist in Clemenceau rose up at this. The newspapers might make mischief, he conceded, but there were ways of limiting any damage that might be done. Meanwhile, the eyes of the world were focused on Paris, and people would expect to see full reports of the discussions that were to determine their future. In any case, there were so many journalists from so many countries covering the peace conference that it would be impossible to prevent articles from appearing in some part of the world, whether they were true or false.

Lloyd George, though, would not be fobbed off. He wanted the flow of information to the press to be controlled by the conference secretariat, and for delegates to be told that they should not speak to reporters. The journalists should also be warned to beware of any communication that did not come from official sources.

For once, President Wilson found himself taking precisely the same view as Clemenceau.

'I'm sorry,' he said, 'but I can't see anything short of complete publicity satisfying the American people. And, after all, we are here representing our respective peoples. Now I know we've agreed that all our decisions should be unanimous, but if that's all we communicate to people, they're naturally going to wonder how that unanimity was achieved – and they surely have a right to know what was said.'

'We all have to defend ourselves in our own countries,' said Lloyd George, 'but I don't see that we have to do it every day. If that were the case, the conference would never reach any conclusions at all. I trust the people. I believe they mean to allow us fair play. But there are newspapers that are more concerned with their own tactics, so I think if we were to issue the sort of public caution I've suggested, it would serve to discredit unauthorised reports.'

Wilson said that meant they must issue official communiqués, with full summaries of their meetings, but Lloyd George did not like that idea. Uppermost in his mind was the thought that if his diplomatic improvisations were to become public knowledge, he might have a difficult time justifying himself in Parliament. He had been forced, during the election campaign, to take up a position on reparations that he did not find comfortable, and he was already worrying about what might happen if the expectations that had been raised were not met – which all his political senses told him they would not be. He was going to have to give way on the point, but he did not want people to be aware of that fact while he was doing it.

The temper of the meeting was against him, though, so he tried a different tack. He was not afraid of the press, he said, but he did not believe that its demands for access to the proceedings of the conference were supported by the public. He did not have reporters at his Cabinet meetings in London, and everybody understood that they took place in private. Was it not the case that the leading powers in Paris for the conference constituted a sort of Cabinet of nations? They had already decided that America, Britain, France and Italy should discuss among themselves the terms of the treaty and present them to the other delegates only when agreement had been reached. It was the only sensible way to proceed if the conference was to complete its work in a reasonable amount of time. That being so, what they were engaged in now were not sessions of the conference, but merely conversations, and all the press needed to know, in the fullness of time, were the details of the decisions they had reached.

Wilson and Clemenceau began to see what Lloyd George was really getting at. This was not to be an international peace conference at all, but a secret negotiation in which the issues would be decided for the mutual benefit of the great powers. It was not just the press Lloyd George was seeking to exclude, but also the representatives of most of the twenty-three other nations gathered in Paris. That suited the French Prime Minister. It did not suit the American President, who was anxious to let his public watch as he took his place in history. But Wilson was not prepared to allow any souring of relations at this early stage, whatever irritation he might feel at a retreat into secrecy. He wanted to press on with the cornerstone of his foreign policy, the creation of a league of nations.

'Oh, very well,' he said. 'I suppose the conference might find it necessary to go into what we call in America executive session.'

The meeting broke for lunch. Clemenceau left the conference room with his Foreign Secretary, Stéphan Pichon.

'Well,' Clemenceau said quietly, 'so much for President Wilson's *open covenants of peace, openly arrived at*. There's the first of the Fourteen Points to fall.'

## II

—

They were crammed, as usual, into the dark, airless conference room on the Quai d'Orsay, only this time there were to be even more of them. Lloyd George's reluctance to accept submissions about the terms of the peace treaty from nations other than the four leading powers did not extend to representatives of the most important members of the British Empire – especially when it was the future of Germany's overseas colonies that was under discussion.

'I thought it appropriate,' Lloyd George was saying, 'that in discussing the future of the former German colonies we should ask each of the British Dominions to present its own case, since most of those colonies were captured by Dominion troops. All I would say on behalf of the British Empire as a whole is that I would be very much opposed to the return of any colonies to Germany. The reason for my opposition is partly that, in many cases, the Germans treated the native populations very badly.'

'I think we're all agreed that no colonies should be returned, aren't we?' President Wilson asked.

Orlando, the Italian Prime Minister, nodded, as did Baron Makino, the representative of the Japanese government, who had been invited to press his country's claim to territory previously leased by the Germans from China and to German island colonies in the Pacific.

'But,' said Clemenceau, who was chairing the meeting, 'it

would probably be wiser not to make any public statement regarding our policy at this point.'

The other disciples of President Wilson's open diplomacy signified their assent.

'In that case,' Clemenceau told Lloyd George, 'let's bring in your cannibals. You did say some of them were cannibals, didn't you?'

Lloyd George laughed. 'What I said was that in some of the islands taken by Australia, many of the inhabitants were still cannibals.'

The Dominion representatives were summoned, led by their prime ministers – Billy Hughes of Australia; the onetime Boer general Louis Botha, from South Africa; the level-headed New Zealand farmer William Massey, and Sir Robert Borden from Canada.

'I hear, Mr Hughes,' said Clemenceau, 'that you are a cannibal.'

The Australian grinned. 'Monsieur Clemenceau, I can assure you that report is grossly exaggerated.'

There had, said Lloyd George, been a suggestion that the former colonies might be administered on the basis of a mandate by the league of nations, which President Wilson insisted should be created as an integral part of the peace treaty. In theory, Britain saw no difficulty with the mandatory system, but the question was: would it work?

'German South West Africa,' he went on, 'borders the Union of South Africa. There is no natural boundary and if the region were not to be colonized by the British and Dutch populations of South Africa, it would remain a wilderness. If

South Africa were merely to be given a league of nations mandate, you would have two territories in one geographical area, each with a different system of administration – and I doubt whether there would be any advantage in that.'

There was a similar difficulty in New Guinea, of which a third was already administered by Australia and the remainder had been captured from the Germans.

'There would be obvious disadvantages in erecting a customs barrier between one part of the island and the other,' Lloyd George said, 'yet if Australia were the mandatory power, under the league of nations, for what was German New Guinea, it might find itself obliged to run the island in a different way from the system that operates in the part it already administers.'

Clemenceau smiled to himself. It was very clear what was in Lloyd George's mind. Britain had already succeeded in neutralizing the German navy and merchant fleet, under the armistice terms, and now it wanted to take over the German colonies. Its navy and its colonies were the very things that had raised Germany to the position where it might challenge the great British Empire.

'Then there is Samoa,' Lloyd George said, 'which, I have no doubt, would be best administered by New Zealand. I must point out that colonies are an expensive undertaking. Our colonial budget in Britain increases steadily. I wouldn't be surprised if New Zealand didn't think it worthwhile to assume responsibility for Samoa only as a mandatory power. You must remember that New Zealand has a population of only a little more than a million souls, yet she put a hundred thousand men into the field and suffered sixty thousand casualties, with sixteen hundred dead. Her war debt stands at a hundred million pounds sterling, and money will have to be spent in Samoa if the island is to be retained.'

Wilson was shaking his head. 'This is not right,' he said. 'I fully endorse the idea that the colonies shouldn't be restored to Germany, but we can't have this process of annexation. If countries simply go about annexing what was previously a German colony, it will challenge the whole idea of a league of nations. The league will be discredited before it even starts.'

Billy Hughes was not impressed. 'The idea of inter-nationalization is all very well in principle,' he said, 'but in the case of Australia and New Guinea, we have to be practical. For a start, we already administer part of the country, which means Australian laws operate there. If the other part were to be controlled by the league of nations, it would not only be confusing but it would also be dangerous for Australia. Our authority would be completely overshadowed, and I doubt whether any country here would agree to be placed in that position. I would go so far as to say that if the league of nations established a mandatory power in New Guinea, Australia would be inclined to regard that power as a potential enemy. Friends in one war are not always friends in the next one.'

Wilson waved away the argument. 'We can't just transfer territory from one empire to another,' he said irritably. 'And in any case, there is no reason why Australia should not be the mandatory power.'

'But that wouldn't work,' Hughes protested. 'As I've said, it would presumably be the league of nations that directed the policy of the mandatory power, and Australia wouldn't be in a position to stand up to the league.'

Lloyd George said: 'There's also the question of money. An organization established in Europe might find it difficult to contribute even a small amount to the administration of these territories we're talking about.'

'That's a good point,' Hughes agreed. 'Our war debt comes to three hundred million pounds sterling, and that doesn't take into account the hundred million we're going to have to spend on repatriating our troops and paying pensions. Australia isn't prepared to stagger along under that load and not even feel safe because the strategically important territory of New Guinea is controlled by somebody else.'

'I'm sorry,' Wilson said, 'but if we were to hand over these colonies to another colonial power, all we would be doing is returning to the status quo ante. The whole of the civilized world would be outraged if the victorious powers simply seized what they had taken from Germany in battle.'

Hughes turned away in disgust, but one of the South Africans, General Smuts, joined the argument.

'South Africa has a similar problem,' he said. 'As you know, I'm a firm supporter of the idea of a league of nations, and I have no doubt that there's a good case for administering some of the German possessions in Africa by mandate. But I don't believe that case applies to South West Africa. It isn't like the Cameroons, or Togoland or German East Africa. It's a desert country that doesn't produce anything of real value, and for that reason it can only be developed from within the Union of South Africa. After all, we've done our best to give a form of self-government to three million natives and we'd do the same in South West Africa. We wouldn't want to be in the position that faced us before, when the Germans tried to provoke a serious rebellion among our own natives.'

'We do have to consider the position of the natives,' said the New Zealander Massey. 'I've received pathetic letters from the native races in Samoa begging us not to let them be returned to German rule.'

'There's no question of that,' Wilson snapped. 'We're all agreed that the colonies shouldn't be returned to Germany. What we have to agree about is the principle of international trusteeship under the league of nations, rather than exchanging one form of imperial rule for another.'

'Well,' Massey said, 'I agree with General Smuts. I hope the league of nations is established and I hope it will be very successful. But I'm not convinced that international control of native races is going to succeed. I think the claim New Zealand is making for Samoa is in the best interests of the native peoples and of humanity as a whole. I mean, I ask you, Mr President, what would have happened after the American War of Independence if it had been suggested to George Washington or Alexander Hamilton that a mandatory power – or even the colonists themselves under the authority of a league of nations – should take charge of the vast unoccupied areas of North America?'

'I hardly think that is relevant,' Wilson replied icily. 'It seems to me that what we are hearing is a detailed negation of the whole principle of mandates.'

'We also have some observations to make on that principle,'

said Clemenceau. 'Monsieur Simon, the Minister for the Colonies, will explain our view.'

The minister cleared his throat and launched into a lecture that cloaked French demands for the annexation of the former German colonies of Togoland and the Cameroons in the trappings of a philosophical argument against the idea of a mandatory system.

'I cannot support an arrangement under which a mandate will be given to one power by the league of nations,' he announced. 'The mandatory system consists of giving one nation the power to act on behalf of another, but because every mandate is revocable, there would be no guarantee that it would continue. Where, then, is the incentive for the investment of capital or for colonization of a country whose future is unknown? No, I must take the view that annexation, pure and simple, is the only solution that will accomplish the development of the country in question and the effective protection of the natives during their development towards a higher level of civilization.'

President Wilson grimaced.

'We are not speaking,' Simon went on, 'of annexation that might be said to lead to the exploitation of a country for the benefit of an individual, a closed door economic policy and the ill-treatment of the natives. Those are elements of a theory which is obsolete today and rightly condemned. France has higher aspirations, and every nation is now guided by higher moral principles. Like all great powers worthy of the name, we consider our colonies to be wards entrusted to us by the world. We accept the duties of guardianship – the maintenance of peace, the protection of the people through limitation of alcohol sales and the prevention of gun-running and so on, the provision of social education. Only a great nation, with a trained administrative service, and with men and money at its disposal, can undertake this work of civilization.'

The minister then treated his listeners to a lesson in the history of French colonialism. France, he said, had spent centuries in exploring and developing the territories of North Africa and the whole world had enjoyed the benefits of this investment.

'We have spent nine thousand million francs on the Mediterranean coast of North Africa, six hundred and twenty-six million on West Africa, and two hundred and seventy-two million on equatorial Africa. In the old colonies, our work appears to be concluded. The inhabitants have equal rights as citizens and send representatives to the Chamber of Deputies. Their system of local government is exactly the same as that in France herself. We rely on these facts in making our case for sovereignty over the Cameroons and Togoland. We ask to be allowed to continue our work of civilization in Africa.'

Wilson sat stony-faced as the minister reached his peroration. When Simon had left the room, the President said: 'This discussion has reached a point where our roads diverge. I'm bound to assume that the French Colonial Office will not see its way to accepting the idea of a mandate and we have Australia, South Africa and New Zealand claiming sovereignty over what were German colonies. If those arrangements were to be part of the peace treaty, the world would say that the great powers first portioned out the helpless parts of the world and then founded the league of nations. The crude fact will be that each of those parts of the world has been assigned to one of the great powers.

'Now, I have to point out, in all frankness, that the world will not accept such an action. It will make the league of nations impossible and we will find ourselves back in the old system of competitive armaments, with accumulating debts and the burden of large armies. But, I tell you, my friends, there *must be* a league of nations – and it will be a laughing stock if it is not invested with the quality of trusteeship. I wouldn't want you to think there is any personal antagonism here, but I feel that most intensely, and I believe no sacrifice would be too great to achieve it.'

Wilson paused and looked at each of the faces round the table.

'The American people,' he said deliberately, 'will feel their sacrifices in coming into the war will have been in vain if the men returning home only come back to be trained in arms and to bear the increased burden of competitive armaments. I tell you, my friends, that in such a case the United States will have to build a greatly increased navy and maintain a large standing army. That is something which will be intolerable to the people of Europe, and you will see a great wave, like the one now sweeping Russia, that will threaten the very existence of society. The people of the world will not permit the parcelling out among the great powers of the helpless countries conquered from Germany. That is my solemn opinion, and I urge you to consider it very carefully.'

He paused again, then pushed his chair back from the table.

'I think,' he said, 'it would be wise to discontinue this discussion. If it continues, I'm afraid it might lead to a point where it will appear that we have reached a serious disagreement. I particularly wish to avoid that. Perhaps we should leave things for a few hours, or possibly until tomorrow.'

A distinct chill settled upon the company. Lloyd George tried to restore a degree of warmth.

'I do think we should try to reach a decision on the principles we adopt in relation to the former German colonies,' he said. 'Are annexations to be allowed, or do we adopt some other method? So far as mandates are concerned, I've had discussions with some officials from the British Colonial Department and, in their view, the difficulties are more imaginary than real. For my part, I don't see any difficulties in laying down general principles, and Great Britain would be prepared to administer territories under conditions laid down by the league of nations. I mean, I don't want us to get into the habit of simply putting off difficult decisions. There are obviously details to be thrashed out on this, but it seems to me the first task is to come to a decision on the principles.'

Wilson was soothed to some extent. 'Certainly there are many aspects of this that need to be cleared up. It is a new idea, after all, and we have to do some work on developing it. But I agree with the British Colonial Office that the difficulties are largely imaginary. For a start, the composition of the league of nations has been left to us in this room, so we ought to be able to settle things among ourselves. The guiding principle is one of trusteeship, and I believe the world will see that as the test of our labours. It would be unfortunate if this matter was to give the world its first cold bath of disappointment. All we have to do is agree on the principles and the rest can be left to the league of nations.'

The Canadian Prime Minister had said little throughout the meeting, since his country had no direct interest in conquered German territory. Now Sir Robert Borden placed himself in the role of mediator.

'I wonder,' he asked Wilson, 'whether we could remove the difficulty, before it becomes acute, by nominating the mandatories *before* the establishment of the league of nations? It seems to me that since the great powers will form a council controlling the work of the league, the difference between making the nominations now and referring them to the council of the league is not great.'

Wilson brightened slightly. 'That *is* a possibility,' he conceded. 'I don't think I would have difficulty with that.'

Clemenceau caught the smell of compromise in the air.

'Well,' he said, 'we've heard the views of the French Colonial Office, but I think President Wilson has interpreted them too rigidly. I am certainly ready to make concessions if reasonable proposals are put forward. I fully accept the gravity of the decision we have to take and the consequences that might flow from it, but while there is danger in refusing a means of salvation, there's an even greater one in adopting the wrong means. I thought the league of nations was being established to ensure the peace of the world, but now it seems we're proposing a league with the power to interfere in internal affairs, with trustees in various places sending reports to . . . well, I don't know to whom. So the idea of an unknown mandatory acting on behalf of some undetermined tribunal does give me some anxiety. However, if Mr Lloyd George is prepared to accept a league of nations mandate, then I won't stand against it for the sake of the Cameroons and Togoland. On the other hand, I would be nervous at the prospect of every question relating to the mandate being referred to the league of nations.'

Lloyd George had also begun to see a way of reconciling the aims of empire with the idealistic ambitions of the American President.

'To me,' he said, 'this trusteeship idea is merely a general system based on defined conditions. The league of nations would only become involved if there were some scandalous abuse of those conditions, and then it would have the power to demand an explanation from the mandatory and the right to insist on a remedy. If we accept this principle, then I do hope President Wilson will not insist on postponing the selection of the mandatories until after the establishment of the league of nations. So long as those questions are unsettled, everything will be unsettled. And, as Sir Robert pointed out, we are, in effect, the league of nations.'

He turned to the French Prime Minister: 'Am I right in supposing that you would be prepared to accept the idea of trusteeship as I have outlined it?'

'I don't approve of it,' Clemenceau grumbled, 'but I'll be guided by the judgement of the majority.'

They both looked at Wilson. The American President, however, remained adamant.

'I don't see that the disposition of the former German colonies is vital to the life of the world,' he said. 'It can wait until we've applied ourselves to the far more pressing questions of what happens now in Europe. With the colonies, the difficulty is that if we assign mandates, and the mandatories are the great powers, it will look to the world as if we're just dividing up the spoils.'

The Japanese minister, Baron Makino, had been silent for some time, though he had earlier made it clear that Japan expected to take over some of Germany's island colonies in the Pacific and its leased territory in China. He now inquired innocently: 'Whether or not mandates are assigned, have we accepted the mandatory principle?'

'No,' said Clemenceau. 'The question has been adjourned.'

The meeting broke up in no very good humour. Wilson returned to the Place des Etats-Unis, refusing, as usual, to walk the short distance from the Quai d'Orsay and insisting on being driven back to his house. As usual, his wife scolded him gently for his failure to take healthy exercise. As usual he smiled indulgently at her.

'You *know* I hate walking, dear.'

He went into his study and impatiently wound the handle on the telephone, asking the operator to connect him to Colonel House on the secure line that had been established to the Hôtel Crillon. There was no smile on his face now.

'I'm very disturbed by the way things have gone this afternoon,' he told House. 'I seem to be in an absolute minority on the colonies. All the others are interested in is dividing the swag and then having the league of nations created to endorse their title. The French came out utterly against the mandatory system and the British lined up their Dominions to support them in expanding their empire – especially the little Australian, Hughes.'

House said: 'I get the impression that the British aren't really behind Hughes on this. I've spoken to the people in their Colonial Department, and they seem comfortable with a mandatory system. I also believe Hughes's claim for annexation isn't supported by public opinion in Australia.'

'Perhaps that's our best weapon,' Wilson mused. 'If they persist in demanding outright annexation, I might warn them that I'll present the whole case to the public.'

'That would certainly flush them out. Hughes would either have to claim the territory by right of conquest, and as a reward for Australia's participation in the war, or else he would have to accept a league of nations mandate for the better government of the backward peoples. I think he'd have a difficult time pursuing the demand for annexation in those circumstances.'

'I'm confident the public will support the league of nations.'

'However,' the Colonel said, 'I think the best way to proceed would be to tell them you don't believe they represent the opinion of all the nations attending the conference, so you propose to raise the matter of the colonies at the next full session. They've already agreed that full sessions should be held in public, so the whole argument would come out, but at the same time the powers couldn't accuse you of threatening them.'

Wilson began to smile again. 'That's an excellent suggestion. I'll keep it up my sleeve to use if I can't bring them to terms.'

'It would be so much better if these things weren't done in the council of the great powers,' House said. 'I'm certain Lloyd George and Clemenceau wouldn't have dared express the views they did today if it had been in public. I wish you'd break away and demand open sessions. I hear a lot of dissatisfaction and criticism about "star chamber" methods.'

'I'm afraid it's the only way they know how to proceed here,' said Wilson. 'Lloyd George twists this way and that, and he's made it very clear that he needs closed meetings so he can say one thing one day and something completely different the next. Clemenceau says he can only make concessions in private. That's what they call negotiation.'

The British Prime Minister, indeed, was busily deploying his negotiating technique among his colleagues from the Dominions. Having begun by justifying their claims to the annexation of German colonies they occupied, he was now arguing forcefully for their acceptance of President Wilson's mandatory principle.

'He's determined to have his league of nations,' Lloyd George said when he met Hughes, Massey, and the others at the Hôtel Majestic, headquarters of the British delegation, the day after the confrontation with Wilson. 'Everything else follows from that.'

'I'd like to know who the hell he thinks he is,' Hughes complained, 'Jehovah, or what? I don't like being lectured to, especially by somebody who doesn't know what he's talking about. And if I hear another mention of the Fourteen Points, I think I'll explode.'

'Look,' said Lloyd George soothingly, 'it would be foolish to wreck the whole conference on a point such as this. I'm perfectly happy to accept the principle of a mandate for German East Africa, and so are the Colonial Office. That's a far bigger and more important territory than New Guinea or Samoa. It's simply a question of framing the conditions of the mandates in such a way that responsibility rests with the mandatory power, not with the league of nations. And there's no better model than the way we run our colonies now.'

'Well, I don't know,' Hughes persisted. 'We Australians don't want people looking over our shoulders at the way we organize our affairs. Seems to me that annexation is a perfectly reasonable solution for countries that can't govern themselves, and I can't see why we need to dress it up in fancy talk about mandates and trusteeship and the like. If we're going to run the place, then let's just run it.'

Sir Robert Borden, always the voice of reason, spoke up: 'President Wilson is never going to accept that. To him, it would be just an expansion of the Empire, and it wouldn't be acceptable to the American people, who still harbour unpleasant folk memories of colonialism. We're going to have to reach a compromise that allows him to present the league of nations as an alternative to imperialism and the old balance of power.'

'I don't give a fig for the league of nations or what President Wilson presents to his people,' Hughes said hotly. 'I'm concerned about Australia and what's best for Australians.

We've made big sacrifices in this war, and *I* have to be able to tell *my* people that those sacrifices have been recognized. The league of nations is going to seem a very long way from where we are.'

Lloyd George leaned forward and placed a hand on the Australian's arm.

'Be patient,' he said. 'President Wilson has been obsessed with the league of nations since before the end of the war. When he came to London last month, it was all he really wanted to talk about. But the fact is that he has no real plan. He hasn't determined how the league will work or how it will be paid for. The same is true of these mandates he's talking about. All we have to do is accept the principle – that's what concerns Wilson most – and then we can work out the details for him.'

Hughes narrowed his eyes suspiciously. 'What do you mean, exactly?'

'I've been giving it some thought,' Lloyd George replied, 'and I've jotted down a few notes for a proposal we can submit to the next meeting. It will satisfy Wilson because it enshrines the authority of the league of nations, and at the same time I think it will meet our needs – even yours.'

Accepting the position of trustees under the league of nations, he explained, Britain, the Dominions and France would undertake the mandates relating to the former German colonies, and the conquered parts of the Turkish empire, on the basis of a series of conditions he had drawn up. In Central Africa, for example, the mandatory would be responsible for administration but would not be permitted to establish military bases or train native troops for anything other than police operations. The mandated power would also guarantee free trade with other members of the league of nations.

'Then,' Lloyd George went on, 'we come to the likes of South West Africa and the South Pacific islands, which, because of local conditions, are best administered under the laws of the mandatory state, of which, in effect, they become a part – though again subject to guarantees given to the league of nations by the mandatory power.'

'Ah,' said Hughes, 'so they're colonies in all but name?'

'I don't think we should use the word colony,' Sir Robert Borden said.

A thought occurred to Hughes: 'But what happens if the mandate is given to some other country? America, for instance?'

Sir Robert shook his head. 'The Congress would never accept it.'

'And,' said Lloyd George, 'who else is there?'

'In addition to which,' added Sir Robert, 'possession is nine-tenths of the law. You're already in New Guinea, New Zealand has Samoa and South Africa drove the Germans out of South West Africa.'

Hughes frowned. 'I suppose it could work,' he said slowly. 'But what if President Wilson won't go along with this proposal?'

'Oh, I think he will,' said Lloyd George. 'As I said, he has no proper plan for his league of nations, and we're very helpfully going to give him one that he'll be able to call his own. The mandates will be its first great success.'

He smiled at Hughes. 'But we'll still be able to go home and tell our people we got what they wanted.'

In the Place des Etats-Unis, President Wilson was quietly playing Canfield, an American version of the card game solitaire, watched by his wife and Rear-Admiral Grayson. In his office, the telephone rang and, after a few moments, one of the President's aides entered the drawing room to announce that Robert Lansing was on the line. Wilson went into the office, leaving the door open behind him.

'What?' Edith and Grayson heard him say irritably. 'Who authorized them to do that? I certainly didn't.'

He listened to Lansing's explanation, then, unusually for him, raised his voice almost to a shout: 'Well, you tell them I don't want to see their draft. I told you before that I don't want lawyers involved. This is going to be *my* treaty.'

*III*
———

Georges Clemenceau found himself left largely to his own devices towards the end of February 1919. The peace conference was grinding slowly on as myriad committees of experts worried over the minutiae of the terms the eventual treaty might contain, and drafts of its various putative conditions were laboriously developed by delegates concerned that their own countries' special interests should not be overlooked. It was work largely in vain, since it was becoming clear that the only real decisions would emerge not from the conference itself but from the secret councils of the main Allied nations. For the moment, however, this clandestine process was held in abeyance as the leaders of the United States, Britain and Italy turned their attention away from the future of the world and towards the somewhat narrower horizons of the future of their own governments.

President Wilson had taken ship for home in response to urgent messages from Washington warning him that significant elements of the new Republican majority in the Congress were ranging themselves against the President's vision of a league of nations. The League now existed – at least in the form of a draft covenant cobbled together by Wilson, House and the British – but leading Republican senators had declared it unacceptable. The League as it was conceived, they said, was at odds with the hallowed Monroe Doctrine, issued in 1823 by the last American president of the revolutionary generation, which asserted that the paramount influence in the western hemisphere was to be America's and that any attempted expansion of European power there would amount to an unfriendly act.

These senators, Wilson had been told, together with others who were concerned about challenges to American trade and immigration policies, were numerous enough to prevent the two-thirds majority that would be required to ratify a peace treaty, and would certainly prevent ratification if the treaty included the League of Nations covenant in its present form.

It was an inconvenient moment. The Allies were discussing whether to continue with their aggressive policy in Russia, where they had sent troops to help oppose the Bolshevik revolution. For Wilson, though, problems in the west were considerably more pressing than events in the east.

'My personal thoughts on Russia,' he told the Quai d'Orsay conclave as he prepared to leave to catch a train for Brest, 'are that our troops there aren't doing a great deal of good, mostly because the anti-Bolshevik forces are ineffective. I believe that sooner or later, we're going to have to withdraw our troops, and my inclination would be to do so now. But I'll leave it to you to discuss the matter and cast in my lot with whatever you decide.'

The League of Nations was to be his legacy to history, and he was not about to lose it to the selfish interests of a group of home-town reactionaries. He would do what he had always done: appeal directly to the people. Russia could look after itself.

Lloyd George, meanwhile, had also been obliged to

abandon his role as a world statesman in favour of a short exercise in political fixing. In Britain, the euphoria of the armistice had evaporated quite quickly, to be replaced by agitation for more rapid demobilization of conscripted soldiers and wholesale industrial reform. During the election campaign, the Prime Minister had promised to make Britain a fit country for heroes to live in. Now the heroes wanted to see some sign of their rewards.

Matters had reached a crisis in the coal-mining industry, which had naturally come under government control during the war as the nation's principal source of energy. When the conflict ended, the government had no wish to continue subsidizing the mines, but, equally, the miners did not want to be left once more to the tender mercies of the coal owners, who had a history of paying poorly, having scant regard for safety and treating their workers badly. The temporary nationalization appeared to have worked well, and there were demands from the trade union that it should become permanent – in addition to which, the miners presented a claim for a thirty per cent increase in wages, a reduction of their working day to six hours, and full pay for workers who had been laid off as a result of the sudden return to peacetime conditions and an accompanying decline in coal output. They threatened to go on strike if they did not get what they wanted.

'This amounts to an attempt at revolution,' Lloyd George told Frances Stevenson grimly when the news reached him at his flat in the Rue Nitot, where Frances was enjoying her temporary status as his *de facto* wife. He was drinking tea and nibbling on the sweet *langue de chat* biscuits to which he had developed something of an addiction.

'We've got to fight it,' he went on. 'It's regrettable, but we'll have to starve them into submission if necessary.'

Frances asked: 'Do you think it will be ugly?'

He smiled. 'I'll go to London and speak to the miners' leaders. I'm sure they'll be willing to listen to me. It will be a salutary lesson for the Tories. They need me to face up to the Labour extremists and their notions of social upheaval.'

Also facing up to extremists, though of a rather different kind, was Vittorio Emanuele Orlando. Certainly, he had his problems with the trades unions, as an economy ravaged by the war failed to cope with the peace. Prices were rising inexorably beyond the reach of wages, and wages themselves were hard to come by as demobilized soldiers and redundant war workers competed for what appeared to be a decreasing number of jobs. But a more serious threat to his government's survival came from the people – including his own Foreign Minister, Sonnino – who saw the collapse of Germany and Austria as Italy's opportunity to take its place alongside Britain and France as one of the leading powers of Europe.

Orlando had already been forced to reconstruct his Cabinet to take account of the popular clamour for Italian expansion, the return of lands to the north formerly held by the Austro-Hungarian Empire, and the annexation of newly liberated territories on the Dalmatian coast of the Adriatic. Some people even demanded that Italy should share in the disposition of former enemy colonies in North Africa, on the ground that they had once been part of the Roman empire. This was not merely an excess of patriotism. Italy was desperately short of industrial resources such as coal and iron, and Sonnino and his supporters saw territorial expansion as the only means of increasing economic power. Most of all, though, Italians felt they had done their part during the war and wanted their reward. They had, after all, been made solemn promises by the British and the French, and many of them did not want now to be told that events had rendered those pledges null and void.

Orlando was no less of a patriot than any other Italian, but he was a cultured, sensitive and reasonable man, prepared to work with the other Allies to reach a fair settlement whatever hostages had been given to fortune under the pressures of war. Unfortunately, he was also a prisoner of forces that were proving extremely difficult to control. It was not simply a question of Mussolini and his Fascisti, who rallied support among the disaffected working classes with their vision of strong government in a powerful Italy, but also of politicians and intellectuals who banded together in an unholy alliance designed to secure what they saw as the just deserts of their country.

'We seem almost oppressed by our triumph,' proclaimed the intensely patriotic writer Gabriele D'Annunzio, attacking Orlando's diplomatic approach. 'We beg for the smile of the arbiter. And what peace will in the end be imposed on us, poor little ones of Christ? A Gallic peace? A British peace? A star-spangled peace? Then, no! Enough. Victorious Italy – the most victorious of all the nations – victorious over herself and over the enemy – will have on the Alps and over her sea the Pax Romana. If necessary, we will meet the plot against us with a grenade in each hand and a knife between our teeth.'

Orlando, since his arrival in Paris, had been looking over his shoulder. President Wilson's visit to Italy had served further to inflame patriotic passions and reinforce the suspicion that the Italians were to be betrayed by the people alongside whom they had fought. Among the Byzantine networks of Italian politics, the Prime Minister had sought to strengthen his hand by removing moderates from his government and packing it with expansionist hard-liners, but that had merely raised questions about how Orlando could remain at its head when the policy it pursued was to be dictated by the obdurate Sonnino. The Prime Minister's sudden return to Rome in the midst of the peace conference was as much to do with preventing his own ousting from office *in absentia* as it was about soothing the growing mood of violent discontent.

This outbreak of domestic disharmony in Italy, Britain and the United States was, for Georges Clemenceau, an additional reason for the frustration he was feeling in regard to the peace conference he had organized and had hoped to direct, at least in some measure. Flushed with the success of having established the conference in Paris, the Prime Minister had set his officials the task of drawing up the schedule of its work in accordance with the traditional principles of French logic.

'We'll start,' he had told André Tardieu, 'with a discussion of the general principles on which the treaty will be based. That will put Wilson's Fourteen Points into some sort of context, because unless we do that, we'll get nowhere. Then we can go on to the territorial settlements, and obviously the first item on the agenda will be to deal with Germany's frontiers and colonies.'

'There could be difficulties with that,' Tardieu said.

'I don't doubt it,' replied Clemenceau. 'But what happens to Germany now is the essential question, and the whole treaty will depend on it. Once the German problem is settled, we can make proper arrangements for future security, demilitarization and so on.'

'And the frontiers of new countries, such as Poland, Czechoslovakia and Yugoslavia.'

'I think,' Clemenceau said, 'the Italians are going to have plenty to say about the last one. It conflicts with the booty that's due to them under the Treaty of London, and they aren't going to be happy at the prospect of an independent nation of Slavs facing them across the Adriatic. But that's precisely why these matters must be discussed first. With them out of the way, we can go on to look at the restitution and reparations the enemy will have to make for war damage and finally set about a proper programme of economic reconstruction.'

'You haven't mentioned the league of nations,' Tardieu pointed out.

Clemenceau shrugged. 'I don't object to the idea at all. Perhaps I don't see it in quite the way Wilson does, but it's something we can talk about at leisure, once the serious business of the conference is over. I don't see how you can build an organization for keeping the peace until you've finally ended the war.'

'Well, it all seems perfectly rational to me,' said Tardieu.

'I'll work on the details and have the programme properly set out.'

The Prime Minister patted him on the back. 'Good boy. I don't want this conference to drag on, you know. People won't stand for it if we don't come to some decisions quickly. They feel they've won the war and they want to enjoy the victory. There'll only be a lot of criticism and simmering dissatisfaction – perhaps not just simmering – if we take too long about it.'

What might have seemed rational to a Frenchman, however, did not have the same appeal for the Americans and the British. To Clemenceau's intense irritation, they rejected his programme as being too systematic.

'What do they mean?' he roared at Tardieu. 'How in God's name are we going to get through this if we don't approach it systematically?'

'It's the way the Anglo-Saxon mind works, I suppose,' the younger man said, ignoring the fact that Lloyd George was a Celt. 'They seem to like muddle and to reach decisions almost by accident.'

'And they're usually late. Have you noticed? Lloyd George was even late for the official opening of the conference. He came in halfway through Poincaré's speech. Not that he missed much, mind you.'

'Well,' said Tardieu, 'I suppose we'll have to go along with them. They're our guests, after all.'

Clemenceau grunted. 'But we'll get the blame, as the hosts, if it doesn't work out.'

There had been no turning President Wilson away from the

obsession with his league of nations. To Clemenceau's mind, it defied all logic, but Wilson seemed to think that, even if nothing else was achieved, the league must be born. Lloyd George, on the other hand, had been fixed on having committees to examine everything. Clemenceau was not sure why, since it soon became obvious that the British Prime Minister paid little attention to what his experts told him, and appeared set on making all decisions on the basis of instinct, according to the way the wind blew in the conclaves of the big powers.

'It was probably inevitable,' Tardieu told his Prime Minister. 'The politics was always going to be more important than the technical details.'

'In which case,' Clemenceau grumbled, 'why can't we just get on with the politics? By my reckoning, we now have fifty-eight expert committees and sub-committees picking over every little detail, and we've hardly begun to agree about the principles on which it's all going to depend. We must get down to some real work.'

Tardieu smiled. 'Work? Is that what you call it? According to Colonel House, it's all a great adventure.'

'Hah! It may be a great adventure when you haven't got a pack of jackals at your heels. All these people shrieking blue murder and throwing out their chests . . . They seem to think they can have one of those merciless peace treaties that Napoleon used to impose when he overthrew an empire in three cavalry charges.'

President Poincaré had been busy whipping up feelings in the Chamber of Deputies and among the press by promoting

Marshal Foch's plan for the covert annexation of the Rhineland, claiming that it was the only way in which the security of France could be guaranteed for the future. He knew that Clemenceau had still failed to raise the matter openly with the other Allied leaders, and his ceaseless championing of the cause soon produced a whispering campaign against the Prime Minister, suggesting that he could not be relied upon to defend French interests to the full. Clemenceau treated this with contempt, but he was more concerned when the newspapers – afraid of attacking *le Tigre* himself – began to accuse President Wilson of standing in the way of what many now regarded as France's legitimate pursuit of self-protection.

The annexationists, though, were not his only problem as he sat in the room at the War Ministry he had used since his call to office in 1917, waiting for Wilson, Lloyd George and Orlando to return to Paris so that the serious work of the peace conference could continue. In France, perhaps more than anywhere among the Allied nations, the war had devastated the economy as much as the countryside, with the government's expenditure by 1918 running at seven times the amount of its revenues. The peace raised popular expectations, but it could not reduce the government's spending because the costs of war still had to be met, and it provoked a sharp rise in prices as the pent-up consumer demand of the war years was released.

'Our total debts are about three hundred thousand million francs,' Clemenceau's Finance Minister, Louis-Lucien Klotz, told the Prime Minister when he came to see him at the War

Ministry. 'The interest payments are huge, and when you combine that with the costs we're facing for reconstruction, the pensions to the war widows and the wounded soldiers, the severance pay for the demobilized troops, the farming subsidies . . . Well, you can see the difficulties. That's why we have to count on reparation payments from the Boche.'

Clemenceau had little respect for Klotz's financial acumen, but he could sympathize with his loyal minister's predicament.

'Well, we certainly can't raise taxes at this stage,' he said. 'That would guarantee our defeat in the elections in November. We'll just have to postpone the budget until after the vote. For the present, we can ask the National Assembly to vote appropriations as and when we need them.'

'But that will make an even bigger mess of our finances,' Klotz pointed out. 'The Socialists are already calling loudly for new taxes. A levy on capital of twenty-five per cent was one demand I heard from them the other day.'

'Ignore them,' said Clemenceau sharply. 'They make a lot of noise, but they've got no real support in the Chamber. And we must keep the support of the centre and right-wing parties. Stick to the line about reparations.'

Klotz smirked. 'Germany will pay, eh?'

'That's it. The Socialists will challenge you, but it'll please our friends who are out for revenge.'

Klotz did as he was told, with enthusiasm, even adding on his own initiative that France would urge the peace conference to give precedence to some of its claims over others. But all round him the clamour intensified, with one side braying that

Germany must be made to pay vast sums in damages, while the Socialists poured scorn on the unfortunate Finance Minister.

'Madness!' they roared in response to his repeated assurances. '*C'est un bluff misérable!*'

As the volume mounted, so did the tension. Clemenceau chafed at his inability to make progress and respond to his growing number of critics because of the absence of the other leaders. He lurked in his office at the War Ministry, avoiding heated debates in the National Assembly as Klotz's promises became ever wilder and the Socialists demanded to know what the government's budgetary intentions were.

On the morning of Wednesday 19 February, the Prime Minister came down from his apartment in the Rue Franklin at about nine o'clock and got into the back seat of a War Ministry car for the short journey to his office in the Rue Saint-Dominique, three blocks back from the Quai d'Orsay and the river.

The army driver pulled away and headed south-west, intending to pass through the Trocadéro Gardens and cross the Seine by the Pont d'Iéna. As the car slowed down to turn left into the Boulevard Delessert, an unkempt-looking man rushed out of the *pissoir* on the corner, pulled a revolver from his coat and fired a single shot through the rear passenger door.

He continued firing as the driver jammed his foot on the accelerator and sped in the direction of the Trocadéro – two, three, four bullets passing through and over the car, smashing the windscreen.

Clemenceau had been hit. He hammered on the window

separating him from the driver. The car screeched to a halt.

'Back home,' Clemenceau gasped.

As the car swung round, a passing air force officer leapt on to the running board, opened the rear door and squirmed inside.

'He was a poor shot,' Clemenceau said weakly.

Back in the Rue Franklin, the driver and the airman helped the bleeding Prime Minister out of the car.

As they crossed the courtyard towards his apartment, he cried out, 'Be careful! You're hurting me.'

Gently, the two men guided him into the flat.

In the Rue Delessert, the would-be assassin had thrown away his revolver as an angry crowd surrounded him before he could escape. Two policemen seized him and fought their way through what threatened to turn into a lynch mob, finally reaching the safety of the Mairie half a mile away.

Clemenceau's doctors were at the old man's apartment within fifteen minutes of the shooting and quickly examined him.

'There's a deep wound in the right shoulder blade,' said the surgeon, Dr Gosset, after conferring with his colleagues, 'but I don't think it's a dangerous injury.'

The news had spread rapidly and the telephone rang incessantly – Poincaré, Foch, the members of the Cabinet, and a host of well-wishers. Jean Martet arrived by car from the War Ministry, where he had been waiting for his boss. He found Clemenceau refusing to go to bed, instead sitting up, yellow-faced and looking very old, in an armchair. The wounded *Tigre* managed a weak smile.

'Well, this is one experience that's new to me,' he said. 'I've never been assassinated before.'

Anxious telegrams began to arrive, then a note from the famous actress Sarah Bernhardt was delivered by messenger: 'I must have news. I'm unnerved by the rumours. Just now, Clemenceau is France.'

Martet turned to Gosset. 'You'd better issue a bulletin, Doctor, to reassure everyone if nothing else.'

Gosset did so, indicating that the Prime Minister was in no danger and that his general condition was good in spite of his wound. But an hour or so later, Clemenceau began to cough up blood.

'There must be lung damage,' the surgeon said. 'We'll have to get him to hospital immediately.'

They found a puncture in Clemenceau's lung, but no trace of any bullet. It must, said one eminent doctor, have struck the shoulder blade and bounced back out through the hole by which it had entered the body.

Clemenceau, as a medical man himself, raised an eyebrow at this diagnosis: 'It's a pretty miraculous bullet to have done that.'

He remained in hospital overnight, and the next day an X-ray finally revealed the mysterious bullet lodged in the membrane between the lungs. The doctors began to discuss whether they should attempt to remove it.

'Will it do any harm if it stays where it is?' Clemenceau asked gruffly.

They thought not. It might cause some minor discomfort, perhaps some slight disturbance in the lungs, a chronic cough, possibly.

'Then leave it where it is,' Clemenceau said. 'I have enough wrong with me, so a little something extra won't make any difference. In any case, I can't be doing with surgery. I have work to do, and it won't wait.'

So they sent him home, where Martet relayed to him the details of the incompetent assassin.

'He's a young man named Emile Cottin, an anarchist apparently. But they're saying the attempt was instigated by the Bolsheviks because they don't like our aggressive policy in Russia. Anyway, he'll come up before a military tribunal early next month. The word is that he's certain to be sentenced to death.'

Clemenceau grunted. 'Don't you believe it, my boy. Remember Jaurès. And in his case the attempt was successful.'

The Socialist leader Jean Jaurès, founder of the newspaper *L'Humanité*, had been assassinated in 1914, a few days before the outbreak of the war, by a young fanatic who believed Jaurès' pacifism was encouraging German aggression. At his trial, the killer had been set free.

'This is different,' Martet said. 'And, anyway, Cottin will face a military tribunal, whereas the man who killed Jaurès went before the assize court.'

Clemenceau waved a hand dismissively. 'I admire your faith, my friend, but there is politics involved here. Oh, yes, they may well condemn this poor fool to death, but you can be sure that the sentence will never be carried out.'

He tapped his chest. 'No, Martet, I'm afraid that Monsieur Cottin has done me the favour, without any request on my part, of thanking me for what I have done for my country.'

Martet asked: 'What are your plans now?'

'I'll rest for a few days,' Clemenceau replied, 'then I'll get back to work. Probably by the end of next week. And my first call will be on the Chamber of Deputies.'

'They'll be relieved to see you back in harness.'

Clemenceau smiled. 'I doubt it, Martet, I doubt it. There are too many of them who won't forgive the victory.'

## CHAPTER 2

# *Four Horsemen of the Apocalypse*

*I*

The early months of 1919 had been cold, wet and miserable on the Western Front. Not that it really was the Western Front any more, of course. The armistice had obliged the Germans to withdraw, leaving large numbers of their men behind as prisoners, and the Allied troops who remained, during this strange interlude between war and peace, now milled about aimlessly, bored and restless, wondering how long it would be before they could go home.

At Blangy-Tronville, a British army brigade headquarters on the south bank of the River Somme, east of Amiens, officers did their best to keep their conscript soldiers occupied while they waited with growing impatience for demobilization. For the most part, they relied on familiar devices such as route marches, parades and drill, but the men resented this, and half-hearted attempts were made to entertain them with a series of lectures and educational courses. Rather more popular were the regular sporting contests that allowed pent-up energy to be released and fostered healthy rivalry with other units.

Occasionally, there were moments of genuine excitement, such as the day two companies were dispatched, heavily armed, early in the morning to round up a band of deserters who had taken up residence on an island in the river, from where they pillaged the surrounding district for food and other supplies. The sortie proved to be more thrilling in the anticipation than in the execution, however, ending quietly with the arrest of two bewildered men in their pyjamas.

The boredom and petty irritations of what seemed now to be a pointless existence was sometimes relieved by a strange form of tourism. Men revisited the battlefields on which so many of their comrades had died, told stories of their exploits to wide-eyed late arrivals from England, and hunted for souvenirs – German helmets, weapons, cap badges, belts, or perhaps more personal items such as cigarette cases. One party came upon an abandoned artillery piece under whose shells they had learned to cower, its barrel so long that more than twenty men could sit astride it.

Between the victors and the remnants of the defeated enemy, there was mutual respect and the peculiar sort of comradeship that can exist between soldiers on opposing sides when their fighting is done. The German prisoners at Blangy-Tronville were housed across the road from their British captors, in identical huts, no less impatient to go home and hardly more uncertain about what might await them when they did. Their officers obviously had even greater difficulty in preventing their men from sinking into lethargy and indiscipline, and one of their remedies had been to form a string orchestra, to whose regular concerts the British were also invited. It did not escape the visitors' notice that the German huts seemed to be warmer than their own, thanks, no doubt, to the influence of the Red Cross in obtaining coal for the prisoners.

While this curious military half-life continued, the supreme commander of the Allied forces was busily engaged in finding more durable and more useful tasks for the large numbers of soldiers still available to him. Marshal Foch had taken advantage of the February lull in the peace negotiations to pursue his plan for the isolation of Germany behind the frontier of the Rhine. Having secured the main Rhine bridgeheads shortly after the signing of the armistice, the dapper little soldier had encouraged his local commanders to canvass the opinions of the populations in the west-bank provinces of Germany about how they might see their future. Among the chaos, confusion and political upheaval that had fallen upon the German people with the sudden realization of defeat, it was not difficult to rouse the disaffected and disenchanted to support the idea of a break with the remnants of the discredited regime that had led them to disaster.

President Poincaré had helped by sending French administrators to undertake the business of local government, demonstrating that the victors had only the best interests of the inhabitants at heart. With the new and unstable German government itself raising the frightening spectre of a Bolshevik revolution, Foch had every hope of a clamour arising in the Rhenish regions for the safer option of throwing in their lot with the Allies.

Until that happened, however, Foch faced the problem of persuading the Americans and the British not only to accept the principle of the Rhine frontier, but also to agree to a military occupation of the 'liberated' provinces until such time as their non-German status could be properly established. The signs had not been very positive thus far. Lloyd George had been cool towards the idea at the first meeting in London, and had then proceeded to shelve Foch's memorandum of justification. For reasons the Marshal could not fathom, Clemenceau had neglected to raise the matter during a month of secret meetings at the Foreign Ministry. It was almost as if the Prime Minister was afraid to provoke a confrontation with the Allies, preferring to confine their discussions to subjects which, so far as Foch was concerned, were peripheral to the main event.

'I can't understand it,' he told Poincaré, who had done his best to ensure public opinion would force the Prime Minister into making a stand. 'This would be the great prize of our victory. All my generals think so.'

'A lot of people in the Assembly, too,' Poincaré said. 'But then Clemenceau has never paid too much attention to what the Deputies say. Look at the way he behaved during the war, even ignoring the members of his own government. The man has the instincts of a dictator.'

For his own part, Clemenceau had made it clear to Foch that, when he had put the Rhineland proposition privately to President Wilson, before the opening of the peace conference, the response he had received had been entirely negative. Wilson had cited both his Fourteen Points and the proposed powers of his league of nations as reasons why he was not prepared to consider at that stage any detachment of German territory in favour of the Allies.

'But did he say he would openly oppose it?' Foch demanded.

'No, he didn't actually say he would oppose it,' replied Clemenceau.

'Then we must press the matter, surely. If this conference isn't about strategical considerations, what is it about? I mean, it's clear from the schedule you had Tardieu draw up that the settlement of the German frontiers is the item upon which all others depend.'

Clemenceau shrugged. 'That programme for the conference wasn't accepted by the Americans and the British, and we have to take note of the wishes of our allies.'

'Not when our future security is involved, we don't,' snapped Foch.

'Look, Marshal, this is a peace conference – that's the important word, "conference". At a conference, people confer. They don't simply make demands and say to the others, "You'd better accept these, or else . . .". It's not as simple as a battle. It's not a question of winning or losing, but of reaching agreement – and in this case, the agreement has to be unanimous.'

Foch raised his arms in a gesture of incomprehension. 'So are you saying that we must be prepared to give way on this for the sake of pleasing our allies?'

Clemenceau shook his head. 'I'm not saying we should give way. I'm as convinced as you are that Germany must be contained, and that France must be guaranteed safety from another attack across the Rhine. What I'm saying is that how we arrange that containment and that guarantee is a matter for negotiation.'

'But we aren't even negotiating.'

'That is precisely what we *are* doing,' Clemenceau insisted. 'I have reported to you and to Monsieur le Président the results of my discussions with Wilson and Lloyd George on the subject of the Rhine provinces. It is clear that they are not sympathetic to the proposals you have put forward. To press them now would be foolhardy – it would only force them into positions from which they would be unable to retreat, and the whole cause would be lost. The point of negotiating is to see what concessions you can obtain on the basis of those you yourself make. These present discussions are a process of feeling our way. You may think the topics are unimportant as against what we do about Germany, but if we can show willing on the unimportant points, it gives us a better chance of winning the important ones.'

'Well, I can't see where all this shilly-shallying is getting us when the only thing that really matters is capitalizing on our victory in strategical terms.'

The Prime Minister was becoming irritated, but he kept his voice even. 'Just think back to the war, and the business over unity of command. That was achieved by several stages. Everybody did his bit. But the difficulty of bringing unity of command into being was much less than the difficulty of making it work. That's because different people think in different ways, and you don't suddenly change just because you've made a temporary alliance with a foreigner.'

Foch left Clemenceau's room at the War Ministry unconvinced. If the Prime Minister was not prepared to raise the issue of the Rhine frontier in an open way, then the Marshal would do it for him. But he needed help. He turned to André Tardieu, who had experienced the horror of fighting the Boche at first hand, but who also understood the ways of diplomacy and politics.

'There's no time to be lost,' Foch told the younger man. 'We achieved our victory in 1918, but it's already 1919, and we must establish that victory by settling the principal peace terms, and especially by disarming Germany and fixing the limit of her power, which means her frontiers.'

'What does the Prime Minister have to say about this?' asked Tardieu, who knew something of Clemenceau's reservations about the Rhine policy, but had not been taken fully into his confidence, as was usual with the old man.

'He agrees with me,' said Foch. 'He said he believed Germany must be contained and that France required guarantees against future aggression across the Rhine. In my view, the only way of securing those things is to have Germany relinquish all rights over the left bank of the Rhine and the bridgeheads, which we occupy now anyway.'

'So what do you want me to do, Marshal?'

'Well, as I said, there's no time to be lost. It seems to me we must urge the peace conference – which really means the big powers – to bring about an immediate and summary settlement with Germany, before it deals with other matters.

So what I want you to do, in your official position as one of the drafters of the French proposals, is compose a memorandum to that effect that can be presented to the Allied council. You know better than I do how to phrase these things.'

'That's straightforward enough,' Tardieu said, 'but, of course, we don't know when the next meeting will be. President Wilson is in Washington and Lloyd George has gone back to England.'

'What better time to act? We'll submit our proposal to their officials, then there'll be no excuse for not discussing it the minute Wilson and Lloyd George return to Paris.'

Tardieu consulted Clemenceau.

'I can't see any harm in submitting a memorandum,' the Prime Minister said. 'Wilson and Lloyd George already know what's in Foch's mind. But, of course, there's no guarantee that they'll want to discuss the Rhineland at this stage, and I'll have to be guided by their wishes. Foch will have to understand that.'

Armed with a note from Foch, in which he stated baldly that the current condition of Germany would ensure that its government accepted virtually anything the Allies sought to impose, Tardieu went to work. His sophisticated mind thought better of demanding an immediate settlement with Germany, as the Marshal had suggested, but he constructed an elegant argument supporting Foch's case, slyly inserting a reference to the peace conference that followed the defeat of Napoleon at Waterloo in 1815.

'I'm inserting a reference from a letter sent by Lord Castlereagh to the Duke of Wellington about the time of the

Treaty of Paris,' he told Foch proudly. 'The Foreign Secretary wrote to the Duke that Mr Pitt had been quite right in 1805 when he had sought to give Prussia more territory on the left bank of the Rhine, because at that time, of course, the British were attempting to weaken France's strategic position.'

'Perfect,' said Foch. 'It's precisely the argument that I'm employing. And it should go down well with the British.'

The memorandum suggested that a mere limitation of Germany's armed forces and reliance on the as yet unproved League of Nations were insufficient to guarantee the future security of France. It proceeded to reprise Foch's case in less militaristic and peremptory terms, concluding that 'the Rhine affords the people on both its banks a natural and equal guarantee against attack'. Finally, conscious of Clemenceau's fears about how the French attitude might be misinterpreted, Tardieu noted:

> *In this question, France asks nothing for herself; neither an inch of territory nor any sovereign rights. France demands only one thing: that the measures, and the only ones calculated surely to prevent the left bank of the Rhine from becoming once more the base of a German attack, should be taken by the powers now assembled at the peace conference.*
>
> *In other words, without any territorial ambition, but convinced of the necessity of establishing protection at once international and national, France expects from an Inter-Allied occupation of the Rhine that which Britain and the United States expect from the maintenance of their naval forces – nothing more and nothing less.*

Foch was delighted.

'It's an excellent piece of work,' he said when Tardieu showed him the document. 'But, more to the point, it is the formalization of our claims in a manner the conference cannot ignore. There'll be no more tiptoeing round the subject once this has been delivered.'

'I'm glad you approve,' said Tardieu. 'I've sent a copy to the President, so all I have to do now is show it to the Prime Minister.'

But it was the day on which Clemenceau had been shot.

'You can hardly show it to him now,' Foch said. 'I know he isn't in any danger, but I don't think we should be troubling him after that terrible experience.'

'Then we'd better wait until he has recovered, I suppose.'

'No, no, we can't do that. I've already spoken to the British liaison officer at Allied staff headquarters, and given him a copy of the memorandum I sent to you. They're expecting your formal document. We can't tell how long Clemenceau will be out of action, and we must strike now otherwise they'll have an excuse to defer the thing again. This is an urgent matter.'

'Well, if you're sure . . .' said Tardieu. 'Clemenceau certainly didn't object to this approach when I mentioned it to him.'

'Of course not. Why should he? This is a subject the conference must discuss. I think you'd better send your memorandum straight away.'

What neither Foch nor Tardieu knew, however, was that Lloyd George was already preparing to block what he still regarded as a blatant French attempt at annexation. The British liaison officer had contacted the Prime Minister in London immediately after his conversation with Foch, and Lloyd George had not liked what he had been told.

'It's an absolute betrayal of the principles on which we all said we were fighting the war,' he complained to Andrew Bonar Law, having averted the threatened miners' strike by promising a commission of inquiry into the state of the coal industry. 'President Wilson and I have discussed it several times, and he completely agrees with our position. The French aren't going to get away with this.'

Tardieu's memorandum, for all its elegance, did nothing to alter his opinion, and when, in Paris once more, he met the now recovered but still shaky Clemenceau, Lloyd George was in no mood for compromise.

'If you persist in bringing this before the council,' he said, 'you're going to risk a serious deadlock.'

'That's the last thing I want,' said Clemenceau. 'I warned them what might happen. I can't think what's got into Tardieu.'

'But I can only assume that the Tardieu document is a statement of the policy of the French government.'

'It's a very delicate matter. President Poincaré . . . Marshal Foch . . . Feelings are running high, you know. We can't simply ignore people's expectations, or their fears. Germany will have to be contained, and there will have to be guarantees for the future security of France. We can't go on bearing the brunt of German ambitions.'

'Well, we certainly can't discuss it now, while President

Wilson is away. But from what I gather, Marshal Foch is demanding an immediate settlement of the German question.'

'People are impatient,' said Clemenceau. 'They expect to see progress. The fighting may have stopped, but the war isn't over until we've built the peace. There are still German armies in the field.'

'As Marshal Foch never ceases reminding us,' Lloyd George said irritably. 'Look, I suppose we have to do something, so I suggest we refer Tardieu's memorandum to a committee – he can sit on it himself, alongside one of our people and someone from the American delegation. I don't think we need to involve other countries in this.'

Clemenceau readily agreed to this suggestion, reasoning that no progress could be made in any case until Wilson's return from America, and that the manoeuvre would serve to maintain his own detachment from the policy of Poincaré and Foch. It was clear that the French claims were now officially on the agenda at the insistence of the Marshal, which meant there was no need for Clemenceau to risk causing a breach by raising them openly in discussion. At the same time, the fact that the proposal was to be considered by a committee would be enough to demonstrate to Poincaré that it was being taken seriously. Clemenceau could not be blamed by Wilson and Lloyd George for taking a position they could not possibly support, and neither could he be accused by Poincaré of failing in his duty to further the interests of France.

In any case, *le Tigre* could not say with certainty that there were no benefits to be gained from the plan for the Rhineland. Though Wilson appeared to have given it short shrift,

Tardieu had received a rather different message, in the President's absence, from Colonel House. It seemed to be that if the proposal could be adapted to take account of the reference in the Fourteen Points to the desirability of self-determination for emerging states – and to offer some involvement to the famous League of Nations – the Americans might well look favourably on the idea of containing Germany behind the Rhine frontier. If that happened, it would definitely help to silence many of Clemenceau's right-wing critics.

But would Lloyd George bend to the combined will of America and France? Tardieu thought he might, on the basis that he would be unable to ignore the anti-German feeling that was rampant in Britain. Clemenceau was not so sure. But then, if the committee that Lloyd George himself had suggested were to support the Foch scheme, how could the British Prime Minister repudiate it?

But Lloyd George and Colonel House knew precisely what they were doing. Unwilling to confront the French himself, House nominated as the American representative on the committee his brother-in-law, Dr Sidney Mezes, an academic who had advised President Wilson on the outlines of a peace treaty. He could be relied upon to uphold the President's principles. Lloyd George had also ensured that his views would be heard by nominating the intensely loyal Philip Kerr, a foreign affairs specialist who had been on the Prime Minister's personal staff since 1916. The result, to the irritation of Tardieu, was that the committee proved to be just the interminable talking shop Lloyd George had intended it to be.

Clemenceau realized he was being outmanoeuvred. He called on the British Prime Minister at his flat in the Rue Nitot.

'I'm sorry,' Lloyd George told him, 'but it would be politically impossible for me to go along with this proposal for the Rhineland, quite apart from the fact that I regard it as utterly incompatible with the cause we all said we were fighting for.'

'Oh, come on,' Clemenceau said. 'We only dreamed up those war aims because the Americans wanted them to justify their joining in.'

'Nevertheless, the British public would, I'm certain, never countenance the separation of the Rhine provinces from Germany against their will. It offends our sense of fair play. And neither would there be support for the entanglement of British forces in any occupation. If I were to agree to what you're asking, the position would very quickly become intolerable, and you can be sure the Germans would exploit it for all it was worth.'

'Well,' said Clemenceau coolly, 'we are given to understand that the Americans take a rather different view.'

'I don't know what you've been given to understand,' replied Lloyd George, 'but I'd be surprised if it were true. Frankly, I'm surprised that the Americans are even listening to your proposals, considering the opinions President Wilson expressed to me on the subject before he went back to Washington.'

'Perhaps he has changed his mind. He'll be here in forty-eight hours, so we can ask him.'

'I think I know already what he'll say, but even if I'm wrong, I have to tell you that I cannot give way on this point. I mean, one thing we haven't even considered is whether the Germans would accept it, and I'm convinced they wouldn't. I can't imagine what would happen if we wrote a treaty the Germans wouldn't sign.'

'Foch thinks the Germans will accept anything we propose.'

'And is Marshal Foch ready to go to war again if they don't? More to the point, are the French people ready?'

Clemenceau stood up and began to pace about a small part of the over-furnished room. The exertion made him cough a little, with the bullet still between his lungs.

'You must see it from my point of view,' he said. 'I can't present the French people with a peace treaty that leaves our population of forty million still facing a hostile sixty-five million with a presence on both sides of the Rhine. That prospect is the only reason why we're proposing to make the Rhine a barrier. There'll be absolute fury in France if people are told we've fought and won this war only to be left as vulnerable as we were in 1870 and again in 1914. Unless you have any better ideas, I must insist on it.'

Lloyd George sat silent, deep in thought. After a few moments, he said: 'Suppose we and the Americans were to offer you a solemn guarantee of military intervention if there were to be any aggression against France on the part of Germany in the future? That would answer the security problem, wouldn't it? In effect we would be continuing the alliance that took on and beat the Germans. Wouldn't the

French people see it as a positive outcome?'

Clemenceau considered the proposition. 'Well, I suppose it would be something. Whether it would be enough is another matter. And, anyway, you're assuming that President Wilson will be as opposed to our plan as you are.'

'I think you can count on that,' said Lloyd George.

Predictably, it was 13 March – though this time a Thursday, rather than Friday – when President Wilson arrived back in Paris. He could not ignore his lucky number. Lloyd George went to see him at his house in the Place des Etats-Unis the following morning, to outline the discussions he had had with Clemenceau about the Rhine frontier. He found that, as he had suspected, Colonel House had merely been telling the French what he thought they wanted to hear – though he made no mention to the President of the false impression that had been created.

'The whole idea is utterly unacceptable,' Wilson said. 'It's annexation by another name, and it flies in the face of everything we're trying to achieve here.'

Lloyd George told him that he had suggested to Clemenceau there might be an Anglo-American military guarantee in the event of future hostile actions against France by Germany.

'Is that absolutely necessary?' Wilson asked. 'I'd have nothing against it myself, but I'm not sure that it would be warmly received in the United States. As you know, there's already a certain amount of opposition to our involvement in the League of Nations.'

'I think,' Lloyd George said, 'that a guarantee might be the only way out of this impasse. I'm afraid the French position is such that there's a risk of the conference breaking down if we can't settle this dispute.'

'We must avoid that at all costs, I agree,' said Wilson. 'But do you really think the French won't move?'

'I think that if we were dealing with Poincaré and Foch, the answer would be no. But Clemenceau is prepared to make concessions up to a point, so long as he gets something in return.'

Wilson smiled. 'I know what you mean. I see they've already raised the stakes by demanding control of the Saar Basin.'

Lloyd George waved an arm despairingly. 'I really don't know what they think they're doing. I can only put it down to the fact that Clemenceau, Poincaré and Foch have a visceral hatred of the Germans going back to 1871.'

American and British officials had just received a document from the French government outlining its case for annexing the Saar Valley, an area rich in coal deposits adjoining Alsace-Lorraine.

'It's a pretty thin argument,' Lloyd George said, 'based on the fact that a little bit of it was French at the time of the Revolution. And they know it's less than convincing, because they're also arguing for it as part of the compensation they expect from Germany for the devastation of the French coal-mining areas.'

'Is this designed to make us give way on the Rhineland, do you think?' asked Wilson.

Lloyd George shrugged. 'I think it's part of a French list of desiderata drawn up on the basis that they'll take what they can get. At least, I'm sure that's Clemenceau's view. But I don't believe we can give way on any of these demands.'

'Then I suppose we had better tell that to Monsieur Clemenceau.'

A meeting had been arranged at the Quai d'Orsay that afternoon.

'The President and I,' Lloyd George told Clemenceau, 'are agreed that we cannot consent to any occupation of the left bank of the Rhine, except as a temporary measure to act as a guarantee for the payment of war reparations by Germany. However, we are prepared to make a formal offer of an immediate military guarantee against any unprovoked German aggression against France. We could even consider the possibility of building a tunnel under the Channel to make it easier for our army to come to the aid of France in an emergency.'

Clemenceau was clearly disappointed. 'Is that as far as you can go?' he asked. 'Am I expected to go to the French people with nothing more than a military guarantee and a tunnel under the Channel – an idea that was ours first, anyway?'

Lloyd George and Wilson again explained the reasons for the inability to agree to the French claims. Alsace and Lorraine had been returned, as was only right, but there the acquisition of territory – whether it was formal annexation or not – would have to stop.

'But what about the eastern frontier of Germany?' demanded Clemenceau. 'You're perfectly prepared to hand over the German populations of Danzig and Upper Silesia to the Poles.'

'As a matter of fact,' Lloyd George said, '*I'm* not prepared to do that, any more than I'm prepared to hand over German populations in the Rhineland to France.'

'We could hold a plebiscite,' Clemenceau suggested.

'I think not,' Lloyd George replied. 'I've already had reports from our people in the Rhineland that the French army is fomenting discontent among the population, and I must tell you I think that is a very dangerous game to play. We are supposed to be making peace here, not creating the conditions in which another European war will become almost inevitable.'

'Well,' Clemenceau said, 'suppose I were to accept your offer of a guarantee, could you go any further? I'm thinking, for instance, of the creation of a demilitarized zone on the *right* bank of the Rhine. That would perhaps serve to make any future German attack less likely.'

The three leaders discussed this idea for some time, and finally Wilson and Lloyd George agreed to the possibility.

Clemenceau was satisfied. It seemed that his ploy of using Foch's plan to obtain more practical guarantees of French security had been successful.

'I might be able to settle for that,' he said. 'But, of course, I can't be sure that President Poincaré and Marshal Foch will.'

'If they don't,' said Lloyd George, 'we'll have reached deadlock.'

*II*

—

'I'm beginning to get tired of this. It's high time we did something about it.' It was the middle of March. The peace conference, in so much as it could really be called a conference, had been going on for two months, and very little seemed to have been achieved. What worried Lloyd George more, however, was the fact that so many details of supposedly private negotiations were still being leaked to the press.

'If this sort of thing goes on, I'll have to stop taking part in the work of the conference,' he told Frances Stevenson angrily one evening, as he sat brooding after dinner at their apartment in the Rue Nitot. 'We agreed in January that the press should not be party to our discussions, only our agreements, yet the papers here are full of the difficulties we're having over the Rhineland. They're just stirring up trouble, as I knew they would.'

'But surely nobody at the meetings is talking to journalists,' Frances said.

'I'm not accusing Clemenceau. But there are too many other people involved. In fact, there are too many people involved altogether. You've seen the London papers – especially Northcliffe's. They're picking up all sorts of tittle-tattle from the delegations, and they're using it as a stick to beat us with. I see the *Mail* has started its campaign about reparations again, accusing us of being soft on Germany.'

'What will you do?'

'Oh, I don't know, Pussy. I've already stopped the journalists listening in to our telephone conversations with London by insisting that everyone speaks in Welsh.' He laughed suddenly. 'Some of our people tell me there are rumours going round that the British have invented a new code. But it isn't funny, really. We're never going to be able to reach agreements in the way we should if every little point is picked over by the papers. It's really getting on my nerves.'

'Well,' Frances said, 'Welsh or not, I'm not sure that all the people you have on your staff entirely deserve your confidence.'

'What the devil do you mean?'

'I mean that man Sylvester, for a start, the shorthand-writer you're always using.'

'But he's from the Cabinet Office staff,' Lloyd George protested. 'If I can't trust him, who can I trust?'

'I don't mean you can't trust him,' Frances said defensively. 'It's just that I think he has ideas above his station because he works so closely with you. He's always scuttling about making notes, and coming in with little pieces of information he has heard and jotted down. I believe he thinks he's your private secretary.'

Lloyd George's eyes twinkled. 'Ah, so that's it. You're just a little bit jealous, my Pussy, aren't you? But you know he could never replace *you*, don't you?'

Frances lowered her eyes demurely. 'Well, not in some ways, perhaps.'

'Not in any way, my little love. You know how much I depend on you for everything.'

She fixed him with her gaze again. 'You don't always show it. Sometimes you seem to take me for granted.'

'Not at all, dearest, not at all. I rely on you to keep me organized and on the straight and narrow. And I always listen to your advice. Sylvester is just a civil servant who happens to be very useful.'

'But he always seems so puffed up with himself that I can't help thinking he pretends to know more than he really does, and we can't tell what he might be saying to other people – not out of disloyalty, I'm sure, but perhaps to try to let them know how important he is. And, don't forget, you suspected that it was a civil servant who was keeping Lord Northcliffe supplied with information. People like to feel they're in the know.'

Lloyd George sighed. 'Ah, you may be right, Pussy, dear. Not that I have the slightest suspicion about Sylvester, mind you. But there are too many people taking down too many notes, and there's no doubt that some of their contents are finding their way to the journalists somehow.'

He stood up, walked to the fireplace and leaned on the mantelpiece. 'The other thing that irritates me, you know, is that we're making such slow progress. We seem to be going round in circles endlessly discussing the same subjects. All President Wilson wants to think about is the League of Nations. He keeps redrafting the terms in spite of the fact that we've already agreed roughly what they should be. As for Clemenceau, I'm not sure he's the man he was during the war. I'd swear he sleeps through most of Wilson's rambling lectures. Perhaps it's since he was shot.'

'Isn't there something you can do to hurry things along?'

'Oh, it was so much simpler when we were at war. There were decisions that had to be made then and there. We cut out a lot of the usual formalities. There was just the War Cabinet . . .'

He stopped and stood upright.

'That's it! I've got it. We'll form a sort of Cabinet – Wilson, Clemenceau and me. Well, I suppose we'd better include Signor Orlando, though he doesn't seem to have much of an opinion on anything except Italy's territorial claims. The foreign ministers can go on having their council meetings and talking to their hearts' content, but we four will meet informally, every day if necessary, and hammer out the main details of the peace treaty. The others can deal with the details, then we'll present it to the full conference.'

'That should save a lot of time,' Frances said.

'Not only that, Pussy, but it will ensure that nothing gets out to the press. We won't even go to the Quai d'Orsay, where the reporters are always hanging about. We can meet here, or at the President's little White House round the corner – Wilson won't even allow ordinary pedestrians to walk past his house. Only our own staffs will know where we are, and only we will know what we're discussing. No shorthand-writers, no notes.'

'Do you think the others will agree?'

'I'm certain of it. Wilson hardly consults anyone else anyway, and Clemenceau has made it clear from the start he speaks for France, whatever Poincaré and Foch might think. As for Orlando, if he believes he'll be able to come to some sort of accommodation in secret, he'll be only too pleased. I'll put it to them tomorrow. Then Northcliffe and his pals can whistle for their leaks.'

He glanced at the clock on the mantelpiece and rubbed his hands together.

'Well,' he said, 'I think it's time for bed, don't you?'

Next morning, he was in good heart as he returned to the dark, airless room on the Quai d'Orsay that he had almost come to dread. The proceedings droned on much as usual, without form and with little substance, as the leaders and their foreign ministers all attempted to have their say on whatever subject happened to be uppermost in their minds – Russia, reparations from Germany, the Rhineland, Italy's claims in the Adriatic, German disarmament, the frontiers of Poland, Japanese ambitions in China, the League of Nations.

The Belgians had proposals to make for amendments to the charter of the League of Nations, a draft of which had been circulated among the conference delegates. Their Foreign Minister, Paul Hymans, had been invited to the Quai to explain their position, and he stood up and did so at great length in a rambling speech which he punctuated by banging his fist on the table. The minds of his listeners began to wander as the dissertation went on; Clemenceau's eyelids drooped, only to snap open again with a start as Hymans reinforced what he regarded as an important assertion. At length *le Tigre* lost patience.

'For God's sake get to the point!' he roared. 'And if you go on hitting the table like that, not only will you hurt your hand, but we won't be able to hear the point when you do eventually get there.'

Undeterred, Hymans ploughed on through the speech he had prepared, evidently fixed on covering every argument in order and in detail. Finally, he stopped speaking and looked round the room.

'Do you think,' he asked the company, 'there is any further service I can give my country?'

'You could always try drowning yourself,' snapped Clemenceau.

The morning's tedium provided Lloyd George with the opportunity, when the meeting broke for lunch, to press his new plan on his colleagues.

'We can't go on like this,' he told President Wilson. 'We directed the war by means of a supreme council, and we must direct the making of the peace in the same way.'

'You're right,' Wilson said. 'I wouldn't want to go through many more sessions like the one we've just endured.'

'Of course, all the delegates and their secretariats are doing invaluable work,' Lloyd George went on. 'But if we convene, the four of us, as I suggest, we can call for their papers at any time, so their concerns will still be heard. What I fear is, that if we go on as we have been doing since January, we'll spend our time arguing about details and that will divert us from serious consideration of the main questions. It would take months to reach a final settlement.'

Wilson nodded in agreement. 'The people want the peace to be made and, in the United States at least, I know they want to see the League of Nations established as a guarantee against future wars. We can't afford to delay too long. And the more people that are involved, the longer it's going to take.'

'This process is too formal,' Lloyd George went on. 'It encourages people to speechify rather than engaging in discussion, and that means positions are taken from which it is sometimes difficult to retreat. It's obvious to me that we are all going to have to make concessions on some things, and I think the informal talks I'm proposing, where we can settle things among ourselves, will make it so much easier to reach compromises.'

Wilson appeared to see no conflict between what Lloyd George was suggesting and the very first of his by now notorious Fourteen Points – *Open covenants of peace, openly arrived at, after which there shall be no private international understanding of any kind, but diplomacy shall proceed always frankly and in the public view*. He seemed, if anything, relieved at the prospect of retreating even deeper into secrecy than he had already agreed to do on the question of relations with the press.

'The fact is,' he said, 'that we are the people who bear the responsibility for making the peace. The world is expecting us to do so. It's logical that we should reach agreement among ourselves, because that will naturally give a lead to the others. And, for my own part, as the young men at Princeton used to say about their cigarettes, "I prefer to roll my own." '

Assured of Wilson's support, Lloyd George repeated his arguments to Clemenceau and Orlando, adding, for their benefit, a further tempting prospect.

'It seems to me,' he said, 'that there are some matters which are primarily the concern of the European powers.' He glanced at Orlando. 'I think, for example, that the position of

Italy in regard to the Treaty of London is one of those matters. Now, I don't believe that we necessarily need to trouble President Wilson every time we discuss that subject.'

'I'm all for that,' said Clemenceau. 'I get tired of being lectured at.'

'But, of course,' Lloyd George continued, 'under the present system of formal meetings, every subject has to be discussed formally by everyone present. That would not be the case if we were to meet informally, without secretaries and other officials, without notes and minutes, and – if I may say so – in more congenial surroundings.'

'There would have to be a translator, though,' said Orlando, who spoke French but not English, and for whom Clemenceau was translating this conversation.

'I can't see any difficulty with that. His work could be quite unofficial.'

'In that case,' Orlando said, 'let's proceed as you suggest. If it offers a chance for us to present a united front to President Wilson on the question of the treaty territories, that will be a great help to me.'

Clemenceau said: 'I can't see that there's anything wrong with the surroundings. It's what is going on in them that's the problem. But your suggestion is an excellent one. Let's be frank about this. We are all bound to pursue the interests of our own countries, but we have to do it in the spirit of our alliance, and I'm sure we have a better chance of doing that away from all the posturings of the conference.'

'We're all agreed, then,' said Lloyd George. 'I thought we'd better let the usual council run through next week, so what do you say we fix our first private meeting – all four of us, that is – for the twenty-fifth?'

The delay was not entirely a matter of courtesy on the part of Lloyd George, as he explained to Frances Stevenson that evening.

'Someone has got to take a grip on this peace treaty. Drafts are flying about all over the place, but we have no sense of what people will really agree to. And some of the things I'm hearing would mean that the Germans certainly wouldn't sign, no matter what Marshal Foch says about their state of desperation.'

Frances said: 'But surely your new arrangement will make it easier to agree on the main points?'

'In the end, perhaps, but what it will do first is make each one fight all the harder for his own point of view, now that the bystanders will have been removed. The French won't budge on the Rhine question so far, and neither will President Wilson, nor I, for that matter. And you can be sure that Orlando will struggle to his last breath for what he – or at least Sonnino, anyway – already sees as Italian territory. Then there's the little matter of reparations, which we've hardly even begun to discuss. Make no mistake, this conference could still break down if somebody doesn't knock heads together.'

Frances smiled. 'I'm sure you have a plan.'

'As a matter of fact, I do. What we need is a framework that makes sure we keep the discussion to the main points.'

'I thought the French had already done that, but you and President Wilson rejected it.'

'Oh, that was just a bit of French list-making. They love

laying down rules, you know, even if they don't actually stick
to them. No, what I have in mind is a series of definite
proposals that make clear what the terms would be of the
peace treaty we would be prepared to sign. Then we can argue
constructively and reach an accommodation.'

Frances smiled again. 'You mean, you're going to write the
peace treaty and persuade the others to agree to it.'

'I wouldn't say that. I'm simply going to set out in
unambiguous terms what we, the British Empire, would like
to see in this treaty. Then the others will have their say, and
eventually we'll reach a conclusion we can present as a treaty
to the whole conference. Now, obviously, I can't produce the
sort of paper I have in mind by myself, but I've thought of
that, too. We'll lock ourselves away in the country, just a small
group, over a weekend, and we'll return to Paris with a
complete outline of the peace terms we believe are acceptable.'

'In the country?'

'Yes. I think the Forest of Fontainebleau would be perfect.
Not too far away, but nice and secluded, especially at this time
of year. See if you can find a hotel there that would
accommodate us, next weekend – Saturday to Monday.'

'How many people?'

He would take Philip Kerr, who had spent the past few
weeks wrestling with the problem of the Rhine provinces, to
no good effect, thanks largely to the implacable Tardieu.
There would also, of course, be Sir Maurice Hankey, the
Cabinet Secretary, who was now acting as the British
secretary-general at the conference. A military mind would be
essential, so he would need Sir Henry Wilson, Chief of the

Imperial General Staff, one of the few generals Lloyd George both liked and trusted – perhaps, Frances suspected, because he was an Irishman rather than an Englishman. And finally, Lloyd George would need a man upon whose advice he had learned to rely heavily, the South African general turned politician, Jan Smuts, who had represented his country with great intelligence and distinction as a member of the Imperial War Cabinet.

'Smuts has remarkable gifts of the mind,' Lloyd George told Frances, 'but, most importantly, he has been clear from the start about the need to build a peace without rancour and without humiliation. That's going to be important when you have Clemenceau and Foch determined to rub the Germans' noses in their defeat and leave them powerless for evermore. Not to mention the Northcliffe crew at home, of course, who are baying for blood.'

The little party was booked into the Hôtel de France et d'Angleterre, in the Boulevard de Magenta, facing the west gate of the vast Château de Fontainebleau. It was not, perhaps, as grand as the ninety-room Savoy, with its magnificent view over the forest, or as the Aigle-Noir in the Place Denecourt, directly opposite the château. Nevertheless, it was a fine eighteenth-century building, reflecting the period when Fontainebleau had been Napoleon's favourite residence – and it had an excellent à la carte restaurant.

As it happened, there were just four of them, General Smuts having been omitted at the last moment. This was, in the end, to be an all-British affair, its aim a settlement that

Lloyd George hoped would suit not so much the British government as the British people.

There had been worrying developments back in England. Northcliffe's campaign to punish the Germans continued unabated, its implicit suggestion that the Prime Minister might be disposed towards leniency incensing growing numbers of Conservative and Unionist members of the coalition on which Lloyd George's power depended. Almost daily, reports reached Paris of discontent among the Tory ranks that threatened at any moment to flare into full-scale rebellion. In the country at large, however, the inconsistency of Northcliffe's position produced an effect very different from the one The Chief desired. His support for Labour during the December election campaign was out of step with his demand for harsh peace terms because it flew in the face of socialist internationalism. Labour supporters were almost to a man Wilsonians, seeing in the President's notions of liberty, justice, openness and fairness a reflection of their own ambitions for social and political reform. As a result, while Northcliffe whipped up the urge for revenge among the more rabid members of the government parties, among large sections of the public, his extremism seemed to be helping to foster opposition to the coalition.

'We're doing badly in by-elections,' Lloyd George muttered anxiously to Frances Stevenson shortly before the planned excursion to Fontainebleau. 'In the two recent polls, our majority has been halved. I'm afraid people are beginning to turn against us. Northcliffe isn't helping by making mischief, of course, but that's mainly a parliamentary problem. What worries me is that the people, the ordinary working people, think we aren't progressive enough.'

'But the coalition has a very large majority in the House,' Frances pointed out.

'I know, but everywhere you look the pressure is building for change, and that means support for the Labour Party is growing. The unions are becoming impatient – and it isn't only the miners. There's industrial unrest everywhere. Oh, I'm sure we can deal with it, but what we don't seem to be doing is tackling the causes of popular dissatisfaction. We have to find a way of inspiring people, of showing them we're in sympathy with the progressive forces that are making themselves felt all over the world now. Perhaps the peace treaty will be the key to it. We have to show we're firm but moderate.'

'Perhaps President Wilson can help,' Frances suggested.

'I'm sure he can. You saw the way the people took him to their hearts when he was in England. He'll certainly help more than the French will. I'm beginning to wonder how far we can support them at all. But Wilson is obsessed with the League of Nations and his airy-fairy ideas of international co-operation. We're going to have to produce something more practical than that if peace in Europe is to be maintained.'

The peace of Europe became an even more urgent problem as the Prime Minister and his party prepared to leave for their forest sojourn. News reached Paris that Bolsheviks had taken advantage of the collapse of the Austrian empire to stage a successful coup in Hungary. An atmosphere bordering on panic spread through the delegations at the peace conference.

Would Austria be next? Or Germany? Would the treaty be signed in time to prevent the spread of revolution across Europe?

In Fontainebleau, by contrast, the atmosphere was both serene and invigorating. The British group at the Hôtel de France et d'Angleterre gave no indication of the seriousness of their mission, or, indeed, that they had any mission at all. Saturday was spent in the idle pursuits most visitors enjoyed: viewing the picturesque town from the Croix-du-Calvaire, marvelling at the magnificent trees of the Nid de l'Aigle and the Gros-Fouteau, taking the short carriage ride to the white sandstone Gorges de Franchard, with a break for refreshment at the little restaurant off the sylvan Route de Milly. Back in the privacy of the Prime Minister's sitting room that evening, however, they settled purposefully to their self-appointed task.

'We must be absolutely thorough,' Lloyd George told them. 'The future peace of Europe, and, indeed, the world, may depend on the conclusions we reach. We must consider the implications of the treaty from all points of view, and for that reason I think it will be helpful if you assume the roles of both the Allies and the enemy.'

He turned to the balding, gentlemanly Sir Maurice Hankey, the former Royal Marines colonel whose clear thinking, efficiency and unflappability had helped to turn the War Cabinet into an effective decision-making body.

'Maurice, I want you to represent the British position, which you are eminently well-qualified to do.'

Next, he asked Sir Henry Wilson, whose clipped

moustache and military bearing belied his Irish charm and most unsoldierly flexibility of mind, to take the roles of both the French and the Germans.

'You've worked closely with Foch, obviously,' Lloyd George said, 'and probably nobody knows better than you the strategical thinking behind the harsh attitude of the French to the peace terms. As for the Germans, well, I saw during the war that you had an instinctive understanding of the way their minds worked – if I recall, it was you alone who predicted the great offensive that almost undid us in the spring of 1918.'

'What about the American position?' asked Sir Maurice's protégé, Philip Kerr.

'I think we're clear enough about President Wilson's view,' said Lloyd George. 'He is fixed on his Fourteen Points and the League of Nations. Those are the only things we have to take into account to accommodate the American position, and it seems to me that if we can translate the principles of the Fourteen Points into practical proposals, we'll have a treaty that will commend itself to reasonable opinion as a fair settlement. You, Philip, must take careful notes of all that is said. I want to be able to circulate a document to Wilson, Clemenceau and Orlando as soon as we return to Paris.'

'Ah,' said Sir Henry, 'the Italians. We aren't representing them, of course.'

'That's a different problem,' Lloyd George replied. 'What we're considering here is the treaty with Germany, which is the key to the entire peace settlement. Italy's claims have more to do with Austria and Turkey, and they must be considered separately.'

'Well, considering the German treaty,' Sir Henry said, 'and speaking as a Frenchman, I think we must be wary of following President Wilson's principles too closely. Quite frankly, it seems to me that the President's obsession with international co-operation will lead us into disaster. The German threat must be removed, and the best way to do that is to restrict Germany's frontiers, limit her armaments and impose heavy indemnities for the war she started as a deterrent for the future.'

Lloyd George inquired: 'And if you were to speak as yourself for a moment, would that still be your view?'

'I have a great deal of sympathy with the French case. It seems to me that the detachment of the provinces on the west bank of the Rhine would offer a reasonable guarantee of security. At the same time, firm action against the Bolshevists in Russia and the creation of new barrier states, such as Poland and Czechoslovakia, in the east would prevent Germany from looking eastward to regain the power she once had.'

Sir Maurice Hankey objected: 'I think you have the danger the wrong way round. Speaking generally, I believe the greatest menace to Europe in the years to come is Bolshevism, spreading from Russia throughout neighbouring countries and as far as the Mediterranean. Already we've seen it triumph in Hungary and take hold in Vienna. In those circumstances, it is surely in our interest not to cripple Germany, but to give her the power to resist Bolshevism.'

Lloyd George nodded his assent. 'There is unrest throughout Europe,' he said, 'sometimes in the form of open revolution and in other cases, such as Britain, France and

Italy, it shows itself in strikes and a general disinclination to settle down to work – which has as much to do with a desire for political and social change as with wage demands. Now much of that unrest is healthy, and we won't make a lasting peace if we simply try to restore the conditions of 1914. But then there is Bolshevism.'

He turned to Sir Henry. 'Imagine the situation if Germany were to throw in her lot with the Bolsheviks and put her resources, her brains and her vast organizing power at the disposal of the revolutionary fanatics who dream of conquering the world by force of arms. It might happen. The present government was given a popular mandate in January, but it's weak, it has no prestige, and its authority is constantly being challenged. Probably the only reason it's there is that there is no alternative but Spartacism, and the Germans aren't ready for that yet. But the day might come when they are.'

'Especially,' Sir Maurice added, 'if we were to pursue a policy that would leave Germany helpless both militarily and economically.'

'Well,' Sir Henry admitted grudgingly, 'I suppose you Frocks' – it was his term for politicians, because of their habit of wearing frock coats – 'I suppose you Frocks do have a point there. But that doesn't mean I am in favour of peace terms that are too lenient.'

'Take up your other role,' said Lloyd George, 'and put yourself in the position of the Germans. Suppose you find yourself faced with a peace treaty that robs you of your territory on the left bank of the Rhine, that places severe restrictions on your military capability, that removes two million from your population and places them under Polish rule, and that demands crippling reparation payments to your former enemies.'

Sir Henry thought for a few moments, then rose to his feet, picked up his field marshal's cap and placed it backwards on his head, simulating the traditional peakless headgear of the Prussian officer class. The others laughed at this piece of showmanship.

'With this oppressive treaty,' he said, forbearing to assume a German accent, 'you propose to occupy or subvert our lands in the west and to force our people into foreign servitude in the east. You wish to humiliate what was formerly one of the most powerful nations in Europe and place upon it financial burdens which are both unfair and impossible to meet. In short, you put us in an untenable position. The only possible response is for us to turn towards Russia, to help that unhappy country restore law and order and recover its stability by supporting the Bolshevists, and in due time to form an alliance with her.'

He took off his cap and sat down. 'Yes,' he said, 'I'm afraid that *would* be the Germans' response if we squeezed them too hard.'

'They wouldn't sign the treaty, would they?' said Lloyd George.

'No, I suspect they wouldn't. I certainly wouldn't sign in those circumstances if I were a German.'

'The point is,' said Sir Maurice, 'that while every demand we have spoken of making on Germany is perfectly justified on its own merits, if we take them all together, they place the

Germans in an absolutely impossible situation. I cannot disagree with the view that the enormity of their crimes must be brought home to them, but at the same time we must try to build up their self-respect so that they have faith in themselves that will enable them to resist Bolshevism.'

Lloyd George stood up and walked over to the window, hands clasped behind him under the tails of his coat. After parting the heavy curtains and gazing across towards the dark bulk of the château for a few moments, he turned and said: 'You know, we've been concentrating so far on building up the power of France in relation to Germany, very much as we adopted precisely the opposite policy after 1815. That approach might have been justified in 1815, when the revolutionary spirit had exhausted itself in France, and Germany had reformed herself in order to satisfy the legitimate demands of her people. But today's revolutionary spirit, born in Russia, is still in its infancy, and it expresses itself in the burning desire of working people not to return to pre-war conditions. I can't help feeling that Sir Maurice is correct, and that while we certainly do want to support the position of France, there is a good case for having a reasonably strong German state in the present condition of Europe.'

The discussions continued late into the night, and throughout the following day. By Sunday evening, Philip Kerr had been able to construct the document Lloyd George required, setting out what would, for better or worse, become the terms that the British wanted to see in the peace treaty. Its preamble was almost Wilsonian in its tone:

We ought to endeavour to draw up a peace settlement as if we were impartial arbiters, forgetful of the passions of war. This settlement ought to have three ends in view. First of all, it must do justice to the Allies by taking into account Germany's responsibility for the origin of the war and for the way in which it was fought. Secondly, it must be a settlement which a responsible German government can sign in the belief that it can fulfil the obligations it incurs. Thirdly, it must be a settlement which will contain in itself no provocations for future wars, and which will constitute an alternative to Bolshevism.

'I wish you luck,' Sir Henry Wilson told the Prime Minister, 'in persuading Messieurs Clemenceau and Poincaré to accept that they cannot have the Rhineland, that the Saar will be merely on loan for ten years, and that reparation payments will be both lower than they expect and of limited duration.'

'No doubt we'll have to make concessions,' Lloyd George said, 'and no doubt there will be inequities in the final document because of that. But, to tell you the truth, I'm less concerned about the diplomatic and military consequences of this treaty than I am about the combination of a settlement that would enrage the Germans and the seeds of revolution that are now being sown across Europe.'

Sir Maurice Hankey and Philip Kerr had gone out for a walk in the crisp night air with its woody scents of early spring.

'This strikes me as a remarkable change of heart by the Prime Minister,' Kerr said. 'I've been arguing on behalf of this sort of approach for weeks without appearing to get anywhere.'

Sir Maurice smiled. 'You grow accustomed to it in time. He's never afraid to change his mind, or suddenly to embrace a position directly opposed to the one he passionately advocated only the day before. He reaches his conclusions entirely by instinct and, of course, what his instinct tells him depends very much on his mood at the time.'

'And what do you think has prompted this sudden flash of instinct?'

'What I suspect is that the Prime Minister has one eye on French ambitions in Europe and the other on the Labour Party, which seems to be starting to make an impression on the radical votes that used to go to the Liberals. The coalition will not go on for ever, and the Prime Minister is still relatively young for a politician. He wants this to be *his* peace treaty.'

'Well,' Kerr said, 'it's quite clear that he very much enjoys his personal power. What worries me, though, is that he has begun to act as if he were the source of it.'

*III*

——

Predictably, it was Lloyd George who was the last to arrive. The meeting was at President Wilson's house in the Place des Etats-Unis, a gathering of what would shortly become known through the press as 'the Big Four'.

Wilson, Clemenceau and Orlando were standing close together, apparently in the midst of a disagreement, when Lloyd George was shown into the room.

'I'm sorry to be so late,' he said. 'What am I missing? It looks as if I've walked in on an argument.'

All three men turned to look at him.

'How old are you?' asked Clemenceau.

'I'm fifty-six,' Lloyd George replied, 'but what's that got to do with it?'

'Everything,' said Clemenceau. 'You're just a baby. We were talking about our ages, and I said you were a young man. I was mistaken. You're a child.'

'Well, child or not,' Lloyd George said, 'I've written the peace treaty. I take it you've all read my memorandum.'

'I've glanced through it,' said Clemenceau, 'and I'll respond in writing after your memorandum has been translated and President Poincaré has had the opportunity of studying it.'

Wilson said: 'But you must be able to respond to the principles expressed at the beginning of the document. They're clear and unambiguous. For example, do you agree that, in general, we ought to be moderate and fair in our treatment of Germany?'

'As I say,' replied Clemenceau, 'I would rather respond in writing when the document has been carefully studied.'

'Well,' Wilson persisted, 'I think you should give us some idea of what France's position is going to be. We are concerned that the peace treaty should give Germany no excuse for resentment or revanchism. Do you agree with that? I must say that, for my own part, I do have a worry about future wars arising from popular dissatisfaction.'

'Don't forget,' Lloyd George put in, 'that even in 1815, when Napoleon had been defeated, we managed to persuade the Prussians that a strong and stable France was essential to order and security in Europe.'

'Very well,' Clemenceau said. 'If you're pressing me to respond now, without the benefit of a considered statement of our position, I'll do so. I can begin by saying I am in complete accord with the general aim set out in the memorandum, which is for a peace that is both just and lasting. I quite accept that we must not abuse our victory, because it is important to avoid an upsurge of nationalist sentiments in Germany. And, before I continue, I want to say that France has no differences with its allies about the principles of the peace. Do I make myself clear?'

The others nodded.

'Where there are differences,' Clemenceau went on, 'is in the matter of how those principles are applied. In fact, I would go further and say that, while we agree with the objectives Mr Lloyd George expresses in his note, we do not believe that the principles necessarily lead to the conclusions he reaches.'

'What exactly do you mean by that?' asked Lloyd George.

'Well, to begin with, I think your fear of German threats is unwarranted. Of course they're going to challenge every point we put to them. Of course they're going to rage at the impositions we place on them. Of course they're going to threaten that they won't sign the treaty. Wouldn't you do the same in their position?'

'I'm sorry,' Lloyd George retorted, 'but I can't accept the rather childlike view of Marshal Foch that the Germans are so desperate they'll sign anything we care to present to them.'

'That's as may be,' said Clemenceau, 'but I think it's equally naïve to assume that unless we appease them in some way, they'll embrace Bolshevism. In my judgement, they're emphasizing the threat of revolution for the precise purpose of making us moderate our peace terms, and events like the Bolshevist uprising in Budapest are being used to support their case. Now, I have no doubt that such dangers do exist, but I don't think they should be exaggerated.'

Wilson broke in: 'Well, my friend, Bolshevism is not the only threat. As Mr Lloyd George says in his note, the maintenance of peace will depend to some extent on there being no conditions in the treaty capable of stirring up the spirit of patriotism or justice.'

'Look at it this way,' added Lloyd George. 'I cannot imagine any more likely provocation for a future war than to have the German people – who've proved themselves one of the most vigorous and powerful races in the world – surrounded by small states, of which many have never had their own stable governments, all containing large numbers of Germans clamouring for reunion with their native land.'

'But you're looking at this too much through the eyes of Europe,' Clemenceau protested. 'You're saying that the settlement of Germany's European frontiers should be, as you put it, fair so that she won't harbour feelings of resentment. Well, that might be a sensible policy if what we have endured had been, for Germany, just a European war. But it wasn't. Before the war, Germany was a great world power, and she took great pride in that fact. Remember what the Germans always said – "our future is on the water". That's the loss Germany will resent most deeply.'

'What do you mean?' Wilson asked.

'Look, we've taken away, or we're going to take away from Germany – apparently with no fear of any resentment it's going to cause – all her colonies, her entire navy, a large part of her merchant marine as compensation and the foreign markets in which she was dominant. That's the worst blow we could deal the Germans, and to believe that it would be softened by a few territorial concessions in Europe is pure illusion.'

'So what,' asked Lloyd George, 'would you suggest we do instead?'

Clemenceau waved a hand in the air. 'If we were to decide that, for reasons of general policy, we wished to give certain concessions to Germany, then there would be no use in our looking for them in Europe. It would be a vain gesture so long as we insisted on cutting off Germany from world politics. If we really want to appease the Germans for some reason – and I'm speaking completely hypothetically here – then the only way of doing it that will succeed is to give them concessions on their colonies, on their navy, and on trading throughout the world.'

'Well, that's completely ridiculous,' Lloyd George said.

Clemenceau nodded.

'Your argument, then,' said Wilson, 'is that, having agreed to strip Germany of her status as an international power, we might as well severely limit her influence in Europe as well?'

'The reasons for confining the Boches in Europe are at least as good as those for limiting their international power. The most important one, so far as we are concerned, is the matter of our security. It's not a big question for Great Britain and the United States. Your navies are your guarantee – and in the case of Britain, you made the surrender of the German fleet part of the armistice terms. But we have land frontiers, so our requirements are different. It's not as if we don't have experience of our vulnerability. I'm sorry to keep harking back to it, but some of us remember 1871.'

Lloyd George snorted. 'That's no excuse for making the same mistakes that were made in 1871. Don't forget, it was the army that persuaded Bismarck to settle on the idea of the strategic frontier, and you yourself are living proof of the foolishness of that policy.'

'But the question of Germany's frontiers, both east and west, is a very important one,' Clemenceau said doggedly. 'You can't ignore strategical considerations when it comes to constructing a new balance of power in Europe.'

Wilson said: 'Well, my friend, it seems to me that in the modern world, the idea of creating a balance of power is outmoded . . .'

'For God's sake stop saying "Well, my friend",' Clemenceau snapped. 'Every time you do it, I feel a cold shiver down my spine.'

Wilson leaned back in his chair. Lloyd George continued the argument.

'I come back to the fact that we must have an agreement that the German government will sign. If our terms are too severe, that government will be overthrown – and then, look out for Bolshevism.'

Clemenceau sighed. 'But Germany is not the only country that could be overtaken by Bolshevism. In fact, if, for the sake of satisfying the Germans, you sacrifice some of the new states we want to create – Poland, for example, or Bohemia – by determining their frontiers in a way that is unacceptable to them, they are just as likely to fall prey to the Bolshevists. It's only their nationalist sentiments that have given them the strength to resist Bolshevism so far. Damage that spirit of nationalism, and you might end up destroying the barrier between Russia and Germany. The result of that would be either a confederation of central and eastern Europe under the leadership of a Bolshevist Germany, or else the enslavement of that vast territory by a Germany that reverts to its old ways after a period of general anarchy. In either case, the Allies will have lost the war.'

'But,' Lloyd George countered, 'if we offer Germany a peace that everyone can see is just, and our terms are moderate and reasonable, all sensible men will regard it as an alternative to Bolshevism. And as for your argument about Germany losing her position in the world, I would propose that – if she accepts our terms, especially in regard to reparation – we should open to her the raw materials and markets of the world on equal terms with ourselves. That will help the Germans to get back on their feet again.'

'I'm afraid,' Clemenceau said, 'that you misunderstand the German mentality. I'm not at all sure that the Germans will have the same idea of what is just as the Allies have.'

Lloyd George said: 'But that's no excuse for crippling her and, at the same time, expecting her to pay. We stand a much better chance of addressing all the difficulties you've mentioned if we're fair.'

'The fairness,' Clemenceau retorted, 'must be on both sides. Germany was our enemy, after all, and it surely isn't right that we should be fair to our enemy at the expense of our friends. However important our post-war relations with Germany might be, they are considerably less important than relations among us as allies, and if you insist on placing the solution of the German problem before the solutions relating to the countries that bore the cost of the war, it could be disastrous.'

Wilson felt able to join in again, remembering this time not to address *le Tigre* as his friend: 'We will never be able to establish and maintain peace if we proceed solely on the basis of our own selfish interests. There must be a spirit of international co-operation, embodied in the League of Nations. Of course there will be disputes that arise, but these will be dealt with by the League.'

'But in the meantime,' said Clemenceau, 'there is no better way to encourage the spread of revolutionary sentiments than to foster national disappointment. And I'm not just talking about Bolshevism. Feelings are running high in France, as I know they are in England, too. If the expectations our people have for the peace treaty are not met, there could well be serious trouble. And, frankly, if there are going to be revolutionary upheavals, I'd rather they were in the enemy camp than in ours.'

'That's nonsense,' fumed Lloyd George. 'You're confusing the threat of disorder on the right with that on the left. I can tell you from personal experience that it's the left we have to fear, and the way to meet the threat is not to resort to force, but to do our best to satisfy the legitimate aspirations that generate such revolutionary sentiments. Yes, it's true that in Britain there is pressure for a settlement that is harsh towards Germany, but the sort of hatred that pressure reflects is most common among the upper classes. The British worker doesn't want to weigh down the German people with excessive claims, and, so far as I can see, it would be an oppressive treaty rather than a more lenient one that would be likely to provoke the rise of Bolshevism in England.'

'Well,' said Clemenceau, 'you wanted me to respond immediately to this note, without waiting for a more considered judgement, and that's what I've done. I shall let you have a written response, but don't expect it to be very much different from what I've said today, except, perhaps, in one or two matters of detail. I know you Anglo-Saxons like a direct and overall approach to problems, and I respect that, as you see. It's not the Latin way, but so be it. To put it concisely, we take the view that we were attacked and we were victorious.

We represent right, and we have might. That might must be used in the service of right.'

'Whatever the consequences?' Lloyd George asked tartly. 'Would France, for instance, be prepared to send her soldiers to prevent Germany from supporting her own kin in a rebellion against the Polish state? I doubt that Britain would, and I think public opinion in the United States simply would not allow the President to do so.'

'That's absolutely correct,' added Wilson. 'Using armies to try to stop a revolutionary movement is like using a broom to stop a great flood.'

'The plain fact is,' Lloyd George went on, 'that the terms we intend to put to the Germans are already severe. As you yourself said, Germany is about to lose her colonies, her fleet, six or seven million of her citizens and much of her natural resources. Militarily, she is being reduced to the level of Greece and, in naval terms, her status will be comparable to that of the Argentine Republic. On top of all that, she will have to pay substantial reparations – upon which, incidentally, France will have the first call if my proposals are accepted. The territorial demands you are insisting on would be the final drop of water that causes the pitcher to overflow.'

He paused, then continued: 'Let me ask you a question. In 1871, which did France resent more: the loss of Alsace and Lorraine or the obligation to pay an indemnity of five million francs? You don't even need to answer, because I think I already know. I remember very well that, on my first visit to Paris, I was struck by the sight of the Strasbourg memorial, draped in black. We mustn't give the Germans cause to build such monuments in *their* cities.'

Clemenceau acknowledged the point. 'As I said, I completely support the intentions that inspired your note. What we must agree about is the best way of achieving the results we all desire.'

The meeting broke up, but Lloyd George lingered after Clemenceau and Orlando had left.

'Well,' said Wilson, 'what do you make of that?'

'I'm inclined not to take it too seriously,' replied Lloyd George. 'Clemenceau is irritated because he was completely unprepared for my note, and he suspects it is a part of a plot to outmanoeuvre him. I have no doubt he sees it as an attempt by the Anglo-Saxons, as he calls us, to impose their preferred settlement without due regard for Latin sensibilities. In addition, of course, he has Poincaré and Foch and large sections of the French press watching him.'

'Ah, those two,' said Wilson. 'I don't trust them at all. I believe Poincaré is a liar. He says one thing and does something else. And Foch has displayed a certain disingenuousness in his assessment of the Germans' remaining military strength, in order to support his plan for an occupation force.'

'I have the impression that Clemenceau is really no more enamoured of Poincaré and Foch than you are, though he does have a high regard for the Marshal as a military man. But he's caught between the Socialists on the one hand and the right-wing nationalists on the other, and he seems to fear the latter more.'

Wilson said: 'But we can't let them get away with their plans for the Rhineland and the Saar.'

'Still less with their idea of handing over to Poland the two million Germans in the Danzig region,' Lloyd George said grimly. 'But, as I say, I think it would be better on the whole not to place too much weight on what Clemenceau has said today. He'll be prepared to compromise so long as we hold our position firmly.'

Clemenceau had gone away to confer with André Tardieu and prepare his written response to the Lloyd George memorandum. It was presented to the Big Four a few days later, serving only to formalize what Clemenceau had already told them.

Lloyd George was ready for this, brushing it aside with the levity he had urged on Wilson.

'I appear to be in error with regard to the French position,' he observed acidly. 'Until I read this document, I was under the delusion that France attached importance to the rich German African colonies she is now in possession of, to ships, to disarmament, and to indemnity and compensation. It seems I was mistaken, and I regret that. France attaches no importance to the fact that she has Alsace-Lorraine, with most of the iron mines and a large proportion of the potash of Germany. She attaches no importance to receiving a share of the German ships for the French ships sunk by submarines, or to receiving any part of the German battle fleet. She attaches no importance to the disarmament of Germany on land and sea. She attaches no importance to a British and American guarantee of the inviolability of her soil. What she really seems to care about is that the Danzig Germans should be handed over to the Poles.'

Then he delivered his final blow.

'And, by the way, I suggested in my document the temporary ownership of the Saar coalfields, with guaranteed permanent access to the coal. However, that proposal was made as an alternative to another one, which I placed first – and that was the restoration of the frontier of 1814. And since Monsieur Clemenceau appears to treat my suggestion as proof of British selfishness, I now withdraw it.'

Clemenceau sat stony-faced, but said nothing. Instead, he ushered in the implacable Marshal Foch, who diligently rehearsed yet again his arguments for the occupation of the Rhineland, and in the process worked himself into a passion that was impressive in a man usually of so few words.

'It would be monstrous to give up the Rhine,' he cried, almost incoherently. 'It would be admitting that Germany, although she is beaten . . . Germany, steeped in blood and crime . . . Germany, responsible for the deaths of millions of human beings . . . Germany, which tried to destroy our country . . . which sought to dominate the world by force . . . Germany would be maintained in such a position, by our withdrawal from the Rhine, that she might as well have been victorious. It's unthinkable!'

Wilson and Lloyd George, though, remained unmoved.

'I've said it before,' the Prime Minister intoned, 'and I must say it again. The British public will not accept any repeat of the mistake Germany made in annexing Alsace-Lorraine.'

Foch tried once more: 'The Allied governments entrusted

me with the leadership of their armies and the welfare of the common cause in the most critical hours of the war. I'm now pleading with them to understand that the welfare of our cause can only be ensured by making the Rhine our military frontier.'

Wilson said: 'Well, my friend . . .' Clemenceau rolled his eyes, '. . . we've consulted the other commanders-in-chief of the Allied armies, and not one of them supports your position. We have also sought the views of the King of the Belgians, and I'm afraid he, too, is opposed to your plan for the Rhineland.'

Foch remained determined. 'Our position on the Rhine is indispensable to our policy,' he said.

Clemenceau, however, could see that they were making little impression. He retreated to the War Ministry to consult with André Tardieu.

'We're getting nowhere against the opposition of Lloyd George,' the Prime Minister said wearily. 'It looks as if we're going to have to make some sort of concession.'

'What about Wilson?' Tardieu asked.

'A case of Anglo–Saxon solidarity, I fear. Lloyd George has been very clever in couching his memorandum in phrases that sound as if they could have come from Wilson himself. I think there may be a ray of hope there, though.'

'What do you mean?'

'Well, look, it's obvious to me that we are not going to convince them, either of them, that the Boches should be contained behind the Rhine. We can argue until we're blue in the face, but they will stick to their point of view – and why shouldn't they? Their resistance is not surprising.

Lloyd George says, "I'm English", Wilson says, "I'm an American", and they have as much right to do so as we have to say we're French. And we all see things in the light of our history – living dead men's lives, as Auguste Comte put it. But that doesn't mean we give up and walk away. Not at all! We simply find a way to shift the balance as far in our favour as we can.'

'What do you suggest?'

'As I said, the scheme Foch and you cooked up for the Rhineland is clearly not going to win agreement.'

'What do you mean, Foch and I cooked up? It was you who asked me to draw up the document in the first place.'

'It was a position, my boy, and none the worse for that. It gave us a stance from which we could negotiate. Now it's time for the negotiation. That's what Foch doesn't understand. He's a soldier, so to him it's just a matter of attack or retreat. You and I know better. If we had got what we wanted, all well and good, but in this situation, it's a question of seeing how far we can go, how we can achieve something close to our objectives and being prepared to accept that. Now they won't countenance the annexation – let's not beat about the bush – of the Rhineland, so what will they accept?'

'It looks to me that Lloyd George won't accept anything on that matter. He's too afraid of British public opinion.'

'Yes, but at present he has the unwavering support of President Wilson. What we must do is put forward a proposal that the President can agree to but that also goes as far as possible in achieving our aims. Then the balance will be in our favour.'

'I assume,' said Tardieu, 'that you have such a proposal in mind.'

Clemenceau gazed up towards the ceiling. 'Look at it this way. Lloyd George and Wilson have already proposed a military guarantee of intervention if France is threatened by Germany, and I have indicated that such a guarantee might be acceptable to us. That encouraged Lloyd George to propose it formally in his memorandum. Fine. We gratefully accept Mr Lloyd George's proposal – but, in return, we require for our own security the military occupation of the Rhine bridgeheads to continue for a defined period. *Voilà*! Germany is contained behind the Rhine, at least for the foreseeable future, and, if she becomes aggressive after that, we have our Anglo–American guarantee.'

Tardieu was doubtful. 'Do you think Lloyd George will agree to that?'

'I think,' Clemenceau said, 'that he might be made to. For one thing, we can offer him his way on the Saar. Again, it isn't quite what we wanted, but he himself proposes giving us access to the Saar coalfields for ten years. I think we might settle for fifteen.'

'But you said he had just withdrawn that proposal.'

'It's in his document, which has been formally presented. If we accept it and President Wilson accepts it, how can Lloyd George then withdraw it? And if he agrees to the occupation of the Saar, how can he then continue to stand out against an occupation of the Rhineland?'

Tardieu was still to be convinced. 'The problem is, this all depends on gaining the agreement of President Wilson.'

Clemenceau smiled. 'I think that might be arranged. You

yourself have spoken to Colonel House on the subject, and he has not been unsympathetic.'

'Quite the opposite. In fact, he gave me to understand that the Americans would not oppose our plans for the left bank of the Rhine and the Saar.'

'Ah, but he speaks *to* the President, not *for* him.'

'Yes, but he said that the spread of Bolshevism in Europe was the President's greatest fear.'

'That may be, but, as I said, Lloyd George has been clever. He's convinced Wilson that the separation of the Rhineland would drive Germany towards Bolshevism and persuaded him that appeasement is the best way of stopping it. On the other hand, Wilson said only the other day that Bolshevism was no concern of ours so long as it remains behind its own frontiers. He doesn't know what he wants, and that makes him suggestible. He's also beginning to resent the attacks on him in our newspapers, and I think we could put a stop to them if he were to move some way towards us on the Rhine and the Saar.'

'And you really think Lloyd George would give way if the President supported the occupation of the Rhineland you're proposing?'

'Like the rest of us, Lloyd George is a politician,' said Clemenceau. 'Politicians are judged on what they deliver to satisfy the public, and from what I read in the press, the demands on Lloyd George to deliver something to the British are growing every day. My proposal will enable him to placate the left with the idea that he has moderated the peace terms, but at the same time he'll be able to tell his right-wing critics that he's being hard on Germany.'

'And what,' Tardieu inquired, 'will you tell the French people? President Poincaré and Marshal Foch, and all their supporters in the Assembly, are not going to be happy if you retreat from the separation of the Rhineland.'

Clemenceau shrugged. 'What's the alternative? I can't go into the Chamber and say, "I've made our demands, the others have refused them, so I'm breaking off the negotiations." They would certainly turn on me then, and quite rightly. The public's patience is wearing thin here, too. It's April already, and so far as the people are concerned, we've delivered them nothing. A compromise on the Rhine and the Saar – if it's the best we can achieve in the circumstances – is surely better than nothing.'

*IV*

——

Lord Northcliffe was watching closely the proceedings of the peace conference – by coincidence, from the same hotel where Lloyd George had composed his Fontainebleau memorandum. Although he chafed at his exclusion from British official circles in Paris, The Chief was not the sort of man to let that stand in his way, and he cultivated a variety of sources in order to keep himself fully informed and, he hoped, to be in a position to stiffen the resolve of the unreliable Lloyd George.

'The trouble with the Prime Minister,' Northcliffe confided to Henry Wickham Steed, who had replaced the too pro-government Geoffrey Dawson as editor of *The Times*, 'is that he lacks that high moral courage which enables a man to stand alone. The most dangerous defect in his character is that he isn't sure of himself.'

The editor was even more dismissive. 'Lloyd George and Wilson are mere amateurs,' he said, comparing the Paris proceedings with the last great European peace conference, the Congress of Vienna. 'They simply don't stand up alongside men such as Castlereagh, or Talleyrand, or Metternich.'

Steed was sending his boss private briefings about the news and gossip his correspondents gleaned in Paris, and these filled Northcliffe with forebodings that Lloyd George was going soft on the question of the reparations Germany would be made to pay for war damage. The impression was reinforced by The Chief's contacts with Sir George Riddell, the man the Prime Minister had chosen over Northcliffe to take charge of the British negotiators' relations with the press. Though a friend of Lloyd George of some years' standing, Sir George was becoming increasingly dismayed at what he saw as the Prime Minister's developing tendency to follow President Wilson's lead at the conference, and such was his alarm that he was prepared to apprise his fellow newspaper proprietor about this apparent departure from the line Lloyd George had taken during the general election campaign.

'It's the pressure of the Jewish financiers on the Sacred Four, you know,' Sir George complained, confirming the suspicions that had nagged at The Chief for months. He had always believed that Lloyd George was surrounded by the wrong sort of people, especially his Jewish financier friends.

Northcliffe also remained close to Colonel House, from whom he learned that Lloyd George, unlike Clemenceau, had been persuaded to accept what President Wilson saw as the fundamental principle of the reparations issue – that the payments extracted from Germany should be limited to the 'actual damage' caused, rather than the full cost of the war, for which The Chief had been campaigning almost since the armistice.

The last straw was an article in the *Westminster Gazette* at the end of March, which quoted a 'high authority' in terms that left no doubt in the reader's mind that a retreat from the policy of making Germany pay in full was in progress.

The burden of the message from the 'high authority' was:

There will be some disappointments, but this is inevitable. We want a sane peace. We have to face realities and prepare a practical treaty, whether it disappoints Allied peoples or not. You cannot go on stripping Germany bare. We shall get something, and I think it will be something worth having, but certainly the question of indemnities, in the sense of going beyond the mere repairing of material damage, is not even posed. We must be moderate. Consider what would happen if we were not – a large occupation army for over thirty years, and who is going to pay for this occupation?

When Northcliffe was told by Steed that the 'high authority' in question was Lloyd George himself, The Chief decided to act.

His first course was to put the Prime Minister on notice that he would not be allowed to resile from the policy he had espoused at the election. Northcliffe's nephew, Esmond Harmsworth, was a member of Lloyd George's staff in Paris, and to him went a letter from his uncle pointing out that people all over England were contacting *The Times* and the *Daily Mail* to express their worry that the Prime Minister was giving away the show. Why, Northcliffe asked – with his customary inconsistency, but echoing perfectly the fear that was in Lloyd George's mind – did the Prime Minister, having won the election, now seem to be expressing the view of the left-wing parties that had lost it?

Naturally, though, it was through his newspapers that The Chief felt he could exert most influence. Still at the Hôtel de

France et d'Angleterre in Fontainebleau, he sent a telegram to the editor of the *Mail* making clear his anxiety about reparations and warning him that unless Lloyd George was placed under very strong pressure, the burden of costs from the war would fall not upon the Germans but on the backs of British workers and businessmen. There was a budget in preparation, he pointed out, and failure to collect adequate reparation payments for the war would result in a staggering burden on taxpayers. The editor was instructed to insist that Lloyd George carried out his election promises.

Next day, the *Daily Mail* launched a frontal attack, with the slogan THEY WILL CHEAT YOU YET, THOSE JUNKERS!

Northcliffe also turned his attention to mobilizing opposition in Parliament to any attempt at the sort of moderate settlement the 'high authority' had been suggesting in the *Westminster Gazette*. The very Tory reactionaries whom he had criticized and urged Lloyd George to drop from his government were the men most likely to support the campaign to squeeze every last penny from Germany, but in The Chief's mind the end justified the means. He lit the blue touch-paper under William Kennedy Jones, an Independent Unionist who represented the London constituency of Hornsey. Jones, who had worked with Northcliffe in the early days of his halfpenny newspapers, was a populist Hun-hater who had entered Parliament as an official Unionist during the dark days of 1916, after first contesting a by-election as an independent candidate under the bellicose, if somewhat vague, banner of 'Do It Now!'. He was an ideal conduit for Northcliffe's message.

The Chief passed on to Jones the secret reports he was

receiving from Wickham Steed, and the MP showed them to selected Unionist members of the coalition. He swore them to the strictest confidence, sometimes embellishing the material with hints that leading members of the French government – including President Poincaré – were deeply annoyed by Lloyd George's attempts to undermine their position on reparations, which was as punitive as, if not more so than, the stance demanded by Northcliffe and his allies.

These tactics raised the political temperature so high that when details of the recommendations on reparations in the Fontainebleau memorandum were leaked to newspapers – both by the French, attempting to raise opposition to them, and by Lloyd George himself, in the hope of gaining their acceptance – the lid blew off the pressure cooker.

In his note, Lloyd George had asserted that the treaty would oblige Germany to undertake to pay full reparation to the Allies. The question was, what did 'full' mean? The memorandum said:

> It is difficult to assess the amount chargeable against Germany. It certainly exceeds what, on any calculation, Germany is capable of paying. It is therefore suggested that Germany should pay an annual sum for a stated number of years. This sum to be agreed among the Allied and Associated Powers. Germany to be allowed a number of years within which to work up to payment of the full annual amount.
>
> It has been suggested that a Permanent Commission should be set up to which Germany should be able to

appeal for permission to postpone some portion of the annual payments for adequate reasons shown. This Commission would be entitled to cancel the payment of interest on postponed payments during the first few years. The amount received from Germany to be distributed in the following proportions:

50 per cent to France;

30 per cent to the British Empire;

20 per cent to other nations.

Part of the German payments to be used to liquidate debts owed by the Allies to one another.

Although the full details were not published, Northcliffe was informed of them and immediately sent a wire to Kennedy Jones telling him that the situation in regard to indemnities was growing worse. He followed this up with a letter indicating that he believed Lloyd George was allowing himself to be bluffed by the Germans – they were telling him they could not pay much and that, if heavy payments were imposed, they would refuse to sign the treaty, or there would be a Bolshevist uprising in Germany, or the Allies would be forced to occupy the entire country. It was a pity, he concluded, that the sacrifices of our gallant soldiers might be rendered worthless by financiers.

By now, Jones had gathered about him more than two hundred discontented Tories. They had already succeeded in instigating a debate on the reparations question in the House of Commons, and Bonar Law had found himself uncomfortably defending the Prime Minister's position.

He began by denying that either Lloyd George, or any other member of the government, had promised to make the Germans pay the whole cost of the war: 'What he said was that we should exact from Germany whatever Germany was able to pay.'

Referring to the promises that some candidates had made during the election campaign, Bonar Law went on: 'I have no doubt there were differences of opinion among members of the government, as among other people, as to what amount could be paid, and some were more sanguine than others. I was not among the most sanguine, and I said that, whatever amount we got, it would be holding out a hope, the fulfilment of which I could not conceive, to suggest that Germany could pay our whole war debt. There is no change whatever up to this hour in the attitude of His Majesty's Government on this question. The intention is still to obtain, as part of the debt which Germany owes, whatever amount can be got from Germany. That is our case.'

It was not a case that appealed to Kennedy Jones and his friends. Jones sat down and composed a telegram to be sent to Lloyd George in Paris. It was signed by two hundred and thirty-three Unionist MPs, and it read:

> The greatest anxiety exists throughout the country at the persistent reports from Paris that the British delegates, instead of formulating the complete financial claim of the Empire, are merely considering what amount can be exacted from the enemy. This anxiety has been deepened by the statement of the Leader of the House.

Our constituents have always expected – and still expect – that the first action of the peace delegates would be, as you repeatedly stated in your election speeches, to present the bill in full, to make Germany acknowledge the debt and then to discuss ways and means of obtaining payment.

Although we have the utmost confidence in your intention to fulfil your pledges to the country, may we, as we have to meet innumerable inquiries from our constituents, have your assurance that you have in no way departed from your original intention.

Before the telegram had even been tapped out over the wires, Bonar Law had arrived in Paris. So alarmed was he that he had forgone the half-day's journey by train and boat and made history by travelling in an aeroplane.

At the apartment in the Rue Nitot, he found Lloyd George on the edge of fury.

'This is all Northcliffe's doing,' the Prime Minister raved. 'The fellow has been my sworn enemy since I refused him a place in the peace delegation. He does nothing but make mischief. Is there to be no end to this insanity?'

'If you think that opinion in the House of Commons has become more sane than it was, then I fear you're mistaken,' Bonar Law told him.

Lloyd George sighed. 'We'll just have to hope some sense comes out of the peace conference – though, I have to say, I see no sign of it yet.'

*

The question of reparations was also troubling Woodrow Wilson. He had paid little attention to the matter in his Fourteen Points, referring merely to the restoration of invaded territory, by which he appeared to mean that the Germans must meet the costs of returning the parts of Belgium and France they had occupied to the condition in which they had found them at the time of their invasion. The European Allies – including Italy, which wanted to ensure that Germany was jointly responsible with Austria for the costs of restoring Italian territory – had assumed that the President's vague notion of restoration would include compensation for damage inflicted on the civilian population of the areas in question, and pressed him to concede the point during the negotiations that led up to the armistice.

On 5 November 1918, Wilson had instructed his Secretary of State to send a reassuring note to the European leaders. Robert Lansing explained:

> When the President formulated his peace conditions, he declared that the invaded territories must be not only evacuated and liberated, but restored. The Allies think that no doubt should be left as to what this stipulation means. They understand by it that compensation will be made by Germany for all damage done to the civilian population of the Allies and their property by the aggression of Germany by land, by sea and from the air. The President is in agreement with this interpretation.

That had settled things so far as Wilson was concerned, but

what the Allies had not told him was that they were also considering reclaiming from Germany the costs they had incurred in fighting the war. Clemenceau had even insisted on the inclusion of a clause in the armistice, which was not shown to the Americans before being presented to the Germans:

> *With the reservation that any subsequent concessions and claims by the Allies and United States remain unaffected, the following financial conditions are imposed:*
> *Reparation for damage done;*
> *While the Armistice lasts, no public securities shall be removed by the enemy which can serve as a pledge to the Allies to cover reparation for war losses.*

With the stroke of a pen, reparation for damage done had become reparation for war losses, and it was the interpretation of the last phrase that was to come as a shock to President Wilson. So far as the French were concerned, and they were supported by Italy, the losses included what fighting the war had cost them – and there were many in Britain who were inclined to the same view, as Lord Northcliffe made clear in his newspapers. To the dismay of the Americans, the question became not what Germany *could* pay, but what it *should* pay.

The extent of the Allies' claims had become obvious in February 1919, in the absence of Wilson and Lloyd George, and as Clemenceau recovered from the attempt on his life. The British delegation to the peace conference issued a document that outlined what it considered to be the basic formulation for calculating German financial responsibilities: shipping losses – ships sunk or damaged, loss of user, loss of cargoes, loss of life; loss of property in Allied countries through operations of war; losses through bombardments and air raids; cost of war pensions; subventions to food costs and increases of old-age pensions; separation allowances; external war debts; advances to Allies and Dominions, and finally, the additional budgetary cost of the war.

The British were demanding total reparation payments of twelve billion pounds, which was at least a retreat on the twenty-four billion suggested by Lloyd George's expert committee in London before the election, but Wilson knew nothing of that. All he understood was that his own financial advisers had estimated Germany's capacity to pay reparations as thirteen billion pounds at the maximum – and even then it would take thirty years for the payments to be completed. When the French went even further than the British demands with an estimate of thirty billion pounds for the total cost of the war, it became clear to the President that his just peace was running into serious trouble.

Wilson, still in Washington, prompted his advisers to remind the British and the French that their position was clear: no claim for reparation would be considered unless *it is clearly due in accordance with international law, or it is stipulated for in the understanding embodied in President Wilson's points regarding restoration of invaded territories, and in the qualification of these clauses by the Allied governments conveyed to Germany in the note of the Secretary of State of the United States of 5 November 1918.*

Lloyd George tried to defuse the situation by going to see Colonel House.

'Look,' he said, 'I know that Germany can't pay anything like the sort of indemnities we and the French are demanding, but we have to go for a large sum because that is what our people expect.'

'It's not what the President expects,' House replied. 'Our people have made very clear what the limits are, taking Germany's financial situation into account, and the President thinks it would be extremely dangerous to go beyond those limits. What your financial advisers are suggesting alone is close to the total amount ours believe is possible without seriously damaging the German economy.'

'I'm well aware of that, Colonel, but what is demanded and what is paid are not necessarily the same things. It would be perfectly possible to include in the treaty a sum for reparations beyond Germany's capacity to pay, and to reduce it later.'

'I'm afraid I can't see the President agreeing to that,' House said stiffly. 'He certainly doesn't want a treaty that depends on secret deals.'

A week or so later, after the President's return to Paris, Lloyd George had tried another tack. Bonar Law had made a brief visit to acquaint the Prime Minister with the worsening industrial unrest in Britain, but he was pressed into service on the reparations issue.

'Why don't you go and see the American financial experts,' Lloyd George suggested. 'Tell them that if we settle the total figure for reparations at nine billion pounds, as against the six billion or so they have proposed, we might accept payment in

German marks. You could also hint to them, very confidentially, that we might not expect to receive payment in full.'

Bonar Law failed to convince the Americans, so Lloyd George himself approached them in the hope of enlisting their aid in finding a way out of his difficulties.

'I agree with you,' he told them, 'that five or six billion pounds is the most we can reasonably expect Germany to pay, but the governor of the Bank of England is the leader of our financial delegation, and he's holding out for twelve billion. If we settle on a figure that doesn't agree with the one my experts have suggested, I'll be crucified at home. I'd very much appreciate it if you would speak to our people and do your best to convert them to your point of view.'

The conversation was reported to Colonel House, who naturally passed on the details to the President.

'Lloyd George is twisting and turning towards our position,' House said. 'I think he really wants to go along with us. I know he has told his financial advisers that attempting to recover the whole cost of the war is out of the question. Of course, we're in a rather different position with the French.'

Wilson, emboldened by the fact that Lloyd George put no figure on reparations in the Fontainebleau memorandum, raised the matter during a meeting of the Big Four at the end of March, in Clemenceau's room at the War Ministry.

'This is not just a financial problem, my friends, but a political one,' the President said. 'We simply cannot impose crushing financial penalties on the Germans for a period of thirty years or more. That would drive her straight into the arms of the Bolshevists.'

Clemenceau shrugged. 'But it's a political problem for us, too. We've made solemn promises to our people, and however much we might wish to accept the figures your advisers are proposing, our hands are tied by the expectations of our electors.'

Lloyd George was in one of his philosophical moods.

'It's true,' he said. 'It will be as difficult for me as for Monsieur Clemenceau to dispel the current illusions about reparations. Four hundred Members of Parliament have sworn to extract from Germany every last penny she owes, and I'm going to have to face them. But it's our duty to serve our country for the best. If I'm overthrown because I haven't done the impossible, my successor can do no better, and if he makes extravagant promises without keeping them, within a year he'll be declared mad and we'll be vindicated.'

Wilson smiled approvingly. Clemenceau scowled, wondering what Lloyd George was up to. That soon became obvious, as the Prime Minister repeated the argument he had employed at Fontainebleau.

'I'm convinced,' Lloyd George went on, 'that the Germans won't sign the terms which are being envisaged. I wouldn't sign in their place. Germany will go over to Bolshevism, Europe will remain mobilized, our industries will be paralysed, our states will go bankrupt, and we'll be held responsible for not having known how to make peace.'

'I couldn't have put it better myself,' said Wilson. 'And I must say how much I admire the spirit of your words. Could there be anything more honourable than to be chased from office for standing up for what is right? But, you know, I don't believe any parliament in the world would dare to oppose reasonable financial arrangements with Germany so long as we took the trouble to explain them properly.'

'There is another point, too,' Lloyd George said, 'and it's this. For Germany to pay the sort of amount we have been talking about – and which I know it's only fair that she should pay – she'd have to occupy a position in the market place even bigger than the one she had before the war. I mean, it's a question of our own self-interest.'

Clemenceau had been muttering to one of his financial advisers, whom he had brought to the meeting to talk figures, a subject the old man found boring. Now he said: 'Well, there might be a way round this difficulty. Suppose we were to agree on the minimum and maximum amounts the Germans were to pay annually, something in keeping with what your experts have already done, Mr President – I believe the sum of twenty billion gold marks by 1921 has been mentioned. We don't need to specify an overall figure in the treaty, but we could establish a commission to work it out.'

Wilson shook his head. 'I don't believe that would be at all satisfactory. Public opinion would want to know how many annual payments there were to be, which would mean establishing a total figure.'

'Oh, I don't know,' said Lloyd George. 'It would be an excellent way of avoiding ugly debates in Parliament, where the die-hards seem to hold sway at present. From a political point of view, at least in Britain, it's essential that we don't abandon our claim to the whole cost of the war, but we must explain that circumstances have compelled us to moderate our demands.'

'But the treaty must be clear,' Wilson insisted. 'People are not going to accept subterfuge. We have to stand up for our convictions, and if we believe that moderate demands are appropriate, that's what we must write in the treaty.'

The meeting adjourned. Wilson returned to the Place des Etats-Unis, where he found Colonel House waiting for him.

'I'm tired of this,' the President said, 'and it's getting on my nerves. They're playing politics, and it's holding everything up. There seems to be no common ground on this reparations business.'

'I think Lloyd George is on our side,' said House, 'but he's under a lot of pressure in London. Clemenceau, too. I hear from one of his financial advisers, who privately agrees with us about imposing terms that are too harsh, that President Poincaré and a large number of deputies in the Assembly are fixed on recovering the full cost of the war.'

'Well, I'm not inclined to go along with them for the sake of their domestic politics. We're dealing with large international questions here. The future of the world is in the balance, and we can't let greed and petty self-interest stand in our way.'

'On the other hand,' House said, 'we are going to have to reach an accommodation with the British and the French. I know, for example, that the British are making a connection between the reparation payments from Germany and the war debts they owe to us.'

'What does that mean?'

'Well, they're saying quietly that if we were to cancel the Allied war debts, the question of reparations would no longer be an issue.'

'But we can't do that,' Wilson protested. 'The Treasury . . . the Congress . . . Wall Street . . . they'd never allow it.'

'Then we're going to have to agree a position on reparations that may be harsher than we have in mind.'

The President frowned. 'Yet if Lloyd George is moving closer towards our position, as he seems to be, and is demanding more moderate terms . . .'

'Lloyd George is afraid of left-wing reaction on the one hand and the fury of the right on the other. He doesn't know where he's going. One minute he's suggesting a figure of fifty billion dollars, which is more than our people think is appropriate or possible, and the next minute he's proposing we fix no figure at all. The key to the whole thing is in the hands of the French.'

'But their figure bears no relation to reality.'

'Then we must make them agree to a figure that does, and maybe the way to do that is simply to increase their share of what we think may be available.'

The President ran the fingers of his right hand across his lips. 'Well, Clemenceau did propose today that, instead of fixing a figure, we agreed on annuities.'

'That may be the way out,' said House. 'All we have to do is produce a reasonable figure for a down payment by the Germans, and let the French think they can collect whatever they want later.'

Wilson said: 'Hmmm. I suppose that *is* what you might call open diplomacy.'

# CHAPTER 3

# *Artillery of Words*

## I

In the bare, blasted wasteland a few kilometres south-east of the River Somme, not far from what had been the Allies' stronghold at Amiens, small groups of soldiers picked their way among half-collapsed trenches and rusting barbed wire, or slithered up and down the treacherous slopes of vast shell holes. They were Australians, come to claim their dead, who had lain for months in makeshift graves, or simply where they had fallen as their battalions had spearheaded the Allies' 'big push' in the summer of 1918. Now, as the spring persuaded grass to push up once more through the scorched earth, and the few trees that had not been blown to splinters produced tentative leaves, the pathetic remains of those hundreds of sacrificed soldiers were painstakingly collected by young men who had never fired a shot in anger.

'Look at them,' observed a battle-hardened sergeant to his corporal, as they stood on a little hill violently created from earth shifted by tons of high explosives, and watched their new troops – faces covered by scarves or gas masks – going about their grim business. 'Bloody Rainbows, they ought to be called.'

'Rainbows?' queried the corporal.

'Well, they've come out after the bloody storm, haven't they?'

'Good luck to them,' said the corporal.

The two men had been there in the misty dawn of 8 August, when the engines of hundreds of tanks suddenly roared into life and the whistles sounded to send the infantrymen over the tops of their trenches to follow the monstrous war machines towards the German dugouts a few hundred yards away. This time, there had been no preliminary bombardment, but the noise of the tanks was more than sufficient to warn the enemy of the approaching attack, and the soldiers had barely begun to pick their way across no-man's-land when the shelling began in response.

In the swirling mist, it was difficult to see where you were going, and the tanks were soon too far ahead to follow. They had smashed down most of the barbed wire protecting the German positions, driving many of the defenders in front of them, but those who remained on the flanks raked the advancing lines with machine-gun fire, sometimes even catching them from behind as they pressed on. And all the while, shells rained down from the enemy guns dug in well behind the front line. Eerie shapes seemed to float through the fog – were they friend, or foe, or just shattered trees? And that cloud rolling towards you, was it gas or merely more water vapour?

By noon, they had advanced fourteen kilometres – but the

ground between them and the trenches they had left that morning was littered with the corpses of their comrades, many more of them than of the enemy they had overrun.

Finally, like hundreds of thousands of others who had never left the Western Front, those dead men were to receive the full measure of the respect they deserved. But, on this April morning, as their earthly remains were being gathered for burial in one of the vast war cemeteries marked out in the valley of the Somme, came a grim reminder of the horror of their deaths.

The sergeant and the corporal were watching as four men, a few hundred yards away from them, began to make their way up a gentle, grassy slope.

'What the . . . ?' The sergeant shielded his eyes with his hand against the sun, and realized what was happening.

'No!' he roared. 'Stop, you men! Stay where you are!'

It was too late. Suddenly, the sound of a large explosion rent the air. Then another, and another. The two NCOs instinctively dropped to their knees and covered their heads as earth and stones showered on them.

'Christ!' shouted the sergeant. 'The poor buggers have walked into a bloody ammo dump!'

The war that had cost so many lives was not finished with the killing yet.

In Paris, the pale spring sunshine was brightening the city's elegant face, but Bonar Law looked glum as he sat in the armchair by the window at Lloyd George's apartment.

'I did what I could,' he said, 'but I don't think I convinced anyone. I'd say nine out of ten Unionist Members, at the least, are disgusted by what they perceive to be our retreat from the position we took at the election.'

The Kennedy Jones telegram lay accusingly on a desk.

'The latest news from London,' Bonar Law went on, 'is that the sentiments expressed in that telegram would now command three hundred and seventy signatures.'

Lloyd George handed him a single sheet of paper with one typed paragraph on it.

'That's my reply,' he said.

Bonar Law read: *'My colleagues and I mean to stand faithfully by the pledges we gave to the constituencies in respect of the whole of the peace terms and of the social programme. We are prepared at any moment to give an account to Parliament and if necessary to the country of our efforts to loyally redeem our promises.'*

He grimaced. 'I'm not sure that it's a good idea to refer to the social programme in this context.'

'Why not?' Lloyd George asked. 'Don't forget that the coalition is composed of two wings, and my Liberal supporters are as concerned about social reform as they are about the peace treaty.'

'It isn't your supporters we have to worry about just now,' Law replied. 'The mood in *my* party is extremely agitated and dangerous, and to introduce the subject of the social programme at this juncture would merely serve to inflame it.'

'But we aren't simply plenipotentiaries,' Lloyd George protested. 'We are a government elected to carry out a programme for the betterment of our people. Apart from that, if we are to have a more moderate treaty than the irreconcilables want, we'll be depending on Liberal support – including the Asquithians.'

'Nevertheless,' said Law, 'it's the terms of the peace treaty, and especially the matter of indemnities, that are the cause of our present difficulties in Parliament. That's the challenge we must face squarely. Why risk provoking even more violent reaction by going into matters which in themselves might be the cause of dispute? No, I would strongly advise you to confine your reply to the subject of the telegram.'

'Oh, very well,' Lloyd George said grudgingly. 'What do you suggest I say?'

Law rose, went over to the desk and took a pen from the inkstand. On the paper, he placed parentheses round the phrase *in respect of the whole of the peace terms and the social programme*, indicating that it should be excised.

'We'll just say, "My colleagues and I mean to stand faithfully by *all* the pledges we gave to the constituencies."'

Then he scored a line diagonally through the whole of the second sentence, and began to write in the space below it.

'I don't think it should say we'll give an account to Parliament,' he said. 'I think it should be stronger than that.'

He wrote: 'We are prepared at any moment to submit to the judgement of Parliament . . .'

'*And if necessary*,' he said, writing as he spoke, '*of the country*, on our efforts . . . ah, there's a split infinitive here . . . our efforts *loyally to redeem* our promises. There. I think that will meet the case.'

Lloyd George read the revised version of the note. 'All

right,' he said, 'I'll send that. And now I'm going to call a press conference to explain my position.'

Bonar Law drew a breath sharply through his teeth. 'That isn't a course of action I would recommend.'

'No, it has to be done,' Lloyd George insisted. 'Wilson, Clemenceau and I are on the verge of an agreement in relation to the indemnities and I must make the position clear before anything comes out. This whole business in Parliament has arisen because a summary of the memorandum I wrote at Fontainebleau has appeared in the press, but without the details being fully explained. They're accusing me of going soft on the Germans and of acting behind the backs of Parliament and the country, and I must vindicate myself by setting out what is being achieved.'

Bonar Law said: 'Well, unless you're going to say that we intend to claim the whole cost of the war, I fear it'll do more harm than good. For a start, it will provoke a rift in the British delegation.'

'What do you mean, a rift? I've discussed it fully with the delegation. I explained to them that my plan was to increase our share of whatever the final figure might be by claiming reparation for the costs not only of all kinds of material damage but also of war pensions covering injury and death among soldiers and civilians, prisoners of war and so on. I convinced them that we couldn't claim the whole cost of the war, because of the terms written into the armistice, but that my plan would ensure that we obtained a substantial figure.'

'You might well have convinced the governor of the Bank of England and his colleagues,' Law said, 'but I'm afraid your argument made no impression on the Prime Minister of Australia. I spoke to Billy Hughes earlier today. He is still pressing for the recovery of the whole cost of the war. No doubt he's concerned about what Australia might receive if there's any compromise.'

'But doesn't he understand there's absolutely no point in making claims that Germany can't possibly pay? I thought I'd made it clear that, with the new proposal, we actually had a chance of receiving compensation. I thought I'd also made it clear that Wilson simply will not consider any suggestion that we should be indemnified for the whole cost of the war.'

Bonar Law shrugged. 'Hughes says he doesn't give two straws for what the Americans think. Those were his exact words. And, I must say, if I had to go back to the House of Commons and announce that we'd abandoned the principle of reclaiming the costs of the war, we'd be in a hopeless position. But that's precisely what I would have to do if you held your press conference now.'

Lloyd George's arms flailed at the air in irritation and despair. 'But they must be made to understand,' he cried.

'I think they can be made to understand,' said Law, 'but it must be done in an atmosphere of calm and reason. As I said to Hughes, I must be able to go to the House and say we've told the Germans they must recognize their *responsibility* to bear the whole costs of the war, but that *we* recognize they cannot pay the whole, so we insist that they pay every penny of the categories that have been agreed, even if it takes fifty years.'

'You're right,' Lloyd George said grimly. 'There's only one

thing for it. I'll have to come back to London and tackle the extremists in your party on the floor of the House. This will have to be made an issue of confidence in the government.'

'In the circumstances, that's the wisest course. As we now say in the reply to Kennedy Jones, we're prepared to accept the judgement of Parliament, and I think the very fact that we put the matter to the House will go a long way towards cooling tempers.'

'They've listened to Northcliffe long enough,' said Lloyd George. 'Now they can listen to me.'

'Might I suggest that you come over by aeroplane? It really is very quick, and not nearly so uncomfortable as you might imagine.'

'I don't think so. I rather enjoy the train journey and the sea voyage. Look, why don't you go back and arrange a debate for some time next week?'

The day appointed for the debate was Wednesday, 16 April. The House was packed, and abuzz with excitement. Six days earlier, the coalition had suffered another setback at a by-election. The faction of the Liberal Party that did not support Lloyd George had overturned a huge Unionist majority from the 'coupon' election – and had done it by demanding, among other things, that the peace terms offered to Germany should be moderate and just.

'This is a message for you,' the successful Liberal warned Lloyd George in his victory speech. 'Don't allow yourself to be bullied by the reactionaries who signed the Kennedy Jones telegram.'

In the corridors of the House, the 'bullies' were

unrepentant. Kennedy Jones himself continued to expound his view that the question was not what Germany could bear, but what the British taxpayer could not bear.

'I'll resign my seat,' threatened a Unionist Member from Cornwall, 'if the Prime Minister fails to exact the uttermost amount of the bill.'

'It's those damned Americans,' snorted another. 'Subversives, I call them. It's them and their friends the professional money-getters.' By that he meant Jews, whom the temper of the times viewed with suspicion. 'They call themselves Englishmen, but they aren't, you know. They change their names from the Biblical ones they started out with.'

Some said openly they would have preferred Winston Churchill to have taken charge of the peace negotiations – 'He's a fighter. He'd stand up for us.'

But the by-election result had reinforced Lloyd George's fear of a left-wing backlash at peace terms designed to satisfy the wild men of the right, and that stiffened his resolve to see off his critics. With a single bound, he would escape from the trap the Unionists had laid for him.

The chamber fell silent as he rose to make his speech. It began quietly enough, as he sought to emphasize the enormity of the task that faced the peace conference, answering complaints that it was all taking far too long.

'No conference that has ever assembled in the history of the world has been faced with problems of such variety, of such complexity, of such magnitude, and of such gravity,' he declared. 'The Congress of Vienna was the nearest approach to it. You had then to settle the affairs of Europe alone. It took eleven months. But the problems at the Congress of Vienna, great as they were, sink into insignificance compared with those which we have had to attempt to settle.'

In the press gallery, Henry Wickham Steed could not resist a wry smile. It was not only the problems, he reflected again, that sank into insignificance when compared to the Congress of Vienna.

After following this tack for some moments, Lloyd George raised the question everyone wanted to be answered.

'The question of indemnities,' he said firmly, 'like other questions affecting the peace of the world and the destiny of the human race, is not an easy one . . . and it is not going to be settled by telegram.'

And there he left it, turning to the situation in Russia and the emerging policy of containing Bolshevism within the borders of the country that had spawned it. Yes, there had been an attempt to intervene in order to bring peace to Russia – which some Members had deplored – but, no, there was no question of recognizing the Bolshevist regime, and its dreams of international revolution would be held back by a *cordon sanitaire* stretching from the Baltic to the Black Sea. (The concept belonged to Marshal Foch; the phrase Lloyd George had borrowed from Stéphan Pichon, the Foreign Minister. The British MPs were as impressed by the new piece of jargon as the French deputies had been.)

Wickham Steed began to wonder whether the Prime Minister would ever get to the point that had so inflamed the Unionists. He never really did.

'There are some who suggest that at the last election I and my colleagues were rushed into declarations of which we now are rather ashamed, and wish to get out of. I do not wish to get out of them in the least. So far from my coming here to ask for reconsideration – to ask release from any pledge or promise which I have given – I am here to say that all the outlines of peace that we have ever given to the public and asked them to make sacrifices to obtain – every pledge we have given with regard to what we pressed for insertion in the peace terms is incorporated in the demands which have been put forward by the Allies.'

It was, thought Wickham Steed, clear and unambiguous, and it said virtually nothing at all.

But there was a nod to the constituency Lloyd George was now anxious to reclaim, having to all intents and purposes abandoned it for the sake of election victory.

'We want a peace which will be just, but not vindictive,' Lloyd George intoned. 'We want a stern peace, because the occasion demands it. The crime demands it. But its severity must be designed, not to gratify vengeance, but to vindicate justice. Every clause and every term in the conditions must be justified on that ground. Above all, we want to protect the future against a repetition of the horrors of this war, by making the wrongdoer repair the wrong and the loss which he has inflicted by his wanton aggression, by punishing any individual who is responsible, by depriving the nations that have menaced the peace of Europe for half a century with a flourishing sword, by depriving them of their weapon . . .'

'What about the Kaiser?' roared one of the irreconcilables.

'I stand by my pledges,' Lloyd George retorted.

His next tactic was to invite the House to replace him if it did not approve of what he was doing in Paris.

'But whoever goes there is going to meet the emissaries of the enemy, the enemy with whom we have been confronted for five years, and who has inflicted terrible wounds upon humanity. Whoever goes there must go knowing that he has the fullest confidence of Parliament behind him.'

But if they did want Lloyd George to go back, they should stop bothering him.

'You cannot be always clearing up misconceptions. You cannot always be leaving the conference to come home to deny or to explain this or that. You cannot conduct negotiations under those conditions.'

Wickham Steed marvelled at it. Here was a prime minister telling the House of Commons that it had no business interfering in what he did in its name, and here were the members of that House sitting quietly and apparently accepting this arrogant dismissal of their rights as elected representatives.

Lloyd George was not finished yet, though. He blamed Lord Northcliffe for much of his troubles, and it was for Northcliffe that he reserved his vitriol. He did not mention any names, but no one was left in doubt.

'At the beginning of the conference, there were appeals to everybody all round to support President Wilson and his great ideals. Where did those come from? From the same "reliable source" that is now hysterically attacking all those great ideals. Just a few weeks ago there was a cartoon in one of these papers representing Bolshevism as a mere bogey, and me as a person trying to frighten the working classes with that mere bogey. Now it is no longer a bogey; it is a monster, and I am doing my best to dress it up as an angel. That is the same "reliable source". Reliable! That is the last adjective I would use. It is here today, jumping there tomorrow, and there the next day. I would as soon rely on a grasshopper.'

Wickham Steed was disgusted. He telephoned Northcliffe and relayed to him some of the Prime Minister's choicest phrases – 'diseased vanity', 'ridiculous expectations', 'the crime of sowing dissension between great lands'.

'This is not a statesman,' Steed told The Chief. 'This is a low demagogue. And his speech! It was an apologia full of half-truths and palliatives, false analogies and cheap rhetorical effects.'

'How did they take it?' Northcliffe asked.

'Like lambs, Chief. A little buzz of appreciation, waving of order papers. Not a word of dissent, not a complaint, not a demand for a clear statement. Even Kennedy Jones was quiet. And the little Welshman loved every minute of it. You should have seen him when he sat down – eyes blazing, flushed face, hair falling everywhere over his ears.'

Northcliffe laughed. 'I always said he looked like a dishevelled conjuror.'

'Well, this is one trick I don't think he'll get away with,' said Steed. 'I think, for all his sleight of hand, the effect of that telegram will be to force him to begin to play a straight game in Paris at last.'

*

'The final figure,' said President Wilson, 'is thirty billion dollars, or about six thousand million pounds sterling.'

Clemenceau asked: 'And how, pray, do you arrive at that sum?'

'Our financial experts have examined the position in detail. They believe it would be reasonable and practicable to expect Germany to pay in a relatively short period – two years, perhaps – a total of between four and five billion dollars in reparation. The experts further believe it reasonable to expect, over a longer period, that Germany would be able to pay an additional five to ten billion dollars, making a grand total of fifteen billion, or approximately three thousand million pounds sterling.'

'And the rest?' inquired Clemenceau. 'That is, assuming we accept your experts' assessment.'

'Well,' said Wilson, 'that is dependent upon how the reparations are made. If we were not to insist on gold, and to accept payment in German paper currency, we think it probable that they could transfer a further fifteen billion, thus bringing the full amount to the thirty billion I have suggested.'

Clemenceau pulled at his lower lip. 'It's a very long way from the one hundred and twenty to one hundred and fifty billion dollars our people think Germany is capable of paying – and even from the forty billion that's now being talked about between your advisers and mine.'

Lloyd George agreed: 'Even if the Germans were to agree to pay six thousand million pounds today, there would be an outcry. It would barely cover twenty per cent of the financial burden the Allies have incurred through this war, so it certainly wouldn't satisfy the sort of demands being bandied about in London.'

'Be that as it may,' said Wilson, 'but the figure of thirty billion dollars is the one our experts believe should be inserted in the treaty, and even at that they suspect there might be difficulties. Germany might refuse to sign a treaty with such a clause in it, or might well repudiate the treaty at a later stage. Furthermore, my advisers suggest that the demand for such a sum could force Germany to compete with the commerce of the Allies on a scale that would damage us.'

'The way to overcome those problems would be to fix a sensible level of annuities,' Lloyd George said, 'but the simple fact, so far as I am concerned, is that there just isn't time properly to investigate either the levels of compensation or Germany's ability to pay before the treaty has to be signed. We haven't fully assessed the damage, and we can't be certain about the prices we'll have to pay to put it right.'

This was the moment Wilson had been waiting for. He said quickly: 'That's absolutely correct. Perhaps, then, it would be better *not* to include an overall sum for reparations in the treaty.'

'We've already suggested that,' Clemenceau grumbled.

'No, forgive me, my friend, but what was suggested was fixing a sum for annuities without saying what the final figure would be. That would be unacceptable.'

'Listen,' said Lloyd George, 'it seems obvious to me that we are not going to be able to agree on an overall sum for reparations, and in any case we do not have the information on which to base realistic estimates. Furthermore, it's becoming obvious to all of us that Germany cannot possibly indemnify the Allies for the cost of the war, whatever other people might believe. The only sensible course for us is to appoint a reparation commission which will determine the amounts to be paid, the time in which they should be paid, and the way in which they should be paid.'

Wilson waved a hand. 'But surely we must include in the treaty a *maximum* sum to be paid by Germany. Otherwise the reparation commission could fix upon a ridiculous amount.'

'I doubt that,' said Lloyd George. 'Tempers are running high at present, but if we allow the commission time to do its work properly, passions will have cooled and wise counsels will prevail.'

'But what,' asked Clemenceau, 'are we to have the Germans sign up to in the treaty?'

'Well, there could be some sort of down payment,' Wilson suggested. 'Our people have calculated that it would be possible for Germany to pay twenty billion gold marks by 1921. That's about five billion dollars.'

'It's the sort of figure I had in mind,' said Lloyd George, 'but it seems to me that there could also be payments in kind, such as coal, or machinery, or livestock, to replace what France has lost during the war. The main benefit of the cash payment would be to silence the critics who believe we intend to let Germany off her debt.'

'I'm all for that,' Clemenceau said warmly, 'but one thing we must agree about is the terms of reference for the reparation commission. How will the total sum be apportioned, for example? I mean, it's clear that France has suffered by far the greatest war damage of all the Allies.'

'On the other hand,' Lloyd George put in, 'the burden of the cost of fighting the war has weighed more heavily on the British Empire than on any other belligerent. It would clearly be unfair to weigh indemnities too heavily in favour of material damage. I think a large part of the settlement should involve war pensions and allowances for the wounded, the widows and the orphans.'

Wilson said: 'There may be difficulties with that. Our people advise me that the logical basis for such claims is hard to establish.'

'I don't see why,' said Lloyd George. 'As a lawyer, I can say with certainty that in any civil action there would be a legitimate claim.'

'I'm not a lawyer,' Wilson replied, 'but I know that damages in a civil action depend upon the establishment of responsibility.'

'That's easy,' Clemenceau said. 'The Germans were obviously responsible for the war. They started it.'

'That was the first point in the summary of my memorandum of 25 March,' Lloyd George added. 'It seems to me that the whole legal basis of the treaty hangs upon the admission of German responsibility for the war. So far as I'm aware, no one has ever been in doubt that the Germans must be made to recognize their guilt.'

'Even so,' Wilson said, 'it is difficult to argue that even an admission of responsibility for the war would justify claiming compensation for the way it was fought. It's one thing to point to the loss and damage caused by German action, but quite another to include death and injury that might be said to have arisen from our own actions. That sounds very much like claiming the whole cost of the war, which we are now agreed is an untenable position.'

Clemenceau bristled. 'It's easy for you to say, Mr President. You have already made it clear that America wants nothing for herself from Germany, and that is a noble sentiment, but the plain fact is that America has suffered nothing in war damage compared with France.'

'I think,' Lloyd George said, 'that I'd like to draw to your attention a memorandum I received from General Smuts, whom I know you admire, and who is the last person to seek a vindictive peace.'

'The general is a great man,' Wilson affirmed. 'His advice on the covenant of the League of Nations was of enormous value.'

'I'm sure you'll find his thoughts on reparation equally helpful. They represent a clarification of the position you yourself adopted on the matter of civilian damage, as described in the note we received from Mr Lansing in regard to the armistice. If I might read just a little of what General Smuts said . . .

> 'Common sense leads to the conclusion that, while direct war expenditure (such as the pay and equipment of soldiers, the cost of rifles, guns, and ordnance and all similar expenditure) could perhaps not be recovered from the Germans, yet disablement pensions to discharged soldiers, or pensions to widows and orphans,

or separation allowances paid to their wives and children during the period of their military service, are all items representing compensation to members of the civilian population for damage sustained by them, for which the German government are liable.'

Lloyd George went on: 'Soldiers, too, of course, are often civilians when they are not fighting a war, and many return to civilian life afterwards. If they are killed or wounded by enemy action, where is the difference between them and civilians who are killed or wounded by enemy action, or whose homes and businesses are damaged?'

'Well,' said Wilson, 'I admit it's a powerful argument, but, if you don't mind, I really must consult my advisers before reaching a conclusion.'

When the President had left the meeting, Lloyd George said to Clemenceau: 'I believe we'll reach a satisfactory compromise on this reparation business.'

*Le Tigre* smiled. 'It was a master stroke to bring up the Smuts memorandum. That's probably done more than anything else to change his mind.'

'I thought it might impress him. Smuts more or less wrote the covenant for the League of Nations, even though the President claims it as his own.'

'I also like the idea of the reparation commission,' Clemenceau said. 'Of course, since France suffered the greatest damage, it will have to have a French chairman.'

*11*
—

Baron Sidney Sonnino was a patient man, but a determined one. 'It's his parentage, I suppose,' Lloyd George told Clemenceau after yet another gruelling session of negotiations with Sonnino and Prime Minister Orlando about Italy's claims to former Austrian territory in the eastern Adriatic. 'A Jewish father and a Welsh mother – that's quite a combination. They're both stubborn races, resistant to persuasion.'

Clemenceau grunted. 'And which one of them,' he asked, 'is the more cunning?'

On this occasion, they had not thought it appropriate to include President Wilson in their deliberations.

'Wilson,' Lloyd George had told Clemenceau, 'seems to be trying to apply the Fourteen Points to the whole peace settlement, whereas, in fact, they only apply to Germany, since they were the basis on which the armistice was agreed. Italy's claims are against Austria, and they must be treated in an entirely different way. Germany still exists, but the Austro-Hungarian empire doesn't, and Italy clearly has an interest in what happens to neighbouring territories that have suddenly been liberated. It's a question of policy involving relations among the nations of Europe.'

'I agree with you,' Clemenceau said, 'but that doesn't mean Wilson isn't going to want to play his part in the settlement. He's fixed on this idea of self-determination for the liberated peoples, and he's convinced that any problems arising can be solved by the League of Nations.'

'But in this case, the problems don't lie in the future, they're with us now. We signed the Treaty of London, and we ought to honour it, but what we have to decide is whether we're going to give the Italians our wholehearted support, and risk setting the Slavs against us, or whether we're going to try to persuade Italy to reduce her demands for the sake of an international settlement which will have the approval of the Americans.'

'Well,' said Clemenceau, 'so far as I can see, there's no chance of Sonnino reducing his demands. Perhaps if it were just Orlando, we might be able to achieve something. He seems to be a reasonable man, and he *has* played some part in the proceedings so far, even though they haven't concerned Italy's position directly. Sonnino just sits there looking either bored or scornful. He cares for nothing but what Italy might be able to get its hands on.'

Lloyd George had some sympathy with the Italian position. 'You can see their difficulty,' he said. 'Austria-Hungary breaks up, and Italy is left facing the prospect of a number of new states, some of which may be friendly and others hostile. There's no love lost between the Italians and the Serbs. Now that Serbia has joined with Croatia, Slovenia and Montenegro to form a new Slav kingdom, Italy might reasonably think it will have an enemy on the other side of the Adriatic.'

'No doubt you're right,' Clemenceau replied, 'but I think the real reason for their intransigence is more to do with France. They're jealous of us, have been for years. Oh, I know the Italians and the Slavs across the water enjoy a cordial dislike of each other, but the real reason why Italy wants control of the Dalmatian coast is to prevent us from exercising any influence there.'

Lloyd George said: 'It's Orlando I feel sorry for. I think he genuinely wants a European settlement, but the Sonnino faction holds the whip hand in parliament, and then he has the extreme socialists to contend with on the one hand and the extreme nationalists on the other.'

'Then why is he holding out for Fiume?' asked Clemenceau. 'You and I would both be prepared to stick to the Treaty of London if it wasn't for the Fiume claim Orlando has now added to it.'

The port of Fiume, at the northern end of the eastern Adriatic shore, had been part of the Austrian province of Slovenia. Even at the time of the Treaty of London in 1915, Fiume had not been included in the territory to be offered to the Italians in return for their participation in the war. The new frontier of Italy, assuming the Austrians were defeated, was to be the Istrian peninsula, west of Fiume, so that the Italians would have a port on the eastern side of the Gulf of Venice, at Trieste. If the Dalmatian coast were also to be handed to Italy, it was assumed that there would need to be a gap that allowed the new states released from Austrian domination to have maritime access.

But, in the euphoria of victory, the twenty thousand Italians living in Fiume had seen their opportunity to be reunited with their homeland. Their demand had been joyfully taken up by the newly confident right-wing parties in Italy – and by Orlando. Baron Sonnino, as foreign minister, was much more concerned to build a barrier against the Slavs in Dalmatia, but he had agreed to support Orlando over the Fiume claim if the Prime Minister coupled it with his demands relating to the Treaty of London.

'Perhaps it's a just a negotiating position,' Lloyd George told Clemenceau hopefully. 'Orlando demands Fiume but is prepared to renounce it so long as, in doing so, he gains everything that was agreed under the treaty. He knows that Sonnino won't give an inch over the territory on the Dalmatian coast, so he's using Fiume as a bluff to put pressure on Wilson to agree to the treaty terms.'

The President had flatly refused to recognize Italy's presumptions under the Treaty of London. And if there were any chances of compromise, when the Big Four, along with Sonnino, reconvened on 19 April for the purpose of settling the Italian question, they rapidly began to fade as the Italians bridled at Wilson in his pedagogic mood.

'I'm sure you'll agree, my friends,' he said, 'that we can't use one set of principles to make peace with Germany and another set for making peace with Austria-Hungary. I would assume that in each case, the principles must be the same. You know, we're trying to construct peace on an entirely new basis and to establish a new order in international relations. So what we have to ask ourselves is whether the lines of the settlements we reach will square with that new order.'

Orlando protested. 'But even if there had been no prior agreements in our favour, you cannot deny that there is a comparison between the claims of Italy and the general principles on which the peace treaty is based. Every time the peace conference has had to determine frontiers, or fix the limits of a new state, it has been recognized that the inclusion of different races is not a reason for overriding strong strategic and economic reasons. We simply desire union with territories on the Italian side of our natural frontiers. Dalmatia, for example, has been connected with Italy since the time of the Roman Empire, and later as part of the Venetian state. The whole culture of Dalmatia is Italian in character.'

Wilson regarded the little Italian dismissively. 'Well, you know, we have to put aside the economic and strategic argument, though I agree that, within limits, natural boundaries must be taken into consideration. The whole course of life is determined by natural boundaries. The slope of mountains not only throws rivers in a certain direction, but it also tends to throw the life of the people in the same direction. For that reason, I have no difficulty in agreeing to that part of Italy's claims. Nature has placed a great boundary round the north of Italy, so that Trieste and the Istrian peninsula are included. Further to the south, however, all the arguments seem to me to lead the other way. It's a different watershed, with different racial units and natural associations between the peoples.'

Grim-faced, Sonnino said: 'I must point out that Italy has never asked for any strategic advantage from an offensive point of view. All we demand is the necessary and indispensable conditions of defence. We want to put an end to the tragic history of Italy as open to attack from across the Adriatic, and for that we need the security of coast on the eastern side. If the situation continues as it is, the temptation to make war remains – or at least to threaten war.'

'I'm sorry,' Wilson responded loftily, 'but I must reject the strategic argument. Military men have led Europe into one blunder after another. It was the military men, don't forget, who were responsible for Alsace-Lorraine. If Italy were to be given a strategic position on the opposite side of the Adriatic, it would be detrimental to the peace of the world.'

'Leaving that aside for a moment,' Orlando said, 'let us look at the position of Fiume. There you have a natural association between the majority of the population, who are Italian, and Italy itself.'

'Well, yes,' said Wilson, 'this is a new claim on your part, which has no connection with the Treaty of London. But, apart from that, Fiume is only an island of Italian population. If that were to be the principle we adopted, there would be spots all over the map. There's no connecting Italian population between Fiume and Italy, so uniting it with Italy would simply be an arbitrary act, completely at odds with the principles we have been acting upon.'

'There's another point, too,' Clemenceau put in. 'In the Treaty of London, it's true, Dalmatia was given to Italy, and we shouldn't forget that. But Fiume was given to Croatia, and Italy agreed to that stipulation. So I can't see how Italy can claim Dalmatia under the treaty and at the same time claim Fiume, which was allotted to Croatia under the same treaty. That must mean signatures don't count any more, which in turn must mean that the treaty no longer applies.'

'That's correct,' Lloyd George added. 'I have here the map

that went with the treaty, and Fiume is clearly shown in Croatia. Are we expected to break faith with the Slavs at this late stage?'

'Well you're breaking faith with us,' Sonnino snapped. 'You're trying to deny us the Dalmatian coast that is ours by right of the Treaty of London.'

Wilson assumed his professorial air again. 'That treaty is clearly inconsistent with the general terms of the peace settlement. Now, I know it was drawn up in circumstances quite different from those in which we find ourselves now, and it isn't my intention to criticize what was done at that time. But if we were to base our decision on the Treaty of London, that would place America in an impossible position. Serbia separated from Austria-Hungary, as we wanted them to, and that makes it not only part of the new order, but also our friend. It's wrong of you to regard the Serbs as enemies. And, in any case, Fiume is not simply a Serbian question, or an Italian one. It's important as an international port.'

'Not only that,' said Lloyd George, 'but you're basing your claim only on the old town of Fiume itself. According to my information, if you were to include the suburbs, which are on the other side of what I believe is a narrow river, the majority would be Slav.'

'That's not true,' Sonnino broke in quickly. 'The majority would still be Italian.'

'A majority of what – eight thousand or so?' asked Lloyd George. 'And what about the surrounding countryside? That's solidly Slav. Just imagine the situation you would create by taking Fiume. We believe you're wrong, so what would the situation be if it provoked a war? There has to be some sanity among statesmen, which is what we're supposed to be.'

Orlando said: 'It's no good. I must maintain my stand on Fiume. It was not included in the Treaty of London because at that time it was considered to be part of Croatia. But now Croatia has joined with Serbia and a new, powerful Slav state is born. The Italian people of Fiume have no wish to live in such a state. I tell you, if Fiume is not granted to Italy, there will be a reaction of protest and hatred among the Italian people so great that it will quickly lead to a violent explosion. What must happen is that the peace conference must guarantee to Italy all the rights given to her by the Treaty of London. Then I won't be obliged to break the Alliance.'

'You're making a serious mistake by threatening to break away from your allies,' Clemenceau warned the Italian Prime Minister.

Wilson put a hand to his forehead. 'I can't believe you're threatening to break the Alliance over this. Listen, New York has a larger Italian population than any city in Italy, but I certainly have no intention of ceding New York to you. I beg you to think this over carefully. Please don't put yourselves in a position where you have no choice but to take an action that would be one of the most tragic consequences of the war.'

As the meeting broke up, Lloyd George took Sonnino aside. 'You realize,' he said, 'that this is the most difficult situation we've found ourselves in since the beginning of the conference. It's not as if it's even a particularly important question.'

'Signor Orlando thinks it's a very important question,' Sonnino countered. 'And so do I.'

'If you persist in this course, Baron, I can't see a way out. We're faced either with Italy refusing to continue her association with us in making the peace, or with the United States refusing to assent to a treaty based on principles that would be a grave departure from those on which she came into the war.'

'I'm sorry,' Sonnino said flatly, 'but you can't blame us. One of the effects of the war has been that of over-exciting the pride of nationality. That isn't Italy's fault. Perhaps we should blame the Americans for putting the principles so clearly.'

The wrangling continued throughout the next day, Easter Sunday, when Orlando restated his case and Wilson delivered a lecture on his principles. Afterwards, Lloyd George and Clemenceau suggested to the Italians that they should have another meeting without the presence of the American President.

It took place the following afternoon, 21 April, and Clemenceau began it by trying to reassure the Italians.

'I've brought Stéphan Pichon with me,' he said, 'because we've been discussing this subject all morning. As Foreign Minister, he agrees with me that because France signed the Treaty of London, we are prepared to stand by it if our Italian friends ask us to.'

'There's no question about that on the British side, either,' Lloyd George added. 'But I think it only right to point out that it will be a very serious matter if the United States doesn't sign the peace treaty.'

Sonnino was unimpressed. 'We joined with Britain and France because we were opposed to the domination of Austria, and that was the foundation of the arrangements we made in 1915. Now a third party comes in and obstructs the agreement we made purely on the ground that it believes in some system that we don't believe in. You don't change human nature with a document prepared by half a dozen diplomats. The League of Nations can try going into the Balkans and seeing what it can do there. No, it's a very simple matter. America has given in to Britain and France on their claims, and because she now feels that was immoral, she's trying to re-establish her virginity at our expense.'

'He's right,' Orlando said. 'If we allow President Wilson to prevail, there'll be a revolution in Italy, make no mistake about that. Italians won't accept a bad peace treaty.'

Clemenceau sighed. 'We must try to find a compromise. Would you, for example, accept a proposal that left out Fiume?'

Orlando shook his head. 'Absolutely not. I might as well make my position absolutely clear. It's better not to equivocate on something like this. We stand apart, and no amount of discussion will make us give way.'

Pichon asked: 'Is there no sort of conciliation you can offer?'

'No,' Orlando replied immediately. 'Italy must have Fiume. Once that's settled, the only question is what we must give up for it.'

'Let's be clear about this,' said Lloyd George. 'Are you seeking a settlement within the Treaty of London?'

'Yes.'

'But you are claiming Fiume, which is promised to the Kingdom of the Serbs, Croats and Slovenes?'

Orlando glanced at Sonnino. 'I'm looking,' he said slowly, 'for a scheme of conciliation outside the treaty.'

Lloyd George winced. It was now clear that, so far as Orlando was concerned, Fiume was a good deal more than a bargaining chip.

'Well, I think that practically puts an end to the matter, at least for the moment,' he said. 'We might as well move on to the details of the other decisions we have to make.'

By this time, Lloyd George had relented and allowed notes to be taken at meetings of the leaders. Sir Maurice Hankey, with his passion for efficiency and order, had complained that the lack of what everyone liked to call, in the diplomatic language of the time, a *procès verbal* made his job as secretary impossible. Lloyd George could never remember precisely what had been said, or by whom, and often he was not sure whether any decisions had been taken, or, if so, what they had been. So Sir Maurice had become the record-keeper at the secret meetings of the Big Four.

'You'd better send the minutes to President Wilson,' Lloyd George told Sir Maurice after the meeting with Orlando and Sonnino, 'but please don't include any reference to what was said about Fiume. I don't want to inflame him any further until we've had a chance to try to find a way out. Just give him the pages dealing with the other things we discussed.'

So it was not until late the following afternoon, when Lloyd George and Clemenceau came to see him, that the President became aware of the sudden raising of the stakes by the Italians. Lloyd George said nothing about the discussions of the previous day, but he had even more worrying news.

'I've just come from a meeting with Orlando,' he said, 'and he told me that he intends to write a letter saying Italy will not be represented at the peace conference when the terms are presented to the Germans unless her claims to Istria and Dalmatia are conceded.'

The muscles in Wilson's jaw tightened. 'Two can play at that game,' he said. 'I have it in mind to publish a statement setting out our position on Italy's claims and appealing directly to the Italian people to support our principles.'

Clemenceau said: 'There are rumours that Orlando is preparing to return to Rome almost immediately and proclaim the annexation of Fiume.'

'And I,' said Wilson, 'have sent word to New York summoning the *George Washington* to sail for Brest at the earliest possible date.'

'Let us try one last time,' pleaded Lloyd George, 'with a direct appeal to Orlando.'

He had conceived the idea of offering a compromise to the Italians by granting them their claims to Adriatic islands and territory in Turkish Anatolia if they would agree to the establishment of Fiume as a free city. There was a precedent in the the decision the Big Four had already taken – over French objections – about the port of Danzig, in the formerly German part of what would become the new independent state of Poland.

'As you wish,' Wilson said. But he published his manifesto

anyway, as he was advised to do by House and Lansing.

'You must make it public now,' the Colonel told the President. 'If you wait for the Italians to live up to their threat of walking out, it will look as if you're simply defending our position. Do it now, before they walk out, and you're stating American principles that will leave the break without any justification in the honest part of the world.'

The Statement Regarding the Disposition of Fiume dismissed Italy's case both for the annexation of the port and the acquisition of territory in the eastern Adriatic. Whatever the Treaty of London had said, the fact was that it had been written at a time when Italy faced the might of the Austro-Hungarian Empire, but that was no longer the case.

> *Austria-Hungary no longer exists. It is proposed that the fortifications which the Austrian government constructed shall be razed and permanently destroyed. It is part, also, of the new plan of European order which centres on the League of Nations that the new states erected shall accept a limitation of armaments which puts aggression out of the question.*

The President appealed to the Italian people to become trustees of the new world order which they had played such an honourable part in establishing. In a flight of academic oratory, he noted:

> *In the north and north-east, her natural frontiers are completely restored, along the whole sweep of the Alps from*

> *north-west to south-east, to the very end of the Istrian*
> *peninsula . . . all the fair regions whose face nature has*
> *turned towards the great peninsula upon which the historic*
> *life of the Latin people has been worked out through*
> *centuries of famous story ever since Rome was first set upon*
> *her seven hills. Her ancient unity is restored . . . It is within*
> *her choice to be surrounded by friends; to exhibit to the*
> *newly liberated peoples across the Adriatic that noblest*
> *quality of greatness, magnanimity, friendly generosity, the*
> *preference of justice over interest.*

Privately, the President's language was considerably less high-flown.

'This old style of diplomacy, where places and people are simply taken over by force, has to be stopped,' he told Colonel House.

Lloyd George and Clemenceau were dismayed. Orlando and Sonnino were furious.

'This is the sort of tactic you use against an enemy, not against a friend,' Orlando snarled as the Big Four, with Sonnino also present, met at Lloyd George's apartment during the late afternoon of 24 April. 'What you have done is to appeal not just to the Italian people, but to people generally, to question the wisdom of the policy of my government. That is offensive and unacceptable. You leave me with no alternative but to return to Rome and explain the situation to Parliament.'

'Does that mean,' Wilson inquired innocently, 'that you're breaking off negotiations?'

'No,' retorted Orlando. 'I am going back to consult the source of my authority. It's useless to continue the present discussions since all three of you are agreed to refuse us Fiume. But in Italy, Fiume is a national question. The people must decide when I explain the situation to them.'

'I hope,' said Wilson, 'you're going to make that clear, and not leave the public with the impression that you're withdrawing from the peace settlement.'

Clemenceau added: 'Now that the treaty is almost complete, we have asked the Germans to attend so that we can present it to them. Will Italy be represented at that meeting?'

'That depends on the decisions that will be taken in Italy,' said Orlando. 'We can't sign the peace with Germany if the questions affecting the peace with Austria-Hungary – the frontiers, that is – are not settled.'

Sonnino fixed his stern gaze on Wilson. 'It seems obvious to me that, by issuing your statement, you made it clear that you were either not aware or did not approve of the additional proposals *made* during the last few days.'

Lloyd George broke in: 'That isn't the case. It's true that the President wasn't keen on the proposals, but my understanding was that he was prepared to accept them if you did.'

'And my understanding,' said Wilson, 'is that you were not prepared to agree to them.'

'Whereas our understanding,' Sonnino said firmly, 'is that, while the sovereignty of Fiume could not be a matter of discussion, if we gave up Fiume, that would form the basis of acceptance of other proposals we had made in regard to our claims elsewhere.'

Wilson frowned. 'Did you get the impression all three of us were in agreement about that?'

'I certainly did,' said Lloyd George.

Sonnino regarded them with scorn. 'The reply was that Fiume was not acceptable, but that the rest might be acceptable. To which our response was that if Italian sovereignty over Fiume couldn't be accepted, what could be substituted for that?'

'Does that mean,' asked Lloyd George, 'that you would be prepared to recommend any arrangement, if it could be agreed, to the Italian parliament?'

'Certainly,' replied Sonnino. 'But so far, nothing has been suggested.'

'What that means,' added Orlando, 'is that I must go back and explain the present situation to parliament and ask for a general authority.'

'Unless, of course,' Sonnino put in, 'we can agree a compromise now that can be placed before parliament.'

Wilson said coldly: 'I have no proposals to make. What you can tell your parliament is that neither the Allied nor the Associated Powers can consent to give Fiume to Italy. You can also say that the British and the French feel bound to stand by the agreement made with Italy in 1915. As for me, you can say that I understand the difficulty of my colleagues and I'm ready to agree to anything that is consistent with my principles.'

Orlando stood up. 'I have a train to catch,' he said.

On the day Prime Minister Orlando arrived back in Rome, Benito Mussolini was leading his Fascisti through the streets under banners proclaiming 'Viva Fiume!' They were not alone. Behind them marched workers, intellectuals, businessmen, housewives – and even a group of parliamentarians. All were united in demanding that Orlando stand firm against what Mussolini denounced as the infamous swindle that a contemptuous and ignorant America was attempting to perpetrate on the proud Italian nation. Woodrow Wilson's appeal to the people had simply served to inflame their patriotic passions, and to destroy the President's reputation among all but a few left-wingers.

Within days, the demonstrations had spread to the industrial cities of Milan and Turin, and also to smaller places such as Bari and Brescia, where there were strong local branches of the *Fascio di combattimento*. Soon, virtually the whole country resounded with the cry that Italy would have Fiume and the Dalmatian coast.

It echoed across the Adriatic, too. In the old town of Fiume itself, a group called the Young Italy Society organized daily marches, watched benignly by the Italian troops who had occupied the place since the Austrians' withdrawal.

'Italy or death!' roared the rabble-rousing speakers. 'We'll destroy Fiume before we submit to the Slav yoke!'

To emphasize their determination, the Italian population passed a resolution announcing the annexation of Fiume to their homeland and giving executive power for the time being to the commander of the Italian garrison. It was the excuse that the heroic poet Gabriele d'Annunzio had been waiting for. Short, bald and effete-looking, d'Annunzio was nevertheless a man of action who thrived on danger and constantly sought glorious exploits for himself. The war had been the most exhilarating period of his life – he had lost an eye serving with the air force – and now, the prospect of an insulting peace offered another opportunity to display his dash and courage.

'Down there, on the roads of Istria,' he declaimed, 'on the roads of Dalmatia, all of which are Roman, do you not hear the rhythmic footsteps of a marching army?'

With d'Annunzio at its head, naturally. He began to raise money to arm and equip a private militia.

'Today, only Italy is great, only Italy is pure,' ran another of his flights of rhetoric, to the ecstatic cheers of a vast crowd. 'In the face of criminal intrigues, Italy must be bold. Annexation! Annexation! That is our battle cry.'

If the Prime Minister could not bring Italy to her destiny by diplomacy, then d'Annunzio, supported by Benito Mussolini, would do it by force.

# CHAPTER 4

# The Mirror Crack'd

*I*

The enemy was within the walls. In the great hall of the Trianon, just beyond the park of the Palace of Versailles, five representatives of the German government faced the plenipotentaries of the Allied powers, and the voluminous document that was to be known as the Treaty of Versailles.

Outside, among the lakes and shrubberies surrounding the great palace of Louis XIV, the signs of war were still visible on this mild May afternoon. Camouflage netting shrouded some of the trees, among which artillery batteries had been stationed, to protect what had been the headquarters of the Allied Supreme Command. Some of the lakes remained hidden under great green tarpaulin sheets designed to disguise them as fields in order to confuse the pilots of German aircraft. A year earlier, the Germans had been just a few miles to the other side of Paris, and the sound of their field guns had reverberated in the ears of the generals gathered at the palace to plan their response to the great and so nearly successful offensive. Now, the Germans – not in the feared grey uniform, but in morning coats – had arrived by invitation, or, more accurately, by order.

These were not the men who had directed Germany's war, or even its surrender. Until a few months ago, they had known little, if anything, about the policies which had promised glory and delivered only bitter defeat. None had ever participated directly in the government of his country, and only one had moved in the official circles associated with the old regime. Germany was now a republic, the Kaiser replaced by a president, the lower middle-class saddler Friedrich Ebert, and a former journalist, Philipp Scheidemann, taking over the office of chancellor from the succession of aristocrats whose preserve it had once been. A whole new political class had emerged, and its representatives were now seated across a table from the leaders against whom the old German political class had pitted itself, and lost. It was not a comfortable position.

So far, the contacts between the governments of the victors and the vanquished had been at arm's length. Their military men met each other regularly at the former German headquarters in Spa, where the progress of the armistice terms was monitored, but the Allied politicians, encouraged by Marshal Foch's assessment of the enemy's disarray and desperation, had determined early on that the only negotiations relating to the peace treaty would be among themselves. They would not be consulting the Germans.

'If we have to debate every point with the enemy, it will take us two years at least to produce a treaty,' Lloyd George had said. 'The cost would be enormous, because during all that time we'd have to maintain great armies to enforce the armistice.'

That, at least, had been the excuse. But Clemenceau had come closer to admitting the truth of the matter when he had told André Tardieu: 'The fact is, we won the war, and that gives us both the power and the right to dictate the peace. The Germans would have done the same if they had won. Remember 1871.'

It had been that memory, too, which had prompted him to insist that the peace conference be held in Paris.

'And we'll make them sign the treaty at the Palace of Versailles,' he told Tardieu. 'In the Hall of Mirrors, among the trophies of Louis Quatorze. That's where *they* chose to humiliate us. The insolence of it. I'll never forget that day – 28 June – when they swaggered into the hall for the proclamation of Wilhelm the First as emperor of Germany. It's only fitting that it should be the place where we stamp the seal on their defeat.'

Thus it was that on 7 May 1919 Clemenceau rose to his feet, not yet in the great palace but, for the moment, in the palatial residence built for a royal mistress. He did not make a speech, but, barely concealing his contempt for the Germans, announced that the day of reckoning was at hand.

'You will, of course,' he told the visitors brusquely, 'be given time to consider the terms of the treaty more fully. We shall expect your written response within two weeks.'

As Clemenceau sat down, an expectant hush fell upon the pillared hall. Every Allied eye turned towards the leader of the German delegation, a tall, moustachioed man of middle age, with a high forehead and short, swept-back hair. Count Ulrich von Brockdorff-Rantzau, once a civilian diplomat of the German Empire and now Foreign Minister of the German Republic, was to be the first enemy voice to be heard in the councils of peace. He had never been a member of the military caste, and he was there genuinely to represent the moderate socialism of the new Germany, but, unfortunately for him, his name and his title resounded with the troubling echoes of the old.

For a few seconds, nothing happened. Then Brockdorff-Rantzau slowly unfolded and arranged the pages of a document he had produced from his pocket.

He knew the main terms contained in the treaty. During the previous few weeks, Allied emissaries had visited the German government in Weimar – the capital of Thuringia and once the centre of German intellectual life, where a new constitution for the republic was being written – and in Berlin, in an attempt to gauge whether it was likely to view the conditions as acceptable. Now, Brockdorff-Rantzau was to read the official response he had intended to send in writing, until he had been peremptorily summoned to Versailles.

'Gentlemen,' Brockdorff-Rantzau said. It was as if an electric shock had sparked round the room. The German had not stood up.

'We are deeply impressed,' he went on, his head bowed over his document, 'with the lofty character of the task which has brought us together with you, namely, to give the world a speedy and enduring peace.'

He paused, and, for the first time, looked up. 'We cherish no illusions as to the extent of our defeat – the degree of our impotence. We know that the might of German arms is broken.'

Some of the Allied delegates nodded in satisfaction. But the Minister's next sentence brought them up short.

'We know the force of hatred which confronts us here,' he said deliberately, 'and we have heard the passionate demand that the victors should both make us pay as vanquished and punish us as guilty. We are required to admit that we alone are guilty in this war.'

Brockdorff-Rantzau's eyes scanned the faces ranged before him. 'Such an admission on my lips would be a lie.'

Germany was not trying to evade its share of responsibility for the fact that war had broken out, or for the way it was fought, he continued. It might be that the attitude of the former German government had contributed to the calamity.

'But we emphatically refute the idea that Germany, whose people were convinced that they were waging a defensive war, should alone be laden with guilt.'

This was not going well. The representatives of the Allies exchanged glances that were pregnant with hostility. The Germans sat very still, their faces betraying no emotion.

It was the mobilization of the Russian armies after the assassination of the Archduke Franz-Ferdinand, said Brockdorff-Rantzau, which had taken the power of decision away from the statesmen and placed it in the hands of their generals. And the crisis might never have arisen had it not been for the imperialism of all the European states, with its policy of expansion and retaliation, that had poisoned the international situation.

His right hand trembled slightly as he went on to refute the charges of war crimes that had been laid against Germany:

'We are ready to acknowledge that wrong has been done. We have not come here to make light of the responsibility of the men who conducted the war, or to disown breaches of international law which have actually been committed. We repeat the declaration made in the Reichstag at the beginning of the war. Belgium has been wronged, and we will make this good. But crimes in war, while they may not be excusable, are committed in the struggle for victory, in anxiety to preserve national existence, in the heat of a passion that blunts the conscience of nations.'

The Allies themselves were hardly blameless. Germany had been forced to wait six weeks to obtain the armistice she had sought, and now six months to be presented with peace terms.

'The hundreds of thousands of non-combatants who have perished since 11 November, through the blockade, were killed with cold deliberation, after victory had been won and assured to our adversaries. Think of that, when you speak of guilt and atonement.'

This was not, Lloyd George thought, the tone of the nation Marshal Foch claimed was so desperate that it would accept any terms the Allies cared to demand.

Brockdorff-Rantzau continued: 'The Allied governments abandoned the idea of a peace of violence and inscribed the words "Peace of Justice" on their banner. The German government put forward the principles of the President of the United States of America as a basis for peace, and was informed that the Allied and Associated Powers had accepted this basis with two specific reservations. President Wilson's principles, therefore, became binding on both belligerent parties – upon you as well as us and our former allies.

'These principles, taken individually, demand of us grievous national and economic sacrifices, but the sacred and fundamental rights of all nations are protected by this agreement. The conscience of the world is behind it. No nation will be permitted to violate it with impunity. On this basis, you will find us prepared to examine the peace preliminaries you lay before us.'

Germany solemnly undertook to restore, in so far as she was able, the devastated territories of Belgium and northern France she had formerly occupied, but the Allies must understand that they shared the responsibility for that. German prisoners of war had begun the work, but that could not be allowed to continue.

'Such labour is certainly cheap,' the Minister said sarcastically, 'but it would cost the world dear if hate and despair were aroused in the German people at the thought of their captive sons, brothers and fathers continuing to languish in their former bondage after the peace preliminaries.'

Then there was the question of the reparations demanded by the Allies: 'Our experts on both sides will have to study how the German people can best meet its obligation without breaking down under the heavy load. Such a collapse would deprive those entitled to compensation of the advantages to which they have a claim, and would involve irreparable confusion in European economic affairs as a whole. Both victors and vanquished must be on their guard against this danger and its incalculable consequences.'

He urged that Germany should be allowed to join the new League of Nations, and ended with the clearest warning he could give in such circumstances:

'The German nation is earnestly prepared to accommodate itself to its hard lot, provided the foundations agreed upon for peace remain unshaken. A peace that cannot be defended in the name of justice before the whole world would continually call forth fresh resistance.

'No one could sign it with a clear conscience, because it would be impossible to fulfil. No one would undertake the guarantee of fulfilment that its signature would imply.'

His message delivered, Brockdorff-Rantzau finally did rise to his feet, then he led his small delegation from the room.

Lloyd George whistled through his teeth. 'It's hard to have won the war and to have to listen to that.'

'Isn't it just like those Germans, though?' President Wilson said.

'It was an insult,' said André Tardieu, who was nearby. 'Especially to Monsieur Clemenceau. And the tone. It was so cold, so harsh.'

Clemenceau shrugged resignedly. 'What have I always told you about Germans, my boy?'

'Do you really think he meant what he said, that they wouldn't sign?' asked Lloyd George.

Outside, in the almost too perfect formal gardens of the Trianon, Brockdorff-Rantzau turned to one of his colleagues.

'I was so nervous in there that my legs wouldn't support me, so I couldn't stand up.'

The official smiled knowingly. 'I think it had the desired effect,' he said. 'By the way, I had a wire from Berlin just before we came here. The government is ordering a national week of mourning, starting tomorrow, against what the Chancellor is calling this "death warrant". There'll be huge protest demonstrations all over Germany.'

They made their way back to the Hôtel des Réservoirs, in a mansion once owned by Madame de Pompadour, opposite the magnificent façade of the palace. Brockdorff-Rantzau found a cable from Reichspräsident Ebert waiting for him. It read: *Request you formally notify Allied and Associated Powers that peace terms presented are unfulfillable, unbearable and ruinous for Germany.*

*II*

—

'I'm sorry,' Georges Clemenceau said, 'but I have no intention of begging pardon for our victory.' The Allies were discussing the German response to the draft treaty that had been presented at the Trianon. Clemenceau was all for ignoring it and insisting on the conditions to which they had all agreed, with the threat of force if necessary.

It had taken some weeks to reach this point. First, the Allies had been deluged by notes from the German delegation – fifteen of them in all – opposing every important condition contained in the draft treaty.

'In the end,' Brockdorff-Rantzau had told his colleagues, 'we're probably going to have no alternative but to sign, because, whatever the President and the Chancellor might think, we simply aren't strong enough any more to resist the Entente if they give us an ultimatum. But what we must do is use every pressure we can bring to bear to gain significant concessions.'

'And how are we going apply that pressure?' asked Edgar Haniel von Haimhaüsen, another experienced hand from the old imperial ministry of foreign affairs. 'They've given us their document and they simply want a written response.'

'You've seen the newspapers,' Brockdorff-Rantzau replied. 'There's outrage in both Britain and France against the treaty, especially among liberal and left-wing opinion. Some of the English papers are calling it a disgrace that violates every principle for which they'd been told they were fighting the war. And, here, in one of the French ones, there's a headline that says "Wilson's Defeat". Even in Italy, the Socialists are saying that it's a betrayal of the Fourteen Points. All this must work in our favour.'

'But the left wing doesn't control the government in any of those countries,' Haimhäusen said. 'Lloyd George, Clemenceau and Orlando will simply ignore it. They're more concerned about their rabid nationalists. That's obvious from the terms they're trying to impose.'

'But don't you see what that means?' said Brockdorff-Rantzau. 'There's a serious political rift right across Europe, and the longer we hold out, the more serious it will become. What we have to do is push them into direct, verbal negotiations.'

'So what's your plan?' asked Haimhäusen.

'The first thing is to refute the treaty point by point. We'll do that with a series of notes, opposing each individual condition. And I'm going to ask for an extension of Clemenceau's deadline for our written response. We've got to rattle them and prolong the negotiations as long as we can. That will be our best chance of overturning the most offensive clauses – especially the territorial demands.'

But the Foreign Minister's ploy did not work. The Allies continued to refuse to negotiate in person.

'I agree that there must be discussions with the Germans,' President Wilson told Lloyd George and Clemenceau as the bombardment-by-note intensified, 'but those discussions should be in writing.'

The three agreed to wait for the written response, and to extend the deadline by one week.

This time, it was not the voice of Brockdorff-Rantzau that was heard in the Germans' reply, but its tone was no less defiant, in spite of the fact that it had been written by the socialist intellectual and pacifist Walther Schücking. The fingerprints of many other hands were visible all over the document, which complained that the draft treaty violated not only the stated war aims of the Entente powers but also the guarantees given at the time of the armistice. It then went into a series of counter-proposals:

> Germany is willing to subject all her overseas colonies to administration by the League of Nations, provided she is recognized as its mandatory power.
>
> Germany is willing to proceed with disarmament in advance of all other nations, to give up compulsory military service and to reduce her army to the 100,000 proposed. She stipulates, however, that all other powers who are parties to the treaty should also abolish conscription and reduce their armaments in the same proportion, and that Germany shall be admitted forthwith as a state with equal rights into the League of Nations.
>
> Germany renounces her sovereign right in Alsace-Lorraine, but wishes a free plebiscite to be taken there. She gives up the greater part of the province of Posen, those districts unquestionably Polish in population. She is prepared to grant Poland, under international

guarantees, free and secure access to the sea by ceding free ports at Danzig, Königsberg and Memel, by an agreement regulating the navigation of the Vistula, and by special railway conventions.

Germany cannot dispense with Upper Silesia. Poland does not need it.

Lloyd George, as he read the document with his Foreign Secretary, Arthur Balfour, felt a twinge of anxiety.

'They definitely have a case on the question of disarmament,' he said. 'In all fairness, we can't disarm Germany while all her neighbours are bristling with weapons that they could turn on her at the slightest sign of dispute.'

'Well, you can't say the same about her colonies,' said Balfour. 'It would be asking for trouble if we were to hand back those naval and aerial bases without being sure that Germany wouldn't attack our lines of communication at some point in the future, when her confidence returned. And, so far as her frontiers in the east are concerned, there has to be some readjustment because of our stated principles of national rights and self-determination.'

Lloyd George re-read the section dealing with Poland. 'But if we look at it impartially, there is a case for making some adjustments. For example, it's hard to see any justification, on the basis of those principles, for taking Upper Silesia away from Germany and giving it to Poland without asking what the inhabitants want.'

They turned their attention to the paragraphs dealing with reparations. The Germans had rejected the principle of

reparations demanded on the basis of their sole
responsibility for the war, but expressed themselves willing
to make reparations on a schedule of their own devising:

> Germany is prepared to make payments up to a
> maximum sum of one hundred thousand million gold
> marks – twenty thousand million by May 1, 1926 and
> the balance in annual payments without interest. These
> annual payments are to be equal in principle to a fixed
> percentage of German revenues, and for the first ten
> years they should not exceed one thousand million gold
> marks a year.

'We can't concede anything on responsibility for the war,'
said Lloyd George. 'If we were to do that, what would we have
been fighting for? There's no escaping the fact that the
Germans attacked Belgium and France, and that we were
dragged in reluctantly.'

Balfour said: 'I quite agree, but once that is accepted, the
liability for the payment of indemnities is established.'

'It's not the liability that worries me, it's how that liability
is met. You know very well that I argued strongly for
moderation in fixing the amount that should be expected,
partly to avoid the charges we see here – that German workers
will become slaves to foreigners – but also to avoid crippling
the German economy, which would do nobody any good.'

'Well,' Balfour said, 'I would just make the point that it's
not only the Germans we have to think about. What about
Belgium, with her factories looted? What about Italy? The

whole of Europe must revive its industries and its economy, and I don't think it's sensible to dwell on the misfortunes of the Germans alone when everybody else has suffered because of their actions. I mean, it's not as if they show any signs of repentance, as is obvious from the speech Brockdorff-Rantzau made and from this note.'

'True,' Lloyd George admitted. 'I suppose any burden that does not fall on the shoulders of German workers will fall on British ones, and others. But I'm not suggesting for a moment we should let Germany off anything. I simply think it would be far better if we came to a sensible agreement with Germany as to the sum that should and could be paid.'

'In short, then,' said Balfour, 'you believe we should be prepared to make concessions as a result of these German objections to the treaty as it stands?'

'I believe we should . . . no *must* . . . we must present the Germans with a treaty they'll sign. At present, everything we hear suggests that they won't sign, and I dread to think what the consequences of that would be.'

'What do you think the attitude of President Wilson and Monsieur Clemenceau will be to this response, and to any possible concessions arising from it?'

'I'll find out soon enough,' Lloyd George said. 'But before I do, I'd like to take the temperature at home and among the Dominions. I'm going to call a special Cabinet meeting.'

'Here?'

'Yes, here, at my flat.'

Two days later, nine members of the British Cabinet and the leaders of the Dominions converged on the Rue Nitot.

Their meeting lasted all that day, and throughout the next. At the end of it, Lloyd George had achieved the consensus he needed, not only to face the other Allies, but also to reassure himself that – whatever the irreconcilables in the House of Commons said – his position would be secure among majority opinion in Britain.

He confronted Wilson and Clemenceau the following Monday, 2 June.

'We believe,' he told them, 'after a great deal of consideration, that the treaty should be amended in order to make some concessions to the Germans and ensure that they sign it.'

Clemenceau stiffened: 'And what might those concessions be?'

'First, there should be modifications to the clause dealing with the eastern frontiers that leave Germany with the districts that are predominantly German, unless there's an overwhelming reason for transferring them to Poland. In doubtful cases, there should be plebiscites.

'Second, we should extend to Germany the offer of joining the League of Nations at a time earlier than the two years envisaged at present, provided she is making real efforts to meet her obligations.

'Third, there should be a reduction in the numbers proposed for the army of occupation and the period of occupation should be made as short as possible.

'Fourth, we should modify the clauses referring to reparations. My proposal is that either the Germans undertake and pay for all restoration themselves, as well as paying to the Allies a fixed sum in the proportions we have agreed, or that they make an offer within three months of a fixed sum in cash or in kind.'

Clemenceau roared: 'Are you out of your mind? Just at the time when we should be standing firm against the Boches, you're suggesting we give in to their arrogant, insulting and outrageous demands.'

It was then that the French Prime Minister made his remark about not seeking forgiveness for having won the war.

'You don't know the Germans as well as we do,' he bellowed at Lloyd George. 'All your damned concessions would do would be to encourage resistance by them. And, incidentally, to rob our own people of their rights.'

'I'm sorry,' Lloyd George said, 'but I disagree. I've consulted the members of my delegation, my Cabinet colleagues, and the Dominions. With one exception . . .' he glanced at President Wilson, 'and that was Mr Hughes . . . they agree that concessions must be made in order to ensure that Germany signs the treaty.'

'But they *will* sign the treaty,' Clemenceau hissed, 'so long as we stand firm and we're united. We've got the military force to support our demands.'

'I am authorized to tell you,' Lloyd George said grimly, 'that in the case of an impasse in regard to the signing of the treaty, Britain will refuse the services of her army to advance into Germany, and the services of her navy to enforce the blockade of Germany.'

Clemenceau sagged in his chair. Wilson regarded Lloyd George with a gaze that felt like cold steel.

'For heaven's sake,' he said indignantly, 'the time for modifying the treaty was when we were writing it. We've spent two months and more on this, and only now are you coming with modifications.'

Lloyd George said: 'The text of the treaty has only recently been published, so it is only now that we can see the reaction of public opinion.'

Clemenceau's heavy moustache twitched with the contemptuous curl of his lip. 'I notice that public opinion in Britain does not seem to be objecting to the fact that Germany is being forced to give up all her colonies and hand over her naval fleet.'

Lloyd George ignored the sarcasm. 'I do apologize for making these proposals so late in the day,' he said, 'but we have reached our conclusions after a period of reflection, and it appears to us that there are certain defects in the treaty that must be put straight.'

'Well, since you've taken the time and trouble to consult your colleagues,' said Wilson, 'it seems only right that we should do the same.'

'We certainly should,' added Clemenceau. 'But I think I know what their reaction will be.' He fixed his eyes on Lloyd George. 'Your people seem to think the way to win the war is to appease the enemy. We, on the other hand, believe the best way to end it is to act quickly and firmly.'

Colonel House arrived at President Wilson's residence in the Place des Etats-Unis and was immediately shown into the study.

'This is a fine old mess,' Wilson complained. 'I've perhaps gone further than I should have done in compromising with the Europeans, and look what I get for it. People overrode our judgement and insisted on having things written into the treaty, and now the things they wrote in are seen as stumbling blocks, and they want them removed. It makes me sick. I say, if those things ought not to have been in the treaty, then we should remove them, but don't let us remove them just for the sake of having the treaty signed.'

House shifted uneasily in his chair. 'There *has* been a certain amount of criticism of the terms among our own delegation, Mr President. I'm sure you've seen the letter from . . .'

'Yes, I've seen it,' Wilson replied testily.

One of the younger members of the American delegation, William Bullitt, who had spent a short time in Russia in a vain attempt to come to some sort of accommodation with the Bolshevists, had resigned his post in disgust after seeing the draft of the treaty.

'We have delivered the suffering people of the world,' he had written to Wilson, 'to new oppressions, subjections and dismemberments – a new century of war.'

Wilson shrugged it off. He told House: 'Bullitt is young and impressionable. I don't think his encounter with the Bolsheviks has improved his powers of impartial analysis.'

'Well, as a matter of fact, there have been others,' House said hesitantly. 'Not resignations as yet, but threats of them.'

'By whom?'

'Some of the younger members of the expert committees

are unhappy about the draft treaty . . . for a variety of reasons.'

'They didn't have to negotiate it,' Wilson said. 'They didn't have to go through the painful process of getting some people to agree in practice to things they had already agreed to in principle. They didn't have to sit for hour after hour going over the same old ground, inching towards a conclusion that somehow had to be squeezed into the principles we set out so clearly before we began this process. And they don't understand what we've achieved here. Oh, I know we didn't keep the Europeans from putting some irrational things in the treaty, but we did manage to force significant modifications out of them. I mean, if we'd written the treaty *they* wanted, the Germans would have gone home the minute they read it.'

'What are you going to do about the British?' House asked.

'Hah! The British! Lloyd George is as slippery as an eel. I never know when to count on him because he turns somersaults all the time. His latest twist is to consult a British group that's made up of every kind of opinion, from reasonable to unreasonable, and they turn out to be unanimous in their funk!' He shook his head slowly. 'It makes me very tired. If they'd been rational to begin with, they wouldn't have needed to have funked at the end.'

'Secretary Lansing has suggested that the best course would be for us to draw up some kind of memorandum of the points that might be conceded in redrafting the treaty. We're only talking about minor modifications, really.'

'I'm not inclined to do that,' Wilson said wearily. 'It would just emphasize the differences between us. Look, if they can show me clauses that are clearly unjust and contrary to the principles we've expressed, then I'm prepared to consider changing them. But I'm not going to change anything just because the Germans think it's too hard on them.'

House sighed. 'It would be a pity if, after all this, we ended up with a bad treaty.'

Wilson regarded him suspiciously. 'I hope you're with us on this, Colonel,' he said menacingly. 'What we're dealing with here is a Europe that is worn out by war, and where popular passions are naturally running high. In those circumstances, what's a good treaty? The main thing is, we achieved the League of Nations. Oh, they tried to separate it from the treaty, but I wouldn't move on that. The treaty is something for today, but the League is the future, and once its power is established the old, destructive style of diplomacy will be gone for ever. It really doesn't matter if some parts of the treaty are bad, so long as we have the League. Rather a bad treaty than a bad peace.'

When he returned to the American delegation's headquarters at the Hôtel Crillon, Colonel House found Robert Lansing waiting for him, anxious to know what had happened at his meeting with the President. House summarized their conversation.

Lansing walked to the tall window and looked out over the Place de la Concorde.

'That's where the guillotine used to be,' he said. 'Louis XVI and Marie Antoinette were executed there, then later Robespierre. I was reading something about it the other day. One of the revolutionaries, it seems, as he was being led to his execution, said to the judges who had condemned him: "I die at a moment when the people have lost their reason. You'll die on the day they recover it." I wonder when people will recover their reason?'

He turned back to face House. 'The Congress will never accept it, you know.'

'What?' House asked.

'The League of Nations, the treaty . . . None of it.'

At the War Ministry behind the Quai d'Orsay, Clemenceau was in conclave with André Tardieu.

'It's unthinkable,' he said firmly. 'We cannot make any more concessions. I've spent weeks defending our interests against the Americans and the British – not forgetting those damned Italians – and I cannot move another inch. I've done the best I can that was consistent with maintaining a balance between what we expected and our relationship with our allies. Unless they stand firm now, I'll have to go before the Chamber of Deputies and resign.'

'Do you think they will stand firm?' asked Tardieu, 'or will President Wilson eventually give in to the pressure of Lloyd George?'

A week had passed since the British Prime Minister had demanded his modifications to the treaty. They had been discussed every day, but no agreement had as yet been reached about how to respond to the German note.

'Lloyd George is almost hysterical,' said Clemenceau. '"But they won't sign, they won't sign!" That's all he keeps saying. I tell you, for the man the British say won the war, he's behaving very much like a man who lost it. I can't understand why he's so afraid of the Germans.'

'I'm not sure it's the Germans he's afraid of,' Tardieu observed. 'I think he's afraid of public opinion in Britain, and I think he's concerned at what he sees as the advantages we've gained from the treaty.'

Clemenceau laughed. 'It's little enough, God knows. I'm perfectly well aware that President Poincaré and Marshal Foch are less than delighted with what I've been able to achieve. But the occupation of the Saar and the Rhineland is important, and so is Poland. I'd rather support the Poles than the Italians, and, as for the Rhineland, well, we're there for fifteen years anyway, and we can stay there for a hundred years if necessary, until the Boches have paid whatever they owe us, thanks to the treaty I negotiated.'

'That,' said Tardieu, 'is what Lloyd George is worried about. He thinks the arrangements give us too much power in Europe.'

'Well, I'm not going to move on the Rhineland, and we must make sure President Wilson doesn't move either. Have you got that letter for Colonel House? . . . Read it to me.'

Tardieu read: 'Very grave mistakes have been made during the past week, and there is only just time to repair them.

'For five months, the heads of governments and their experts have studied the terms of the peace to be imposed on Germany. They have reached an agreement and they have communicated to the Germans a text which, if it does not yet bind Count von Brockdorff-Rantzau, unquestionably binds the Allies.'

'That's good,' said Clemenceau. 'I like that. Go on, please.'

'Could the Allies suppose that this text would be satisfactory to Germany? Of course not. However, they adopted it. Germany protests, as it was certain she would, and immediately a modification of the text is undertaken. I say this is a confession of weakness and of a lack of seriousness for which the Allied governments will pay dearly in terms of public opinion.'

Clemenceau nodded approval.

Tardieu went on reading: 'Is it an impossible treaty? Is it an unjust treaty? Count von Brockdorff-Rantzau believes that it is. If we change it, we admit that we think as he does. What a condemnation of the work we have done during the past sixteen weeks!

'Mr Lloyd George has said, "But they will not sign and we shall have a thousand difficulties." That is an argument we heard so often during the war – after the battle of the Marne, after Verdun, after the German offensive in the spring of 1918, people said in all our countries, "Let us make peace to avoid difficulties." We did not listen to them, and we did well not to do so. We went on with the war and we won it. Shall we have less heart for peace than we had for war?'

'Excellent, my boy, excellent,' Clemenceau said. 'You're right. They're behaving just like the defeatists who tried to undermine us in 1917, in fact almost to the day we won.'

Tardieu's letter went on to refute each of Lloyd George's four proposals in turn, and concluded: 'I would not have the moral position of the Allies sacrificed to the Brockdorff-Rantzau memorandum. I would not have them subjected to the unjustifiable humiliation of admitting that the peace built

by them after more than four months of incessant labour is, as
Germany asserts, an unjust and impossible peace, because that
is the opposite of the truth.'

Clemenceau smiled. 'That, my friend – as President Wilson
is so fond of saying – is the voice of reason.'

'Let's hope President Wilson listens to it,' said Tardieu.

'The President,' Clemenceau assured him, 'is a very tired
man, and, I suspect, a somewhat disillusioned one. He'll
listen.'

Wilson, in fact, needed little persuasion to stand his ground.
Those round him had noticed that, since a mysterious illness
had laid him low for a week or two in April – his doctor had
said it was influenza, but it had appeared to be rather more
serious than that – the President had become even less open to
advice, even more prone to react indignantly to any hint of
criticism, even readier to sense disloyalty. That was why he
had dismissed the opposition to the draft treaty among the
junior members of the American delegation. It was also the
main reason why its senior members were disinclined to
propose any serious attempt to accommodate the objections of
the Germans.

'The problem,' Colonel House said cautiously, 'is that even
if we did concede that certain parts of the treaty were too
harsh, any process of revision might lead to the unravelling of
the whole thing.'

Thus, when the leaders assembled again to discuss the
matter, the President was in no mood to make significant
alterations of the sort Lloyd George was suggesting.

'It appears,' Wilson said, 'that the territorial dispositions are the most serious matter so far as the Germans are concerned.'

He had sent for maps of central and eastern Europe, and these had been spread out on the floor. The President of the United States and the Prime Ministers of Britain and France were on their knees by the maps.

'Especially the case of Upper Silesia,' said Lloyd George, leaning forward to jab his finger on the area of one of the maps where territory that had been part of Germany was now marked as belonging to the new state of Poland. 'That's why I feel offering a plebiscite there might make the Germans more inclined to sign the treaty.'

'I disagree,' Wilson replied. 'I've always regarded Upper Silesia as being unmistakably Polish territory.'

'Well, a plebiscite would determine whether the inhabitants take the same view.'

'But I doubt whether there could be a free vote because of the significant influence of the German businessmen and big landowners in the region.'

'I'm simply arguing the case on the basis of the commitment to self-determination in the Fourteen Points,' Lloyd George said. 'As for the vote, that could be held under the supervision of a League of Nations commission and the presence of Allied troops to prevent intimidation.'

Clemenceau interrupted. 'That would only play into the hands of the Germans. They'd say *we* were preventing a free vote if we had troops there.'

'Of course,' Wilson said, 'there's also the attitude of the

Poles to take into account.'

'The Poles?' sneered Lloyd George. 'What did they do in the war? When they fought at all, it was actually against their own freedom, which they've eventually achieved not by their own exertions, but by the blood of millions of Frenchmen, Englishmen, Italians and Americans. I don't think we need worry too much about satisfying the Poles.'

Wilson snapped: 'And why do we need to worry about satisfying the Germans?'

'For the simple reason that a small concession or two might encourage them to sign the treaty.'

Up to that point, Clemenceau had said little, preferring merely to enjoy the confrontation between Wilson and Lloyd George. Now he saw that there might be an advantage to be gained by intervention. It might strengthen his hand later, when he could not afford to make concessions. With some difficulty, he rose from his kneeling position.

'Look,' he said, 'if it helps to resolve this matter, I'm prepared to support the idea of a plebiscite in Upper Silesia. It might well be the thing that ensures the German government will sign the treaty – and, even if it isn't, it could help gain support for it among the German public, which would make it easier for us to put pressure on the government.'

At this, Wilson and Lloyd George also stood up. The President looked at Clemenceau in amazement. 'But I thought . . .'

Clemenceau airily waved his hand. 'We have to reach an agreement.'

The President considered this for a moment. 'Very well.

We'll bring in experts to consider the arrangements for a plebiscite.'

The next of Lloyd George's proposed amendments to be settled concerned the payment of reparations.

'The Germans,' Wilson said, 'apparently want to fix a sum. My advisers also want a fixed sum. The amounts may be different, but it seems to me there's the prospect of reaching an accommodation. Now, I know the political difficulties you have with this, so we've considered the matter and we would be prepared to go as high as thirty billion dollars, or six thousand million sterling. That's not too far above what the Germans seem to be proposing, though there is a question about interest payments.'

Lloyd George shook his head. 'The simple fact is that any figure we put in the treaty that wouldn't frighten the Germans would be lower than anything the people of Britain or France could accept, given the present state of public opinion in both countries.'

'And,' Clemenceau added, 'there's the little matter of how that sum would be divided, particularly between France and Britain. I don't relish that debate.'

'I think our first proposal is the best solution,' Lloyd George said. 'The Germans undertake all restoration work and we insert in the treaty a figure covering the other aspects of reparations.'

Clemenceau snorted. 'And how do you think we would feel about having gangs of German workmen in northern France for two or three years? I tell you, there would be riots.'

'In that case, we have our second proposal. Germany is to

offer a sum based on a proper estimate of the costs of restoration, or else the clause in the treaty referring to the reparation commission comes into effect.'

Wilson said: 'I still favour a fixed amount. But if you both feel a German offer is appropriate . . .' He looked at Clemenceau, who shrugged. 'Well, I'm prepared to agree to that.'

There was a brief discussion of Lloyd George's desire to admit Germany to the League of Nations at a date earlier than allowed for in the draft treaty. Wilson sought evidence that the new German government was really as representative and democratic as it pretended to be, while Clemenceau required that it prove its stability and promise to honour its international obligations. They compromised on promising the Germans League membership 'in the near future'.

Lloyd George was beginning to feel pleased with himself. The voice of moderation, as represented by him, was making steady progress. But it was about to run into Clemenceau's voice of reason.

'The fifteen-year occupation of the Rhineland is not negotiable,' *le Tigre* said firmly.

'But it's purely a political gesture,' Wilson protested. 'When you think about it, the occupation will come to an end at just about the time when Germany will have recovered her military strength.'

'The occupation is indispensable,' Clemenceau insisted. 'It's our guarantee of payment of the indemnities, a reminder to the Germans of their responsibilities.'

Lloyd George tried one last appeal. 'You have the Anglo-

American military guarantee against aggression, you have the arrangement in the Saarland, you have the demilitarized zone on the right bank of the Rhine . . . I must say, when I go back to Parliament, it's going to want to know why France is granted a long occupation of the Rhineland when the other guarantees are already in place.'

Clemenceau was immovable. 'I've made a concession on Upper Silesia, I've supported the modification to the reparation arrangements, I've agreed to German admission to the League at an early date, even though France would not be comfortable living in such close cohabitation. I can go no further. If, in the course of time, the Germans behave properly and honour their obligations, there might conceivably be a case for ending the occupation . . .'

'Can't we offer them that as a concession?' asked Lloyd George.

'No. That part of the treaty must remain exactly as it is.'

Wilson said: 'Suppose we suggest that the occupation force will be reduced to a minimum as soon as the disarmament of Germany is complete, and that, under certain conditions, we would consider an earlier termination?'

'If that's what you want to tell the Germans, and you think it will make their signature more likely, so be it. But there can be no modification of the terms in the treaty. The Germans will sign it, I assure you. What choice do they have?'

*III*

——

Count Ulrich von Brockdorff-Rantzau and his delegation were on a train heading for Germany. Two days earlier, they had been handed the Allies' response to the objections they had lodged against the peace treaty, and when the contents had been communicated to their government, the order had come for them to return home immediately. As their train rattled northwards, they discussed the four small concessions that had been the sole result of their stay in Paris, their fifteen memoranda and their written statement.

'I'm afraid,' said Brockdorff-Rantzau, 'that it's no more and no less than I expected. I did hope that the Americans and the British might bend, but it was always obvious that the French would be prepared to enforce the severe terms that were presented to us, and it seems they have won the day.'

'Of course, it's still completely unacceptable,' said the Foreign Ministry veteran Haniel von Haimhäusen. 'Even if we did sign it, the treaty is unworkable.'

'I suppose that's an argument for signing it,' Brockdorff-Rantzau replied. 'But I'm still going to recommend to the Cabinet that we don't, unless any of you want to convince me that we should do otherwise.'

The others all indicated that they had no such idea.

'I still think time is on our side,' the Foreign Minister went on. 'You've seen the kind of disturbances that are going on among the workers in France – the strikes, the marches, the demonstrations. In Italy, it appears to be worse, and even in England there's discontent everywhere. The Balkans? Well, anything could happen, and we know that the Bolshevists have taken over Hungary. It seems to me that the Entente powers are in a very precarious position, and the longer we can hold out, the more precarious it might become.'

'You think that might prompt them to offer better terms in the end?' Haimhäusen asked.

'I've always said that what we need is to sit down with them round a conference table. By keeping us at arm's length, they can pretend we're pariahs – that's why they have to block our admission to the League of Nations, to make the rest of the world think we can't be dealt with. We're to blame for the war, they say, so we've put ourselves beyond the pale. Once we can break through that barrier, things could be very different.'

Haimhäusen grunted. 'That might take some doing, if their latest note is anything to go by.' He read from the document they were taking home:

> *The conduct of Germany is almost unexampled in human history. The terrible responsibility which lies at her door can be seen in the fact that no fewer than seven million dead lie buried in Europe, while more than twenty million others carry upon them the evidence of wounds and suffering because Germany saw fit to gratify her lust for tyranny by resort to war.*

'I'll bet that was written by a Frenchman,' Haimhäusen said, 'or at least dictated by one. I mean, it's hardly what we expected from President Wilson's "just peace", is it?'

He went on reading:

> *Justice is what the German delegation asks for, and what*
> *Germany has been promised. Justice is what Germany shall*
> *have. But it must be justice for all. There must be justice for*
> *the dead and wounded and those who have been orphaned*
> *and bereaved . . .*

'Oh, yes, it's *their* justice all right. Don't *we* have dead and wounded, and orphans and widows?'

They fell silent as the train thundered on, and the light began to fade outside the carriage windows. The thought nagged at them that Germany's real guilt lay in her defeat, or rather, and more painful still, her surrender. They worried, too, about what they would find when they reached home. Nobody seemed really to be running the country, except perhaps the army and the Freikorps, who were still hunting down Spartacists and other assorted revolutionaries bent on exploiting the chaos that had spread through the country in the wake of the armistice. The government represented by the Paris delegation had little power, except for the support of the army, and barely more authority as a mass of new political parties struggled for control of the provinces from which they had sprung.

'We don't even really know what the people think about the peace treaty,' Brockdorff-Rantzau said at last. 'They're too busy trying to rebuild their own lives among all the confusion to take much interest in what's going to happen in the future.'

'I think,' Haimhäusen said, 'that the people are beginning to wish for peace at almost any price.'

'That's what we have to avoid,' replied Brockdorff-Rantzau.

It was during the early hours of the morning of Wednesday 18 June that the small group arrived in the old city of Weimar, where the government was still wrestling with its new constitution. After a short rest, a wash and shave, and a change of clothes, Brockdorff-Rantzau led his men to the City Hall to report to Chancellor Scheidemann and his senior ministers. The Cabinet, they discovered, was split down the middle.

'I haven't changed my position,' Scheidemann announced. 'I said the terms of the treaty were unacceptable as soon as I saw them, and there is no reason to change that view in light of the insulting so-called modifications the Entente has now presented to us.'

Matthias Erzberger, the unfortunate man who had been sent to sign the armistice at Compiègne, said: 'Except that time is running out. They've given us a week to sign or suffer the consequences. There are now only five days left.'

'And just what do you think those consequences might be?' asked Brockdorff-Rantzau. 'The Americans aren't going to send troops against us, and neither are the British. Their public wouldn't stand for it.'

'There's still the French,' Erzberger countered, 'and Hindenburg has made it clear to us that, while we could fight on our eastern frontiers, there's no hope of resisting any Entente action against us in the west. And there are our own people to think about, too. More and more of them are saying we should simply accept the treaty and get it over with.'

'I say we can't possibly accept,' von Brockdorff-Rantzau argued. 'We just need another two or three months of negotiation. Probably we won't achieve much in the way of concessions, but we have to salvage what we can. We must delay.'

'Let's vote on it,' said Scheidemann.

But there was no majority.

'We'll have to see what the Reichstag thinks,' Scheidemann said grimly.

That evening, Scheidemann canvassed opinion among the supporters of his Socialist–Centre coalition. Two-thirds of the Socialist deputies were in favour of signing the treaty. The next day, Erzberger found, as he had expected, a huge majority of his Centre Party resolved to accept the treaty, though without clauses that placed an obligation on Germany to hand over men the Allies considered to be war criminals. They, together with the Independent Socialists, who also favoured signing, represented nearly half of German voters. Scheidemann went to see the President.

'I can only be sure of commanding a majority in the Reichstag,' he said, 'if I accept support from the deputies on the extreme right, which I clearly dare not do. I believe that, in the circumstances, I have no choice but to offer the resignation of my government.'

Ebert fiddled with his moustache. 'I think you're probably right,' he said. 'Look, I sympathize with you. I don't believe we *should* sign this damned treaty without serious changes to it. But if we were going to resist, the whole country would have to stand firmly behind us, and everything suggests that wouldn't be the case. Quite frankly, I'm less concerned with what the treaty says than with unifying our people and restoring some order.'

'Then you'd better look for a Chancellor who's willing and able to persuade the Reichstag to give him authority to sign the treaty. In all conscience, I can't do that, and there seems to be no other way.'

Scheidemann, Brockdorff-Rantzau and all the other members of the coalition Cabinet left office on 20 June – though Matthias Erzberger merely swapped one administration for another, becoming vice-chancellor to another former minister, the Socialist Max Bauer. Together, two days later, on Sunday 22 June, they went to the Reichstag to propose acceptance of the treaty with the proviso that the clauses relating to Germany's guilt for the war and the extradition of 'war criminals' were removed.

Even before the votes were counted, Bauer sent a cable to Paris:

> The German Government will sign the Treaty of Peace, without, however, recognizing thereby that the German people was the author of the war, and without undertaking any responsibility for delivering persons in accordance with Articles 227 to 230.

President Wilson's lucky number came up again. Only thirteen members of the Reichstag voted against acceptance of the treaty on the terms Bauer had outlined. Five more abstained, and two hundred and thirty-seven voted in favour of signing.

But the Allies had no intention of letting anything slip through their fingers. They were well aware that the legal designation of Germany as the sole guilty party in the war was essential to their claims for reparations. For the Germans it might be a matter of honour. To the Allies it was simply a question of cash. And if Germany was guilty, it was obvious that she must harbour criminals – public opinion demanded that someone be punished. Bauer's cable received an immediate reply:

> The time for discussion has passed. No qualification or reservation in regard to the treaty can be accepted. Less than twenty-four hours remains for final acceptance or rejection of the treaty.

Bauer had shown his hand too early. He had no mandate for signing the treaty as it stood. He telephoned Haimhäusen, who remained at the Foreign Ministry, and asked him to seek a forty-eight-hour delay to the Allies' deadline. Early in the morning of 23 June the reply came from Paris: *No further extension*.

President Ebert hastily called together all the leaders of the Reichstag parties. Vice-Chancellor Erzberger, who had secured his party's crucial acceptance vote on the basis that the most offensive clauses of the treaty would not be adopted, could not guarantee that the vote would go the same way in this new situation.

'Will anyone,' he asked, 'form a new government that would be prepared to reject the treaty and accept the consequences?'

No one, not even the most extreme nationalists, would rise to the challenge.

'In that case,' Ebert said, 'we must regard yesterday's vote as authorization to sign the treaty as it stands.'

'But I want to make it clear,' Erzberger insisted, eyeing the nationalists, 'that no one should question the patriotism of those who voted for signing.'

The three-day-old government of the as yet immature Republic of Germany, with not even a constitution to its name, found itself with no alternative but to give way to the demands of the two most powerful nations on earth. The pain and humiliation was evident as the new Foreign Minister, Hermann Müller, dictated the cable to be sent to Paris:

'The German Republic is ready to sign the treaty imposed by the Allied and Associated Powers, but in yielding to overwhelming force the German people will not sacrifice their honour, nor will they ever cease to regard the peace terms as an injustice without parallel.'

Five days had passed since the Allied leaders had finally been assured that their victory over Germany was complete. Now it was time to set the seal on that victory. The Parisian sky was overcast, with the threat of rain, but this day – Saturday 28 June 1919 – was to be a glorious one, whatever the weather.

At his apartment in the Rue Franklin, Georges Clemenceau, as he ate his favourite breakfast of porridge with meat – it was a peasant dish from the Vendée that reminded him of his boyhood – could not resist chuckling. He had always resented the fact that the British had insisted on seizing the German battle fleet as part of the armistice terms. Now, through carelessness, stupidity or their sheer arrogance, they had lost it.

After the armistice, the Germans had been instructed to sail their High Seas Fleet to Scapa Flow, a huge, natural deepwater harbour in the Orkney Islands, off the north coast of Scotland. With its narrow entrances, the Flow provided the perfect prison camp for the Germans' eleven battleships, five battle cruisers, eight light cruisers and fifty destroyers.

They were a magnificent sight, these great predators of the seas, as they lay at anchor, the waves lapping gently at their sleek but now utterly unthreatening sides.

'All we need to guard them is three trawlers,' a British admiral had boasted at the time.

But, as the German Cabinet in Weimar discussed the final peace terms Brockdorff-Rantzau had brought back from Paris, the commander of the imprisoned fleet, Vice-Admiral Ludwig von Reuter, was holding a meeting with his senior officers.

'You've seen the conditions the Entente is trying to impose,' he said crisply. 'They are clearly an affront to German honour.'

'Then no doubt our damned politicians will accept them,' one of the captains said sarcastically.

'I don't think so,' Reuter declared. 'No German could sign such a treaty.' Imprisoned on his battleship, he knew almost nothing about what was happening in Berlin. 'We must assume, gentlemen, that the treaty will be rejected by our government and that the war will recommence within a few days.'

His listeners gasped.

'Does that mean, Sir, we must prepare to break out?' someone asked.

Reuter shook his head. 'That would be impossible.'

'But there are only the trawlers guarding us,' said another officer.

Reuter held up his hand. 'Gentlemen, gentlemen! With the skeleton crews we have here, we could barely muster enough men to operate one ship. That would hardly be enough to take on the entire British navy.'

He paused, then said: 'However, it is our duty to ensure our vessels do not fall into enemy hands. I have called you here to issue my last order of the day.'

At one o'clock on the bright, sunny afternoon of 21 June, following Reuter's order, the German navy carried out its last action of the war. The few remaining sailors of the High Seas Fleet scurried about the bowels of their vessels and opened the valves that would flood them and send them slowly to the bottom of the sea.

On the watching British trawlers, it was some time before anyone noticed. One of the deck officers, making his rounds after lunch, glanced idly in the direction of the nearest German ships. He stopped, and frowned. There seemed to be something wrong with the way they were lying in the water. The officer raised his binoculars.

'Good God!' he cried. 'They're sinking! The blighters are

scuttling them! Sound the alarm . . .'

Clemenceau chortled as he imagined the scene. 'I couldn't resist teasing Lloyd George,' he told his secretary, Jean Martet, when the young man called to see him on the fateful morning of 28 June. 'And they call themselves the world's greatest naval power! The whole world is laughing at them now. Lloyd George is so embarrassed. He's been rushing round asking everybody whether they think the British have been careless. Careless? I ask you! I'm furious, of course, and Foch is beside himself. But I can't help seeing the funny side. I told the fellow, when he was trying to water down the peace treaty, that we knew the Germans far better than he did. So much for the spoils of war, eh?'

'Well,' said Martet, 'this afternoon it will all be over.'

'Something will be over, but I'm not entirely sure what,' Clemenceau replied enigmatically.

The ceremony he had begun to arrange even before the peace conference had started, took place, as he had intended, at the Palace of Versailles at three o'clock. Clemenceau was there early, mingling with the assembled dignitaries, the political leaders of the world in their top hats; the generals and admirals, dripping with gold braid and medals; the hundreds of invited guests wearing their fashionable finery. The atmosphere was heavy with the weight of history, symbolized by the blue Napoleonic uniforms of the lancers ranged round the Cour Royale, yet there was an unmistakable air of unreality about it all – and no sign of the euphoria that had accompanied the announcement of the armistice.

Lloyd George arrived.

'This has been a wonderful time,' he said to Clemenceau.

*Le Tigre* regarded him quizzically. Then he said: 'Yes. Happy days, when our opponents were simply those provided by the nature of things. I think we gave to the peace the same measure of effort that the war demanded of us. What an undertaking it has been, and what audacity on our part to have attempted it. I only hope it was worth it.'

Vittorio Emanuele Orlando came, too, on his last day as Prime Minister of Italy. The country was in turmoil, with strikes, riots and marches paralysing an economy crippled by the war, and inflamed by the national sense of disappointment at the fact that, while others had received the rewards for their sacrifices, Italy seemed to have suffered for nothing, humiliated and ignored by the people who called themselves her allies. The Big Three had refused to budge on the extension of Italy beyond her natural borders. They had ceded the formerly Austrian, and largely German-speaking, South Tyrol, which seemed to serve merely to underline the inconsistency of their ludicrous 'ethnic' principles, but so far as the eastern Adriatic was concerned, the new Italy stopped at the Istrian peninsula and did not include Fiume. Orlando had had no choice but to step down. Now, it appeared, the future belonged to the likes of d'Annunzio and Mussolini.

Finally, there was President Wilson, the top hat making him look even taller than usual alongside the three short men in whose company he had spent almost all of the past five months. As he strode proudly into the Cour Royale, the clouds above parted and the whole splendid scene was bathed in sunlight.

The Big Four crossed the courtyard and entered the palace by the Vestibule de Marbre on the left-hand side, passing the apartments of the Dauphin to mount the double flight of marble stairs to the first floor. The staircases were lined with Republican Guards, uniformed in blue and scarlet, with plumed silver helmets and shining steel cuirasses, their swords drawn. The huge Salle des Glaces – two hundred feet long, thirty-three wide and forty-three feet high, with its seventeen arched windows and matching row of mirrors opposite – was hung with the flags of the victors, the French tricolour in pride of place among the mementoes of Louis XIV's seventeenth-century wars against Holland, Spain and, of course, Germany.

The Allied leaders were seated behind a long table on a dais forming three sides of a square, the other members of the delegations, guests and journalists on rows of red and gold benches, though many had to stand. The treaty lay on a rosewood table on the fourth side of the square, where there were empty seats for the signatories. The great hall was abuzz with excited chatter, until Clemenceau rose to his feet, directly below a plaque proclaiming '*Le Roi gouverne par lui-même*'.

In a voice clear and resonant with pride, Clemenceau said: 'Please bring in the Germans.'

A deep silence fell upon the room, punctuated by the clatter of boots as four Guards officers marched in with drawn swords. Behind them came Hermann Müller, pale-faced and bespectacled, his head bowed, and Johannes Bell, long-haired and holding himself perfectly erect – appropriately, a lieutenant of Matthias Erzberger, the man who had signed the armistice. The officers marched out, then the whole room reverberated to the clash of steel as, in a symbolic gesture, every guardsman outside sheathed his sword.

Clemenceau said sonorously: 'We are in complete agreement. I have the honour to ask Messieurs the German Plenipotentiaries to sign the treaty.'

The Germans, unsure of what was expected of them, jumped to their feet and bowed. Clemenceau asked them to sit down, and his words were translated into German.

As Müller and Bell got to their feet again and came forward to sign the document, the silence became oppressive. One of the journalists sitting by the windows turned to a colleague.

'You can almost feel the hatred,' he whispered.

The Germans bowed again, and left the room. As they did so, the cannon at the military academy of Saint-Cyr began to boom and the great fountains in the palace gardens burst into life for the first time since 1914.

President Wilson was the first of the Allied leaders to sign the treaty, followed by Lloyd George, the Dominion prime ministers, Clemenceau and Orlando. The Great War was now officially at an end.

The ceremony over, the leaders descended the ornate staircases and emerged into the sunlit courtyard. They smiled broadly as they accepted the congratulations of many who had witnessed this extraordinary spectacle.

'Well,' said Wilson, 'we now have the means to confront and to settle the problems that may arise in the future. The League of Nations is the practical statesman's hope of success.'

Clemenceau turned to André Tardieu.

'You know,' he said, 'at one time I was afraid of achieving victory without peace. Now I fear a peace without victory just as much.'

Marshal Foch, standing nearby, overheard him.

'You're right,' he said sourly. 'This treaty is far too lenient towards the Germans. We'll be at war again within a generation, mark my words.'

In Germany, the self-styled Independent Soviet Republic of Bavaria was no more – the rogue bands of soldiers who made up the Freikorps had seen to that. Now, in the summer of 1919, although there was a government of sorts, the old kingdom was to all intents and purposes under military rule, administered by a brutal combination of what remained of the regular army and a motley collection of unofficial units such as the *Einwohnerwehr*, or militia, the Oberland League, the Flag of the Old Reich Association, the Iron Fist, the Defence and Defiance League of the German Race, and one or two surviving Freikorps columns.

But the purpose of this ill-assorted junta was not simply to maintain order, as it had been during the days of the 'Red terror' a few months earlier. The officers at the headquarters of Bavarian Group Command IV in Munich had embarked on a determined political campaign designed to restore national pride after the shock of defeat and the humiliation of the Treaty of Versailles. So far as they were concerned, the cornerstone of the new Germany that would be built on the ruins of the old was the army. Bavaria had been the first province to overthrow the old order that had let Germany down so badly. Now, having recovered its senses after a brief and disastrous flirtation with Bolshevism, it would be the first to establish a new order whose courage would not fail.

Political education was the key, and Group Command had created its own Propaganda Department, headed by the energetic Captain Mayr, who, among other things, organized at the university a programme of lectures on 'civic thinking' designed to propagate nationalistic theories of history, politics and economics. One of the most promising students on this course was a thirty-year-old corporal who had served with some distinction on the Western Front, before being sent home suffering from gas blindness just a week or two ahead of the armistice.

The young infantryman – short, slim and with a waxed, Prussian-style moustache – had proved himself enthusiastic in debate and more than capable of holding an audience when he took the floor. Captain Mayr had heard good reports of him from the lecturers, and eventually he chose him to become part of the Propaganda Department's latest project, an 'enlightenment squad' that would work with returning soldiers to make sure they would not be seduced by the undercurrents of Marxism that still swirled through the half-life that was post-war Munich.

The captain soon had good reason to feel pleased with his choice. The corporal had absorbed like a sponge the messages of the army's 'civic thinking', and he was able to reproduce them in a way that both appealed to and seemed to convince his disillusioned fellow-soldiers.

'He speaks in a popular manner that is easily understood,' reported one of the young man's superiors, 'and he has an excellent turn of phrase which resonates with the men. Denunciations of "the November criminals", the "shame of Versailles" and the "corrupt creed of internationalism" go down particularly well. He has a remarkable ability to assimilate ideas one day and transmit them in a very forceful way the next.'

By the end of August, Captain Mayr had singled out this exemplary corporal for special duties. He was to make contact with the bewildering array of radical, right-wing political groups that had sprung up in Munich in the aftermath of the Bolshevist shock, and to try to persuade them to come together in a definite, nationalist movement.

Following orders, the corporal visited a beer-hall on 12 September to attend a meeting of a small, newly formed party that espoused an innovative philosophy combining nationalist sentiments and socialist impulses. He was impressed by what he heard, and took part in the discussion group that followed the meeting. His contribution was notable enough to prompt one of the party's leaders, a machinist named Anton Drexler, to give the soldier a pamphlet he had written entitled *My Political Awakening*.

It proved to be an awakening for the corporal. Before the end of the month, he had been elected to the committee of the party, which intended to put to good use the skills he had learned under Captain Mayr's tuition, by placing him in charge of recruitment and propaganda.

The fledgling movement called itself the *Deutsche Arbeiterpartei*, or DAP – the German Workers' Party.

The little corporal would rise within a few short years to

become the party leader, dedicated to wiping out the shameful memory of the Treaty of Versailles, 'tearing the treaty to shreds', and regaining everything Germany had lost – and more – because of it.

His name was Adolf Hitler.

# The Treaty of Versailles

*The following are the main articles of the Treaty, as they applied to Germany, extracted from the official printed version of the document signed on 28 June 1919.*

## Left Bank of the Rhine

ARTICLE 42: Germany is forbidden to maintain or construct any fortifications either on the left bank of the Rhine or on the right bank to the west of a line drawn 50 kilometres to the east of the Rhine.

ARTICLE 43: In the area defined above the maintenance and the assembly of armed forces, either permanently or temporarily, and military manoeuvres of any kind, as well as the upkeep of all permanent works for mobilization, are in the same way forbidden.

ARTICLE 44: In case Germany violates in any manner whatever the provisions of Articles 42 and 43, she shall be regarded as committing a hostile act against the Powers signatory of the present Treaty and as calculated to disturb the peace of the world.

## Saar Basin

ARTICLE 45: As compensation for the destruction of the coal mines in the north of France and as part payment towards the total reparation due from Germany for the damage resulting from the war, Germany cedes to France in full and absolute possession, with exclusive rights of exploitation, unencumbered and free from all debts and charges of any kind, the coal mines situated in the Saar Basin . . .

ARTICLE 49: Germany renounces in favour of the League of Nations, in the capacity of trustee, the government of the territory defined above. At the end of fifteen years from the coming into force of the present Treaty the inhabitants of the said territory shall be called upon to indicate the sovereignty under which they desire to be placed.

## Alsace-Lorraine

The High Contracting Parties, recognizing the moral obligation to redress the wrong done by Germany in 1871 both to the rights of France and to the wishes of the population of Alsace and Lorraine, which were separated from their country in spite of the solemn protest of their representatives at the Assembly of Bordeaux, agree upon the following . . .

ARTICLE 51: The territories which were ceded to Germany in accordance with the Preliminaries of Peace signed at Versailles on February 26, 1871, and the Treaty of Frankfurt of May 10, 1871, are restored to French sovereignty as from the date of the Armistice of November 11, 1918. The provisions of the Treaties establishing the delimitation of the frontiers before 1871 shall be restored.

## Czecho-Slovak State

ARTICLE 81: Germany, in conformity with the action already taken by the Allied and Associated Powers, recognizes the complete independence of the Czecho-Slovak State which will include the autonomous territory of the Ruthenians to the south of the Carpathians. Germany hereby recognizes the frontiers of this State as determined by the Principal Allied and Associated Powers and the other interested States.

ARTICLE 83: Germany renounces in favour of the Czecho-Slovak State all rights and title over the portion of Silesian territory defined as follows . . .

ARTICLE 84: German nationals habitually resident in any of the territories recognized as forming part of the Czecho-Slovak State will obtain Czecho-Slovak nationality ipso facto and lose their German nationality.

ARTICLE 85: Within a period of two years from the coming into force of the present Treaty, German nationals over eighteen years of age habitually resident in any of the territories recognized as forming part of the Czecho-Slovak State will be entitled to opt for German nationality. Czecho-Slovaks who are German nationals and are habitually resident in Germany will have a similar right to opt for Czecho-Slovak nationality.

Persons who have exercised the above right to opt must within the succeeding twelve months transfer their place of residence to the State for which they have opted.

## Poland

ARTICLE 87: Germany, in conformity with the action already taken by the Allied and Associated Powers, recognizes the complete independence of Poland, and renounces in her favour all rights and title over the territory bounded by the Baltic Sea, the eastern frontier of Germany as laid down in Article 27 of Part II (Boundaries of Germany) of the present Treaty . . .

ARTICLE 91: German nationals habitually resident in territories recognized as forming part of Poland will acquire Polish nationality ipso facto and will lose their German nationality. German nationals, however, or their descendants who became resident in these territories after January 1, 1908, will not acquire Polish nationality without a special authorization from the Polish State.

## East Prussia

ARTICLE 94: In the area between the southern frontier of East Prussia, as described in Article 28 of Part II (Boundaries of Germany) of the present Treaty, and the line described below, the inhabitants will be called upon to indicate by a vote the State to which they wish to belong.

ARTICLE 99: Germany renounces in favour of the Principal Allied and Associated Powers all rights and title over the territories included between the Baltic, the north-eastern frontier of East Prussia as defined in Article 28 of Part II (Boundaries of Germany) of the present Treaty and the former frontier between Germany and Russia. Germany undertakes to accept the settlement made by the Principal Allied and Associated Powers in regard to these territories, particularly in so far as concerns the nationality of the inhabitants.

## Free City of Danzig

ARTICLE 100: Germany renounces in favour of the Principal Allied and Associated Powers all rights and title over the territory comprised within the following limits: from the Baltic Sea southwards to the point where the principal channels of navigation of the Nogat and the Vistula (Weichsel) meet the boundary of East Prussia as described in Article 28 of Part II (Boundaries of Germany) of the present Treaty . . .

ARTICLE 102: The Principal Allied and Associated Powers undertake to establish the town of Danzig, together with the rest of the territory described in Article 100, as a Free City. It will be placed under the protection of the League of Nations.

## German Overseas Territories

ARTICLE 119: Germany renounces in favour of the Principal Allied and Associated Powers all her rights and titles over her overseas possessions.

ARTICLE 156: Germany renounces, in favour of Japan, all her rights, title and privileges . . . which she acquired in virtue of the Treaty concluded by her with China on March 6, 1898, and of all other arrangements relative to the Province of Shantung.

## Military Forces of Germany

ARTICLE 159: The German military forces shall be demobilized and reduced as prescribed hereinafter.

ARTICLE 160: By a date which must not be later than March 31, 1920, the German Army must not comprise more than seven divisions of infantry and three divisions of cavalry. After that date the total number of effectives in the Army of the States constituting Germany must not exceed 100,000 men, including officers and establishments of depots. The Army shall be devoted exclusively to the maintenance of order within the territory and to the control of the frontiers. The total effective strength of officers, including the personnel of staffs, whatever their composition, must not exceed four thousand . . .

## Responsibility for the War
ARTICLE 231: The Allied and Associated Governments affirm and Germany accepts the responsibility of Germany and her allies for causing all the loss and damage to which the Allied and Associated Governments and their nationals have been subjected as a consequence of the war imposed upon them by the aggression of Germany and her allies.

## Reparations
ARTICLE 232: The Allied and Associated Governments recognize that the resources of Germany are not adequate, after taking into account permanent diminutions of such resources which will result from other provisions of the present Treaty, to make complete reparation for all such loss and damage. The Allied and Associated Governments, however, require, and Germany undertakes, that she will make compensation for all damage done to the civilian population of the Allied and Associated Powers and to their property during the period of the belligerency of each as an

Allied or Associated Power against Germany by such aggression by land, by sea, and from the air . . .

In accordance with Germany's pledges, already given, as to complete restoration for Belgium, Germany undertakes, in addition to the compensation for damage elsewhere . . . provided for, as a consequence of the violation of the Treaty of 1839, to make reimbursement of all sums which Belgium has borrowed from the Allied and Associated Governments up to November 11, 1918, together with interest at the rate of five per cent per annum on such sums.

ARTICLE 233: The amount of the above damage for which compensation is to be made by Germany shall be determined by an Inter-Allied Commission, to be called the *Reparation Commission* . . .

This Commission shall consider the claims and give to the German Government a just opportunity to be heard.

The findings of the Commission as to the amount of damage defined as above shall be concluded and notified to the German Government on or before May 1, 1921, as representing the extent of that Government's obligations.

The Commission shall concurrently draw up a schedule of payments prescribing the time and manner for securing and discharging the entire obligation within a period of thirty years from May 1, 1921 . . .

ARTICLE 235: In order to enable the Allied and Associated Powers to proceed at once to the restoration of their industrial and economic life, pending the full determination of their claims, Germany shall pay in such instalments and in such manner (whether in gold, commodities, ships, securities or otherwise) as the Reparation Commission may fix, during 1919, 1920 and the first four months of 1921, the equivalent of 20,000,000,000 gold marks. Out of this sum the expenses of the armies of occupation subsequent to the Armistice of November 11, 1918, shall first be met, and such supplies of food and raw materials as may be judged by the Governments of the Principal Allied and Associated Powers to be essential to enable Germany to meet her obligations for reparation may also, with the approval of the said Governments, be paid out of the above sum. The balance shall be reckoned towards liquidation of the amounts due for reparation . . .

# *Further Reading*

The sources employed as raw material for the creation of *Hall of Mirrors* are too many and varied to list here – often fragmentary or used simply to illuminate some aspect of character or to sketch in elements of background. However, readers who have enjoyed this journey back to the formative years of the twentieth century might be interested in exploring them further, more deeply or in greater detail, in which case the following memoirs and historical works offer a range of information, analysis, perception and valuable insights.

Ambrosius, Lloyd E.: *Woodrow Wilson and the American Diplomatic Tradition*. Cambridge, 1987.

Arendt, Hannah: *Men in Dark Times*. New York, 1968.

Baden, Prince Maximilian von: *The Memoirs of Prince Max of Baden*. New York, 1928.

Baker, Ray Stannard: *Woodrow Wilson. Life and Letters* (8 vols). New York, 1927–1939. *Woodrow Wilson and the World Settlement*. New York, 1923.

Blake, Robert: *The Unknown Prime Minister: The Life and Times of Andrew Bonar Law*. London, 1955. *The Private Papers of Douglas Haig, 1914–1919* (ed.). London, 1952.

Chabod, Federico: *A History of Italian Fascism*. London, 1963.

Churchill, Winston S.: *The World Crisis, 1911–1918*. London, 1941.

Cooper, John Milton, Jr: *Pivotal Decades – The United States, 1900–1920*. New York, l990.

Cowles, V.S.: *The Kaiser*. New York, 1963.

Craig, Gordon A.: *Germany 1866–1945*. New York, 1981.

Dillon, E.J.: *The Inside Story of the Peace Conference*. New York, 1920.

Dugdale, Blanche E.: *Arthur James Balfour*. London, 1936.

Dunn, Captain J.C.: *The War the Infantry Knew*. London, 1987.

Epstein, Klaus: *Matthias Erzberger and the Dilemma of German Democracy*. Princeton, 1959.

Fermi, Laura: *Mussolini*. Chicago, 1961.

Ferrell, Robert H.: *Woodrow Wilson and World War I*. New York, 1985.

Fest, Joachim C.: *Hitler* (trans.). London, 1974.

Gelfand, Lawrence E.: *The Inquiry. American Preparations for Peace, 1917–1919*. Newhaven, 1963.

Goldstein, Erik: *Winning the Peace*. Oxford 1991.

Goodspeed, D.J.: *Ludendorff*. London, 1966.

Grant, A.J. and Temperley, Harold: *Europe in the Nineteenth and Twentieth Centuries*. London, 1939.

Halévy, Elie: *The World Crisis of 1914–1918*. Oxford, 1930.

Hankey, Lord: *The Supreme Control of the Paris Peace Conference, 1919*. London, 1963.

Heckscher, August: *Woodrow Wilson*. New York, 1991.

Hindenburg, Paul von: *Aus Meinem Leben*. Leipzig, 1920. And quoted in John Wheeler-Bennet's *Hindenburg, The Wooden Titan*. London, 1936.

Jenkins, Roy: *Asquith*. London, 1963.

Jones, Thomas: *Lloyd George*. London, 1951.

Keynes, John Maynard: *The Economic Consequences of the Peace*. New York, 1920.

Lansing, Robert L.: *The Peace Negotiations*. Boston, 1921. *The Big Four and Others at the Peace Conference*. Boston, 1921. *The War Memoirs of Robert Lansing*. Indianapolis, 1935.

Liddell Hart, B.H.: *The Real War, 1914–1918*. London, 1930. *Foch – the Man of Orleans*. London, 1937.

Link, Arthur S.: *The Papers of Woodrow Wilson*. Princeton, 1986.

Lloyd George, David: *The Truth About the Peace Treaties*. London, 1938. *Memoirs of the Peace Conference*. Yale, 1939.

Luckau, Alma: *The German Delegation at the Paris Peace Conference*. New York, 1941.

Ludendorff, Erich: *My War Memoirs*. London, 1920.

Martet, Jean: *Clemenceau* (trans.). London, 1930.

Mayer, Arno J.: *Politics and Diplomacy of Peacemaking*. London, 1967.

Monelli, Paolo: *Mussolini: An Intimate Life*. London, 1953.

Nettl, J.P.: *Rosa Luxemburg*. Oxford, 1966.

Nicolson, Harold: *Peacemaking at Paris 1919*. London, 1938.

Nordholdt, Jan Willem Schulte.: *Woodrow Wilson, A Life for World Peace*. Berkeley, 1991.

Owen, Frank: *Tempestuous Journey: Lloyd George, His Life and Times*. London, 1954.

Palmer, Alan W.: *The Kaiser – Warlord of the Second Reich*. London, 1978.

Pound, Reginald and Harmsworth, Geoffrey: *Northcliffe*. London, 1959.

Price, Morgan Philips: *Dispatches from the Weimar Republic* (ed. Tania Rose). London, 1999.

Riddell, George A: *Lord Riddell's Intimate Diary of the Peace Conference and After*. New York, 1934.

Rossi, A.: *The Rise of Italian Fascism*. London, 1938.

Seton Watson, Christopher: *Italy from Liberalism to Fascism*. London, 1967.

Seymour, Charles (ed.): *The Intimate Papers of Colonel House*. Boston, 1926–28.

Smith, Denis Mack: *Mussolini*. New York, 1982.

Steed, Henry Wickham: *Through Thirty Years, 1892–1922*. London, 1924.

Stevenson, Frances: *The Years That Are Past*. London, 1967. *Lloyd George. A Diary* (ed. A.J.P. Taylor). London, 1971.

Sylvester, A.J.: *The Real Lloyd George*. London, 1947.

Tardieu, André: *The Truth About the Treaty*. Paris, 1921.

Taylor, A.J.P.: *The First World War*. London, 1963.

Temperley, H.W.V. (ed.): *A History of the Peace Conference of Paris* (6 vols.). London, 1920–1924.

Terraine, John: *Douglas Haig: The Educated Soldier*. London, 1963, reissued 1990.

Thomson, Malcolm: *David Lloyd George: The Official Biography*. London, 1949.

Toynbee, Arnold: *The World After the Peace Conference*. Oxford, 1924.

Waldman, Eric: *The Spartacist Uprising of 1919*. Milwaukee, 1958.

Wilson, Trevor (ed.): *The Political Diaries of C.P. Scott, 1911–1928*. London, 1970.

Zweig, Stefan: *The World of Yesterday*. London, 1943.

On the Internet, the full text of the Treaty of Versailles, accompanied by many maps and interesting illustrations, may be found on the website of the Historical Department of the University of San Diego:

http://history.acusd.edu/gen/text/versaillestreaty/
vercontents.html

# *Notes on Sources*

*H*all of Mirrors does not pretend to be an historical analysis of the Paris peace conference. It is a dramatic reconstruction of the most significant turning point in the history of the twentieth century, intended for the general reader with an interest in the way the modern world was made. With that in mind, the story is told largely through the characters involved – what they thought, what they said to each other and how they acted and reacted. Most of the dialogue is derived from documentary sources, some listed below and others to be found in *Further Reading*. Some conversations have been imagined, based on exchanges of letters, thoughts expressed in diaries and memoirs, minutes of meetings and the recollections of witnesses. Other dialogue has been adapted from written material for the purpose of allowing the characters to explain key aspects of the story, or to illuminate aspects of their personalities, or simply to help bring events to life. The following notes give an indication of the method employed by the author, who takes full responsibility for his interpretation of the material gathered.

## Part One: 1918

### Chapter 1: Twilight of the Gods

I.    The account of General Ludendorff's fit is based upon a report in a German newspaper, *Rheinische Westf-älische Zeitung*, published on 28 September 1928, which quotes one of the officers who witnessed the incident. Evidence of his state of mind and his actions is taken from Ludendorff's own *War Memoirs*. Material relating to the military situation is derived from various histories of the First World War, from André Tardieu's account of events leading to the German surrender, and from the memoirs of Ludendorff and Hindenburg.

II.    The material in this chapter is based upon contemporary German documents, upon the Ludendorff and Hindenburg memoirs, upon biographies of the Kaiser by V. S. Cowles and Alan W. Palmer, and upon translations of evidence collected in the German official report published as *Die Ursachen des Deutschen Zusammenbruchs im Jahre 1918 (The Causes of the German Collapse in 1918)*.

III.    A large proportion of this chapter is based on *Memoirs of Prince Max of Baden*. Other material derives from the Ludendorff memoirs, contemporary German newspaper reports, Gordon A. Craig's *Germany 1866–1945*, the papers of Woodrow Wilson, Tardieu's *The Truth about the Treaty*, Lloyd George's *War Memoirs* and the recollections of Matthias Erzberger appearing in Klaus

Epstein's *Matthias Erzberger and the Dilemma of German Democracy*.

## Chapter 2: The Man Who Won the War

I.    This chapter draws upon various biographies of Lloyd George, on his letters and on the diary of Frances Stevenson, together with Winston Churchill's *The World Crisis*. Accounts of the Armistice celebrations are based upon contemporary newspaper reports and upon the recollections of army officers collected by Captain J.C. Dunn in *The War the Infantry Knew*.

II.    Material relating to Sir Douglas Haig is based upon his published diaries, edited by Robert Blake. Other sources for this chapter include Lloyd George's *The Truth About the Peace Treaties* and his collected letters, the recollections of Max of Baden and Erzberger, Tardieu, Frances Stevenson's diary, Malcolm Thomson's *David Lloyd George: The Official Biography*, the diaries of C.P. Scott, the Woodrow Wilson papers and newspaper reports.

III.    This chapter is based upon published letters of Lord Northcliffe, upon material in *Northcliffe*, by Reginald Pound and Geoffrey Harmsworth, and upon reports in *The Times* and the *Daily Mail*. Other material derives from Lloyd George's memoirs of the peace conference.

## Chapter 3: The Tiger's Eye

I.    The opening of this chapter is based upon the published recollections of a resident of Paris in 1919.

The conversation between Clemenceau and Tardieu derives from letters written by Clemenceau and remarks made by him to Jean Martet. The account of the Doullens meeting is based upon Tardieu's version in *The Truth about the Treaty* and upon the work of a French general who, in 1931, published anonymously *La Crise du commandement unique: Le conflit Clemenceau, Foch, Haig, Pétain*. Further material derives from various histories of the war, including A.J.P. Taylor's *The First World War*.

II.  The conversations in this chapter are based upon Clemenceau's remarks recorded by Martet and his letters to Tardieu and others, and upon Lloyd George's memoirs of the peace treaty.

## Chapter 4: Pax Americana

I.  The sources for this chapter include American newspaper reports, the Wilson papers, *The Intimate Papers of Colonel House* and *The War Memoirs of Robert Lansing*, with balance added by material based on Robert H. Ferrell's *Woodrow Wilson and World War I* and *Pivotal Decades: The United States, 1900–1920*, by John Milton Cooper, Jr.

II.  President Poincaré's speech was reported in the press at the time, as were French reactions to Wilson's arrival. Wilson's response is included among his papers. Clemenceau's conversation is based upon Martet's records. Other material derives from the memoirs of Lansing, House and Ray Stannard Baker. The discussion of the reparations issue is adapted from Lloyd George's memoirs and from the official biography. The account of Lord Northcliffe's visit to Wilson is his own, published in *The Times*.

III.     Material relating to Lloyd George is based upon his own recollections and those of Frances Stevenson, together with information from the official biography and A.J. Sylvester's *The Real Lloyd George*. Clemenceau's speech was reported in the press. Events and exchanges involving the Americans are derived from the recollections of Lansing, House and Baker, and from material contained in the Wilson papers. Details of Wilson's visit to Italy are based upon press reports and information in Arno J. Mayer's *Policy and Diplomacy of Peacemaking*, together with biographies of Mussolini by Laura Fermi and Paolo Monelli, and Rossi's *The Rise of Italian Fascism*.

## Part Two: 1919

### Chapter 1: Winter of Discontent

I.     The description of events in Germany is based upon press reports, material from Hannah Arendt's *Men in Dark Times*, Eric Waldman's *The Spartacist Uprising of 1919*, Craig's *Germany 1865–1945*, and reports for the British *Daily Herald* by Morgan Philips Price. The second part of the chapter is derived from British government papers, Lloyd George's memoirs, the Wilson papers and US State Department documents, the recollections of Rear Admiral Grayson, and Martet's recorded conversations with Clemenceau.

II.     The descriptions of the meetings at the Quai d'Orsay are adapted from the official minutes of the proceedings taken on behalf of the British delegation, and from Lloyd George's memoirs. Other material is based upon the recollections of Lansing, upon Grayson's diary and upon material in the Wilson papers.

III.    The background to this chapter is adapted from various political histories, including *Europe in the Nineteenth and Twentieth Centuries*, by Grant and Temperley, and from contemporary newspaper reports. The Clemenceau material derives from Martet's account and Clemenceau's own recollections.

## Chapter 2: Four Horsemen of the Apocalypse

I.      This chapter is based largely upon the Liddell Hart biography of Foch and the memoirs of Lloyd George, together with material recorded by Tardieu and the minutes of the proceedings at the Quai d'Orsay. The military situation is derived from the histories of Taylor and Liddell Hart, and the recollections gathered by Captain Dunn.

II.     The early part of this chapter is based upon Lloyd George's memoirs, Frances Stevenson's diary and her book *The Years That Are Past*, also upon *The Real Lloyd George* and official minutes of meetings. The second part relies on material recorded at the time by Hankey, Kerr and Sir Henry Wilson, on Lloyd George's own account, and on Temperley's *A History of the Peace Conference of Paris*.

III. Many of the meetings of the Big Four took place without minutes being kept, so this chapter is based on the recollections of Lloyd George and on the notes of the French translator, Professor Mantoux. Other sources include *The Real Lloyd George*, Tardieu, Martet, and the *History of the Peace Conference*.

IV. Sources for this chapter include *Northcliffe*, the recollections of Henry Wickham Steed, Lloyd George's memoirs and his official biography, the Wilson papers, *The Intimate Papers of Colonel House* and the notes taken by Mantoux.

## Chapter 3: Artillery of Words

I. The opening of this chapter is adapted from material collected by Captain Dunn and from Liddell Hart's *The Real War*. The second section derives from sources including the Lloyd George memoirs, *The Times*, Wickham Steed and the Hansard report of parliamentary debates. The final section is reconstructed from State Department papers relating to the peace conference, Temperley's history, Lloyd George's memoirs and recorded conversations between Clemenceau and Martet.

II. This chapter is based on Lloyd George's memoirs, State Department papers, press reports, *A History of Italian Fascism*, material contained in *Politics and Diplomacy of Peacemaking*, the previously mentioned biographies of Mussolini, and Rossi's book on Italian fascism.

## Chapter 4: The Mirror Crack'd

I.     The main sources for this chapter are Lloyd George, Tardieu, and Alma Luckau's *The German Delegation at the Paris Peace Conference*.

II.    The first section of this chapter is based on Lloyd George, notes taken by Sir Maurice Hankey and Professor Mantoux, and Luckau. Other sections rely on material from Lloyd George's account, State Department papers, Lansing and House, Tardieu and Martet, minutes of the meetings of the Big Four, and Temperley's history of the conference.

III.   The section relating to Germany is based on Luckau, on German government documents, on Craig and on contemporary press reports. The scuttling of the German fleet is based on the recollections of Admiral von Scheer and various other accounts. The signing of the treaty in the Hall of Mirrors is reconstructed from the evidence of several eyewitnesses, from press reports, from the accounts of Tardieu and Martet, from Liddell Hart's biography of Marshal Foch and from contemporary letters.

For more general sources, please see the *Further Reading* section.